The Sermon and The Propers

The Sermon
and The Propers

VOLUME IV

Trinity Season • Second Half

by

FRED H. LINDEMANN

Concordia Publishing House
Saint Louis, Missouri

The Library of Congress has catalogued this book as follows:

Lindemann, Frederick Herman, 1891–
 The sermon and the Propers. Saint Louis, Concordia Pub.
House [1958–59]

  4 v. 23 cm.

  Includes bibliography.

  CONTENTS.—**v. 1.** The Advent and Epiphany seasons.—**v. 2.** Pre-Lent
to Pentecost.—**v. 3.** Trinity season, first half.—**v. 4.** Trinity season,
second half.

  1. Church year sermons. 2. Lutheran Church—Sermons. 3. Sermons, American. 4. Lutheran Church. Liturgy and ritual.   I. Title.

                                    Full name: Frederick Herman Otto Lindemann.

BX8066.L44S4   264.041   57–11909 rev 2 ‡

Library of Congress

Contents

Introduction

The Liturgy and the Reformation

RENEWED INTEREST in liturgical matters is apparent in all branches of Christendom. This revival is to be encouraged among Lutherans, for a more intensive study of the Liturgy can result only in a deeper appreciation of our priceless heritage. The Church of the Augsburg Confession did not originate in the sixteenth century but is the continuation of the Church founded by the Apostles and merely restored and purified by the Reformation. One link with historic Christendom is the Liturgy, first transmitted in the vernacular when Martin Luther introduced the German Mass to the Wittenberg congregation on October 29, 1525. This link has been maintained against seemingly overwhelming odds. From the beginning of the Reformation the Lutheran churches of southern and southwestern Germany did not follow Luther's lead in liturgical matters and yielded in varying degrees to the Reformed spirit of neighboring Switzerland and France. In 1536 the first church order of Wuerttemberg eliminated everything that even remotely reminded of the Roman Mass, except the Epistles and the Gospels. Faithful Lutherans like Erhard Schnepf and Erasmus Albers gave the service a plainness far more Reformed than Lutheran by doing away with the chanting of the Verba, the entire altar service except the communication, and all eucharistic vestments. Johann Brenz and Andreas Osiander, in 1553, reduced the service to a bare Latin introit or German hymn, sermon, hymn and benediction, with a monthly Celebration. In the course of time state churches were formed, various governments attempted to "unite" the Lutherans and the Reformed, and ancient forms and vestments were abolished by civil law. Also Rationalism, Pietism, and Deism strongly opposed retention of the ancient Liturgy.

Lutheran Liturgy in America

In America the Church of the Augsburg Confession faced liturgical problems different from and far more complex than those of any other denomination. The prevailing atmosphere of Calvinistic Protestantism was most unsympathetic to the establishment of a liturgical church. Furthermore, the immigrants from a dozen countries of Europe brought their own peculiar version of Lutheran liturgy in their native tongue. Some of these versions resembled only faintly the historic forms. The liturgical confusion resulting from the retention of the various church orders was only partially relieved, even among the German immigrants, by the appearance of the first American Lutheran Liturgy by Henry Melchior Muhlenberg in 1786 and of the *Agenda for Evangelical Lutheran Congregations U. A. C.* by the Synod of Missouri in 1856 and 1866, the latter combining old Saxon church orders. With the transition to the English language the *Common Service* of 1888, based on German church orders of the sixteenth century, became the accepted Lutheran Liturgy in America. We have it also in *The Lutheran Hymnal* of 1941. The new *Service Book* of the Joint Commission on the Liturgy is based on the *Common Service*. The ancient Liturgy of historic Christendom appears to have become the permanent possession of the Lutheran Church in America, and there remains only that we learn to appreciate it in ever fuller measure and make the proper use of it.

The Purpose of the Liturgy

The Liturgy is worship. The Church exists for the glory of God, and worship is the center of her life. Her every interest centers in her worship, the service of formal praise, adoration, thanksgiving. Worship is the inner movement of the soul, and the Liturgy is its outer manifestation. Through many centuries the Church has found the Liturgy an excellent form of giving expression to what all believers think and feel. However, the Liturgy not only expresses what the faithful think and feel, but it also teaches what they ought to think and feel. Doing or performing the Liturgy together renews the sense of belonging to the Communion of Saints, of the individual believer being a member of Christ's mystical body and of the Ecclesia established by the redemptive acts of God. Corporate worship enhances the sense of brotherhood, of being a member of the community or society that possesses and administers holy things. The thought of fellowship with all believers readily suggests itself to the mind and heart of Lutherans when they do the Liturgy, because the rediscovery of communion in the Lord's Supper is one of the greatest positive contributions of the Reformation.

The Relation of the Sermon to Preceding Parts

If the Liturgy is to serve its purpose of giving expression to what the faithful think and feel and of teaching what they ought to think and feel, the sermon must be regarded as an integral part of the liturgical action. It must, therefore, bear an integral relation to the parts that precede. When it is divorced from its proper context, it is no longer an integral part of the Liturgy. The reading of the Epistle and of the holy Gospel precedes the sermon, and the two must be integrally related. The subject or theme of the sermon dare not be foreign to the pericopes, if the purpose of the Liturgy is to be accomplished. The Epistle and the holy Gospel present to each and all some specific redemptive act of God in Jesus Christ. As a part of the Liturgy, the sermon penetrates behind the day's pericopes to the central redemptive act, the death and resurrection of the God-Man. The sermon extracts the essential core and content of the Scriptures which have been read and relates it to the central truth and central redemptive act. In this way the sermon serves its purpose as an integral part of the Liturgy by teaching the faithful what they ought to think and feel as together they worship in praise and thanksgiving.

The Relation of the Sermon to Following Parts

As an integral part of the Liturgy, the sermon must be integrally related also to what follows. The Liturgy prescribes that the faithful respond joyously and gratefully by proclaiming the central redemptive act, the Lord's death, by eating the Bread and drinking the Cup. The essence of worship is the proclamation of the Gospel and the response of the congregation to the particular truth presented in the Lessons and the sermon. When the Lord's Supper does not follow the sermon, the faithful cannot respond as the Liturgy intends, and there can be no integral relation to what follows in the Liturgy. The art of liturgical preaching has been lost because we have acquired the habit of regarding the sermon not as an integral part of the liturgical action and therefore belonging to the congregation, but as an act of the minister, independent of the work and the eucharistic acts of the faithful. Except on high festivals, the sermon usually has no relation to the pericopes, and only occasionally can it be related to the Lord's Supper. The Roman Church has a liturgy without preaching, the Calvinists have a liturgy with preaching but without the Holy Communion. Within the framework of the ancient and historic Liturgy both these types are impossible.

Nonliturgical Preaching May Become Intellectualism

The Liturgy provides for the proclamation of the Gospel and the response of the congregation to the particular truth presented in the Lessons and the sermon. The purpose of the liturgical sermon is to renew in the individuals the consciousness that they are members of the Ecclesia. When the sermon is divorced from its proper context in the liturgical action and the congregation's response in the Holy Communion is eliminated, preaching is apt to degenerate in one of several directions. One direction is that it becomes intellectualism. This degeneration is obvious in the Lutheran orthodoxy of the seventeenth century, an arid intellectualism which had the quite laudable aim of conveying sound doctrine and securing intellectual assent. We may look for something similar in our day, for we have accustomed ourselves to divorcing the sermon from its liturgical context, and we are content with only an occasional response in Holy Communion. Our sermons usually are not related to the pericopes of the day. Even when, occasionally, the Holy Communion follows upon the sermon, the preaching seldom presupposes and aims at the believing response in the Lord's Supper. However, there is frequently a zeal for intellectual presentation of dogma and a sense of achievement when there is intellectual acceptance. This type of preaching may result in the kind of knowledge that enables members to answer all questions mechanically and by rote according to some acquired formula. But it does not build up the Ecclesia, does not produce a congregation of priests who humbly respond by joyfully accepting the proclaimed truth in faith and by offering praise and thanks, yes, their very selves in the communion act of Christ's mystical body.

Nonliturgical Preaching May Become Moralism

Another direction in which nonliturgical preaching may degenerate is that it becomes moralism. To a degree, preachers are encouraging the world to believe that Christianity is a system of ethical and moral rules, that when one is "good" one is a Christian. Some such conception is not rare. A certain pattern is evolved and accepted. If we are baptized and confirmed, go to church regularly, communicate occasionally, identify ourselves with some form of activity, give a fair proportion of our income to the church, we are good members. This false conception of Christianity is encouraged when the preacher constantly appeals to the will, exhorts to do this and not to do that. If his words fall on good soil, he produces moral individuals, but he does not edify the Ecclesia. The liturgical sermon presents a redemptive act of God. It aims at faithful acceptance. It anticipates the response of the faithful, the declaration of faith and trust by eating the Body and drinking the Blood. Within the context of the Liturgy, the sermon will not be moralistic, for it will recall to the consciousness of the faithful a redemptive act of God and look forward to the response of the congregation, the declaration of acceptance in faith and of confident trust in and reliance on the redemptive act emphasized and the central redemptive act of Christ's death.

Nonliturgical Preaching May Become Emotionalism

Still another direction in which nonliturgical preaching may degenerate is that it becomes emotionalism. The preacher may succeed in producing all kinds of spiritual excitement by playing on the emotions and feelings of his hearers. But this excitement does not edify the mystical body of Christ. St. Paul remarked long ago that, for instance, by speaking in tongues a man may edify himself but not the Church. The temptation to become emotional is minimized when the preacher regards the sermon as an integral part of the Liturgy and strives to accomplish the purpose of the Liturgy. This purpose is not to create and rouse feelings, but to renew and build up faith, to edify the Ecclesia. Preaching that is intellectualism or moralism or emotionalism is individualistic and leaves the individual in his isolation. It does not draw him anew into the Ecclesia. The individual may be "edified" in the popular, non-Biblical sense of the word, but he goes home as an individual; a better person, we hope, intellectually, morally, emotionally, but still an individual. The purpose of the sermon in the Liturgy, however, is to renew in the individual members the sense that they are members of the Ecclesia.

Liturgical Worship Is Sacramental and Sacrificial

In striving to recapture the art of liturgical preaching, we might be distracted momentarily by voices declaring that people should come to church not to get but to give. We are told that coming to get is man-centered, humanistic, subjective, in other words, that it smacks of selfishness and self-seeking, but that coming to give is God-centered and objective; in other words, that it has the odor of selflessness and unselfishness. We may give the appearance of favoring the sacrificial aspect when we speak frequently of liturgical worship as the gathering of the Royal Priesthood for the offering of praise and thanksgiving, and of our eucharistic response as the offering of our own selves. However, the Liturgy is first of all sacramental and only then sacrificial. Sacramental means that God is doing the giving and we the getting. The pericopes and the sermon tell us anew what God has done, is doing, and will do. The Lord's Supper is a memorial and application of God's acts in Christ Jesus. What have we to give? We have nothing to offer but ourselves. All else, our praises and thanks and material gifts of the hands, can be only a token of ourselves. All things belong to God, and we cannot give Him what is already His. Only man was lost. We can offer God only ourselves. But we cannot offer ourselves to God as we are by nature. All our righteousnesses are as filthy rags before the holy God whom we worship. We cannot come trusting in our own righteousness but only in God's manifold and great mercies. In the end, of course, worship is giving, but before we can give, we must get, get the righteousness that is by faith, that righteousness which is Christ Himself. Only then can we give. Only then can we offer ourselves. Worship is a two-way traffic, not only from heaven to earth nor only from earth to heaven. The Liturgy leads us to recall God's redemptive acts and gives us opportunity to respond faithfully to His love by offering praise and thanksgiving, yes, our very selves in and through Jesus Christ.

The Mass of the Faithful in the Early Church

The fact that in post-Apostolic times the Church distinguished between the Mass of the Catechumens and the Mass of the Faithful will not serve as precedent for eliminating the Lord's Supper from the Liturgy. In the early Church the faithful did the entire Liturgy, and only the unbaptized and the penitents not as yet restored to good standing were dismissed before the Mystery of the Lord's Table was celebrated. Our Liturgy is intended to be done by the faithful in its entirety. It would seem unthinkable that when the Liturgy and its purpose and aim is rightly understood, a member of Christ's body should withdraw after the sermon and before the Holy Communion. To invite nonmembers to depart before the Lord's Supper is not practical in modern circumstances. Luther already was disturbed by the presence of the *neugirig Volk,* the curious, but saw no way to separate members from nonmembers and resigned himself to the hope that what the nonmember heard and saw of Christian blessedness might awaken in him the desire to become a partner. This consideration seems to have reconciled him to incorporating the sermon in the Liturgy, as he did in 1526, whereas in his Latin Mass of 1523 and his German Mass of 1524 he preferred the sermon before the Mass, "for the sermon calls to God's Supper, and the Mass is for those who have followed the call, the faithful." Concerning the post-Apostolic era we dare not ignore the fact that the Church did only one Liturgy and that the Mass of the Catechumens and the Mass of the Faithful were parts of one and the same Liturgy for the faithful. The Lord's Supper was not the only Mystery withheld from nonmembers. The Mystery of the Faith, the Creed, was imparted to the catechumens in its entirety only shortly before their Baptism and only after long and careful instruction. This was true also of the Mystery of the Our Father. Some scholars hold that the catechumens were permitted to remain for the reading of the holy Gospel only after a long period of preparation and testing. It appears that the Liturgy of the early Church at no time provided for a separation of the Service of the Word from the Holy Communion.

The Service of the Word Related to the Holy Sacrament

The Liturgy is to be done by the faithful and includes the Service of the Word and the administration of the Holy Communion. There is a close relation between the two. Our Lord instituted two sacraments to take the place of the Circumcision and the Passover. The Lord's Supper was instituted in connection with the Passover. The observance of the memorial meal of the Old Testament was invariably preceded by a discourse relating the meal and its elements to the saving events of the deliverance from Egypt. Before thanks were offered to God for the mighty acts of the Exodus, the participants had these events brought to mind. The earliest Christian liturgies show that the Church of the New Testament followed a similar procedure regarding the Lord's Supper. The reading of the Scriptures, and probably some form of discourse, recalled to mind the saving events of Jesus Christ and related the redemptive acts of the past to the Memorial Feast. The early Church seems to have had a eucharistic prayer which recalled these events. Our present Liturgy summarizes them all in the words of the Narrative: that our Lord Jesus Christ gave His Body and shed His Blood, in which we include every redemptive act from the Conception and the Incarnation to the Death, the Resurrection, the Ascension, and the Parousia. The mighty acts of God in Christ are the material and basis of our worship. The only way to worship God in spirit and in truth is to come before Him rehearsing these mighty acts; therefore the congregation is first confronted anew with these acts before it makes them the material of its worship.

The Service of the Word and Holy Baptism

The early Church regarded each Lord's Day as a minor or little celebration of Easter and the Resurrection. The great Paschal Eucharist was the chief Eucharist and the norm of all others. The Easter observance began with the Baptism of the catechumens and culminated in the Lord's Supper. On other occasions, when Holy Baptism was not administered, the function of the sermon was to reach back to the Baptism of the assembled members, to renew in them the sense of membership in the Ecclesia, and to lead forward to the liturgical action of the Eucharist. To be truly liturgical, modern preaching still serves this purpose and has this aim. The reaching back to Holy Baptism and the rising with Christ to a new life need not be done expressly and stated in words, but this function of the liturgical sermon should be in the preacher's mind and thought as he approaches his task. Holy Baptism is the ground of the Church's existence, the Eucharist is the ground of her continuance. A service ending in a sermon which is related neither backward to Holy Baptism nor forward to the Holy Communion is not the Liturgy.

The Practice of the Primitive Church

To justify the practice of doing the Liturgy up to and including the sermon and of eliminating the Lord's Supper, some have adduced the record of the Book of Acts: "Day by day, attending the temple together and breaking bread in their homes. . . ." This is said to show that the Service of the Word was originally separate from the gathering of the Ecclesia for the celebration of the Holy Communion. The first Christians, former Jews, continued to attend the temple day by day. Now, however, they attended together, probably gathering in some hall of the building. It would have been only natural that they spoke of the Christ and the redemption and atonement wrought by Him. No doubt, they preached and proclaimed His salvation, also to non-Christians who joined their group to inquire and investigate. But they did not celebrate the Holy Communion in the temple. This they did in their homes. The service of the synagog and the distinctly Christian observance were separate. The Service of the Word and the Holy Communion were not included in one and the same Liturgy. However, all this cannot justify the elimination of the Lord's Supper from our Liturgy. The celebration of the Holy Communion was not added to the Jewish service in the Jewish temple, under the very eyes of the hostile and intolerant temple authorities. The liturgy was probably that of the synagog worship. Furthermore, this was a temporary arrangement and soon abandoned as impractical. The Christians soon combined the service of the synagog with the celebration of the Lord's Supper. Our Liturgy today still contains elements of the former. Again, there is no indication that the primitive Church in Jerusalem did not combine the Service of the Word with the Lord's Supper when the Christians gathered in their homes to break bread.

The Record of the Book of Acts

The description of the primitive Church in Jerusalem tells us also: "They devoted themselves to the Apostles' teaching and the fellowship, the breaking of bread and the prayers." The first Christians continued steadfastly in the *Didache* of the Apostles, the instruction in Christian ethics and doctrine imparted to the new converts; in the *Koinonia,* the new relation to each other established by the Holy Spirit; in the breaking of bread, which united them with Christ as members of His mystical body and with one another as members of the same body whose Head is Christ; and in the prayers, the formal and common intercession and thanksgiving. In the original, all four things to which they devoted themselves have the definite article. Without being fanciful, we may assume that all four were integral parts of the Christian service. The Apostles' teaching and instruction was the Ministry of the Word. They practiced fellowship in uniting in praise and giving of thanks, in worshiping together. They entered anew into the fellowship with Christ and with one another by breaking the Bread. They devoted themselves to the prayers, the intercessions and thanksgiving in connection with the Eucharist. In this connection the conclusion of the First Letter to the Corinthians is significant. We have ground here for the surmise that the letters of the New Testament were not only intended to be read at the gatherings of the Christians but were actually so framed as to lead into the performance of the Liturgy. "Greet one another with a holy kiss," suggests the kiss of peace immediately preceding the prayer of thanksgiving. "If anyone has no love for the Lord let him be anathema," reminds of the word of the *Didache:* "If any be holy, let him come; if he be not, let him repent," and of the phrase in later liturgies: "Holy things to the holy." "Maranatha! Our Lord, come!" is a petition for the coming of Christ in the Holy Communion in anticipation of the Parousia. "The grace of the Lord

Jesus be with you," is the salutation introducing the dialog before the prayer of thanksgiving. All this would indicate that the Service of the Word, the reading of the Epistles, was part of the Liturgy that included also the Lord's Supper. In the twentieth chapter of the Acts we read: "On the first day of the week, when we were gathered together to break bread, Paul talked with them." Even if "to break bread" should not mean that they gathered to celebrate the Holy Communion but the Agape, we know nevertheless that the Holy Sacrament was always celebrated in connection with the Love Feast. When the Christians gathered on the first day of the week to break bread, St. Paul preached, prolonging his speech until midnight.

Liturgical Preaching Is Kerygma only Incidentally

Several types of preaching are readily discernible in the New Testament. When our Lord commanded His disciples to go into all the world and preach the Gospel to the whole creation, He had in mind the missionary preaching to the unconverted. We call it Kerygma. It proclaims an Event and a Person, the Event and Person who is Jesus Christ, the appearance of Christ in the flesh and His death and resurrection as the supreme and final redemptive act. The purpose of this proclamation is to bring men face to face with the Person proclaimed and with the Event He is, and to declare that all was wrought by God for men. The aim is not to secure intellectul acceptance of the historic facts but to evoke faith, to bring about a personal encounter with the Person that issues in full reliance on and trust in what Christ did in men's stead. This type of preaching is only incidental in the Liturgy, only a means to an end. As part of the liturgical act of the Royal Priesthood, the liturgical sermon addresses itself to men and women who have had their personal encounter with Christ, have accepted Him as their Redeemer and Lord, and by faith have come into possession of all He purchased and won for them. It deals with people who in Holy Baptism have been joined to His body as members and now live in Him as He lives in them. Since Kerygma is addressed to the unconverted and does not take for granted the individual's membership in the Ecclesia, it should be employed sparingly in the Liturgy, merely as background and basis.

Liturgical Preaching Is Not Evangelistic

What has been said above applies also to the type we speak of as evangelistic, the preaching that is addressed to the outsider and aims at decision and conversion and surrender. There is need for this type of preaching, but the doing of the Liturgy by the Royal Priesthood of God is not the occasion for dealing with the unconverted. Evangelistic preaching should not be accompanied by the Liturgy, for the Liturgy is unintelligible to the outsider and, when used as the prelude to evangelistic preaching, it is inevitably mangled or expunged or edited. This procedure is fair neither to the Liturgy nor to the potential convert.

Liturgical Preaching Is Not Instruction

Another type of preaching discerned in the New Testament is the instruction of the new converts and the already baptized in Christian ethics and doctrine. This type of the Ministry of the Word should not be employed in the Liturgy, for the purpose of the sermon here is not instruction. Teaching is not the direct and immediate aim of the liturgical sermon, but proclamation and the response of faith. The aim of teaching is to secure understanding of the doctrinal, ethical, and devotional implications involved in that response of faith. Teaching may be, and normally is, an indirect by-product of the liturgical sermon, but it can never become its primary objective without so changing the character of the discourse that it is no longer an integral part of the Liturgy.

Proclamation by Eating and Drinking

Parenthetically another type of proclamation may be mentioned. St. Paul wrote to the Corinthians that "as often as you eat this Bread and drink the Cup, you proclaim the Lord's death until He comes" (*kataggellete*). Luther translated, "sollt ihr des Herrn Tod verkuendigen." Since, however, this preaching is done by the faithful communicating, it does not enter into consideration as we attempt to define liturgical preaching in the pulpit.

Liturgical Preaching Is Paraklesis

Finally, there is a type of New Testament preaching that is addressed to the already converted and baptized, and aims to renew and deepen the apprehension of the Kerygma. It is Paraklesis. This word included the idea of supporting, comforting, consoling. In speaking of liturgical preaching we are dealing with a type of preaching that conforms to Paraklesis. When the faithful are assembled to do the Liturgy, of which the Holy Communion is a part, the sermon has the purpose of renewing in their consciousness what they already know and of deepening their apprehension of what they have already accepted in faith. It aims to apply familiar truths that they might give the faithful additional strength, comfort, and reassurance.

The Time and Occasion for Teaching

The fact that liturgical preaching does not aim to instruct in no way implies that no instruction, no explanation, no exegesis is to be incorporated. Possibly the reading of the Lessons could be sufficient proclamation of the Word. However, many parts of Scripture are difficult to understand. Like the Ethiopian eunuch, many members need some one to guide them, to explain the meaning. Unless they have made the Bible the subject of prolonged study, they will find much beyond their comprehension and fail to see many less apparent truths. Yet, teaching and explaining is not the chief aim of liturgical preaching. If it were, the preacher would ultimately be unnecessary, for people would progress sufficiently in knowledge no longer to require exegesis in a sermon. Furthermore, the preacher who aims chiefly or only at teaching would be confronted with the difficulty arising from the varying degrees of intellectual capacity, spiritual experience and knowledge among the members. Since it is an integral part of the Liturgy, the sermon is addressed to the whole body of the assembled faithful with the intention of producing the same response in all. The proper place for exegesis is the church school, the classroom, the group meeting, and private admonition. On nonliturgical occasions the explanation of difficult passages in Holy Writ can be adapted to the needs of the individual or the group concerned, and to the level of their intellectual, moral, and spiritual attainments. In the Liturgy, exegesis is only incidental. It has a liturgical purpose only in showing the relationship of the Epistle and the holy Gospel to the central event of God's redemptive work. All the saints assembled for worship are sinners, even the most spiritually and intellectually advanced. All come to church as the poor in spirit, who hunger and thirst after righteousness.

The Cult of the Relevant

Some may protest that they do not preach liturgically because sermons should be relevant. The word "relevant" is extremely popular in theological circles today. Preachers declare that their one and only aim is to preach the truth. According to Kierkegaard "truth is subjectivity," so they insist on being subjective and relevant in their preaching. The usual argument is that the Scriptures speak to a situation of the past and the preacher's function is to bring the Word out of the past and relate it to the needs of the individuals. The sermon must be subjective, it is said, for a statement is not true unless it can be made true to the individual, and it cannot be true to him unless it concerns his existence and has an answer to the problems his individual life poses. No one will deny that a false objectivity must be avoided, also in liturgical preaching. The value of a sermon that relates the truth of the liturgical lessons to the needs of the congregation dare not be underestimated. The Gospel is not being preached at all if it is preached as an abstraction right over the heads of the people. A preacher need not regard as evidence of having missed the mark when occasionally some member thanks him for having said just what he or she needed personally.

Liturgical Preaching Is Concerned with Ultimate Needs

However, that kind of relevancy and subjectivity is not the purpose of liturgical preaching. If that is what the members are looking for, there will always be many who leave the church saying that the sermon contained no message for them. If the primary purpose is to satisfy the needs of the individual in this way, anyone could declare that there is no point in his going to church at all, since the preacher never has any message for him. The sermon is part of the Liturgy. The preacher speaks to members of Christ's body to edify, sustain, strengthen, renew, and increase faith. His aim is that the hearers recall and accept the redemptive event emphasized in the day's Lessons as having occurred for them. Therefore the preacher cannot be preoccupied with the immediately and directly relevant. The Gospel is concerned with man's ultimate needs, with his need for forgiveness and salvation. As a preacher of the Gospel, the man in the pulpit belongs to the cult of the ultimate and only incidentally to the cult of the relevant. He need not preach to make men conscious of their immediate needs, their need for security, for deliverance from anxiety and frustration, for the attainment of social acceptance and the like. When performing the Liturgy, the Church need not compete with the psychiatrists on their own level and to offer the kind of "comfort" and "release" looked for in needs that are less than ultimate, need not trim down the Gospel to the measure of these needs. In the Liturgy the objective is not the people's temporal needs but the Gospel in its fullness. This Gospel may expose their needs as trivial and even false, and reveal to them in stark reality that they have an ultimate need, a need exposed only when they stand naked at the Last Day before the judgment seat of God.

Preaching on the Doctrinal Epistles

The letters of the New Testament were addressed to people who had accepted the apostolic preaching of Jesus Christ as the Redeemer. The Epistle for the Day then is not Kerygma but assumes a knowledge of God's redemptive acts and from this assumption proceeds to expound the doctrinal and ethical implications. When the Epistle is doctrinal, it is not to be treated as a series of revealed statements proposed for consideration or acceptance, but an endeavor to draw out and present the implications of the surrender to Christ mediated by the Kerygma. The preacher's task is to penetrate behind the doctrinal argument to the Kerygma whose implications are being set forth, so that the hearers might renew their response to it in faith, preparatory to the liturgical action of eating and drinking in memory of Christ's atoning death. The Apostle Paul follows this procedure most admirably in 1 Corinthians 15. He is dealing with problems in connection with the resurrection of the dead. In answering the questions that were agitating the Christians in Corinth, he does not formulate new and unknown propositions but reminds them of what he had originally delivered to them and deduces from this Kerygma its implications for the problem in hand.

Preaching on the Ethical Epistles

When the Epistle for the Day is ethical, the exhortations are not categorical imperatives revealed from heaven but spring out of the new relation with Jesus Christ into which the believers were brought, a relation resulting from their hearing and accepting the Kerygma and being made children of God in Holy Baptism. An example of this procedure is St. Paul's treatment of slavery. He does not lay down a regulation that all slaves are to be emancipated at once, nor does he speculate about their "rights" in the abstract. He starts with the new relation into which Christian slaves and masters were brought. Both are servants of the same Master. The slaves' service to their earthly masters is to be seen as a parable and a means of their service to God in Christ. The masters' treatment of slaves is controlled by the knowledge that they, too, have a Master. Slaves and masters alike are called to obedience to Christ, who purchased them by a real act of redemption. St. Peter proceeds in the same way when he gives injunctions to Christian slaves, starting from the new relation with Christ into which the Kerygma and Holy Baptism have led them. The Christian slave reproduces in his own behavior the pattern of Christ's deportment as the Suffering Servant, bearing our sins in His body on the tree, 1 Peter 2:18-25. In this way a consideration of the slaves' duties leads to the heart of Christ's atoning death. Here is no flat moralism but an ethic that springs direct from the redemptive act of God in Christ and its proclamation in the Kerygma. Ethical Epistles are not to be used for little moralistic exhortations. The preacher penetrates behind the specific ethical admonition to the Kerygma it presupposes and confronts the congregation with that Kerygma, so that it may occasion a renewed encounter with Jesus Christ and indicate the kind of behavior that encounter will imply in the daily lives of baptized people. Incidentally, this is why the New Testament is so disappointing as a handbook of Christian ethics. It passes over so many of the burning issues that beset the modern world. For Christian morality consists in giving effect within human relations to the divine love which is the glory of God disclosed in the work of Christ. The ethical injunctions of the New Testament letters are simply illustrations of the way in which that divine love should operate in terms of human relations.

The Holy Gospel in the Liturgy

In approaching the holy Gospels as bases for liturgical sermons, consideration must be given to the fact that the accounts of the Evangelists are not biographies but narrate a series of incidents. The three Synoptics use the same material, by and large, yet each arranges it as best serves his particular purpose of establishing and demonstrating his own aspect of Jesus Christ, as the promised Messiah, the Son of Abraham, as the Suffering Servant of Jehovah, as the Son of Adam and the Savior of both Jews and Gentiles. The fourth Gospel presents much distinctive material to awaken faith in Jesus as the Son of God. From this collection of recorded incidents the Church has chosen the holy Gospels of the Church Year. Each incident is an illustration of the central message of the Kerygma, each proclaims the redemptive act of God in miniature. The holy Gospels of the Nativity Cycle are prefaces to the Kerygma, testifying to the supernatural origin of Christ. Those of the Paschal Cycle, including Easter Day and Ascension Day, are parts of the Kerygma itself. All that is required of the preacher is that he relate the particular event to the Kerygma of the redemptive act as a whole. The majority of the holy Gospels for ordinary Sundays and for the Trinity Season are pronouncement stories or miracle stories or parables. The only other major class are the discourses from St. John's Gospel, from the Second Sunday after Easter to the Festival of Pentecost. The Church had a profound insight when she treated these discourses as testimonies of the risen Christ.

Liturgical Preaching on the Holy Gospels

In dealing with the various types of holy Gospels in the liturgical sermon, the preacher's task is to relate the pericope to the Kerygma it proclaims and then to link it with the liturgical action which is to follow. For example, turn to the traditional holy Gospel for the Later Service on the Feast of the Nativity, unfortunately not listed in *The Lutheran Hymnal*. "The Word became flesh and dwelt among us" (John 1:14). The Incarnation is part of the total movement of God to man in Jesus Christ. It is not to be considered in isolation from the Kerygma as a whole. "The Word became flesh" is God's initiation of a movement which is to culminate on the Cross. That is why the climax of the Christmas Festival is not a pretty devotion round the crib and the singing of carols, but the Christ-Mass, the Christmas celebration of the Holy Communion, in which we proceed, as the Proper Preface declares, from the commemoration of our Lord's birth, "in the mystery of the Word made flesh, Thou hast given us a new revelation of Thy glory," to the commemoration of His death, "My Body given for you, My Blood shed for the remission of sins." The liturgical sermon announces the action of God around which the whole eucharistic action is built. The faithful respond in words by offering praise and thanks in prayers and hymns, in token by presenting a material offering, and their response culminates in the offering of their person as they communicate at the Lord's Table. Frequently the divine action proclaimed in the pericope will be related to the Holy Communion as an anticipation of the Parousia. Liturgical preaching is practically impossible when the culminating response in the Lord's Supper is eliminated, for the preacher cannot point forward, and the faithful cannot look forward to the response required by the Liturgy.

The Minister and the Liturgy

Every minister who contemplates the demands of the ministry of the Word must feel constrained to exclaim with the Apostle Paul: "Who is sufficient for these things?" It is easy to reply: "Our sufficiency is from God." But we can make that reply only after we have put forth our own utmost effort. Like so many things in our religion, the grace of God is always a paradox. Where men strive with all their might, there they can recognize in retrospect that it was "not I, but Christ in me." The minister's striving to be sufficient for the things required of him should take two forms, the one spiritual, the other intellectual. The focal point of his spiritual preparation to equip himself for his task will be his continuous identification of himself with the Word he is commissioned to proclaim as that Word is expressed in the Liturgy. He must himself constantly live in the Liturgy, especially in the frequent celebration of the Eucharist. In this way he will learn to bring every thought into captivity to the obedience of Christ. His personal, private devotions will not be the occasion of cultivating his own soul but will spring from the Liturgy and lead back to the Liturgy again. He will make the liturgical Scriptures the constant theme of his meditation. For his intellectual preparation he will strive to carry out his ordination vow and diligently read and study the Bible. This study and reading also may be linked with the Liturgy by following one of the Church's lectionaries, with its association of various books of the Scriptures with the different seasons. At the other end of the communication line, he will be constantly among his people, so that, like the Great High Priest in whose Name he preaches, he may be able to sympathize with their weaknesses.

NOTE. A number of sermons are submitted in translation from the German. The present generation of preachers generally is disinclined to read such material in the original, yet would profit by acquaintance with noted preachers of the past, although the sermonic style is poorly suited for our day. In translating, every effort was made to retain something of the original. This naturally resulted in a Germanic and often stilted type of English. The sermons by Johann Gerhard are not intended for imitation as to style or length, but they illustrate the style and method of this Lutheran dogmatician of the early seventeenth century and demonstrate how Lutherans observed Saints' Days and other Feasts two hundred and fifty years ago.

GENERAL RUBRICS

THE FOLLOWING RUBRICS are from the Common Service Book and were selected as a directory for the performance only of The Service, The Communion, and not of Matins or Vespers or a preaching service.

A Hymn of Invocation of the Holy Ghost may be sung at the beginning of all Services. A hymn may be sung after the Benediction at all Services. Silent Prayer should be offered after all Services.

The Introit, Collect, Epistle, Gradual, and Gospel, the Propria for the Day, shall be used throughout the week following, except on those Days for which other appointments are made. When a greater festival falls within the week, the Propria for the Festival shall be used until the following Sunday.

Whenever the Collect for the Day is said, the full termination as appointed shall be used. If other Collects are said after it, as at Matins and Vespers, the full termination shall be used with the Collect for the Day and with the last Collect only. When the Petition is addressed to God the Father, the full termination is: "through Jesus Christ, Thy Son, our Lord, who liveth and reigneth with Thee and the Holy Ghost, ever one God, world without end. Amen." When the Petition is addressed to God the Son, the termination is: "who livest and reignest with the Father and the Holy Ghost, ever one God, world without end. Amen." When mention is made of our Lord in the body of the Petition, the termination is: "through the same Jesus Christ, Thy Son, our Lord, who liveth and reigneth with Thee and the Holy Ghost, ever one God, world without end. Amen." When mention is made of our Lord at the end of the Petition, the termination is: "who liveth and reigneth with the Father and the Holy Ghost, ever one God, world without end. Amen." When the Petition is addressed to God the

Holy Trinity, the termination is: "who livest and reignest, one God, world without end. Amen."

At the Hymn of Invocation of the Holy Ghost the congregation shall rise. For the Invocation, the Confession, and the Declaration of Grace the minister may stand in the chancel before the altar. At the Introit he shall stand at the altar. When the Service begins with the Introit, the minister shall go immediately to the altar. Beginning with the Versicle, "Our help is in the name of the Lord," the congregation may kneel for the Confession of Sins and until the Introit. The Versicles and Amens in the Confession of Sins may be said by the congregation instead of being sung.

The Introit for the Day with the Gloria Patri should be sung by the choir; but the Introit may be sung by the choir, the congregation uniting in the Gloria Patri; or the Introit may be said by the minister, the choir and the congregation singing the Gloria Patri. The Kyrie may be sung or said responsively by the minister and the congregation; or the minister may say the first petition, the choir and the congregation singing the entire Kyrie in response. The Gloria in Excelsis shall be used invariably on all Festival Days or when there is a Communion.

Before the Epistle for the Day, other lessons of Holy Scripture may be read, but the Epistle and the Gospel for the Day shall always be read. The Gradual for the Day or Season should be sung by the choir; or, instead thereof, the simple Alleluia or the Sentence for the Season may be sung. The Nicene Creed shall be used on all Festivals and whenever there is a Communion.

Before the General Prayer the minister shall make mention of any special petitions, intercessions, or thanksgivings which may have been requested. He may also make mention of the death of any members of the congregation. The General Prayer appointed in the Service shall always be used on Festivals and whenever there is a Communion. The Lord's Prayer may be omitted after the General Prayer when there is a Communion; but it shall be omitted at this place when one of the Occasional Offices is used in connection with The Service. The Proper Preface for a Festival shall be used throughout the Festival Season.

When The Service has been completed, a deacon or other officer shall remove the Sacramental Vessels from the altar to the sacristy and dispose of that part of the Bread and Wine which remains as follows: He shall carefully remove the Bread from the Paten and Ciborium to a fit receptacle, there to be kept against the next Communion. He shall carry the Chalice to a proper and convenient place without the church and shall pour the Wine upon the ground.

PRECEDENCE OF FESTIVALS AND DAYS

I. The following days shall be observed invariably as appointed in the Calendar. A Day or Festival concurring with any of these here noted may be observed the first open day thereafter.

Greater Festivals and Days

The Sundays of Advent   Ash Wednesday
The Nativity   The Sundays in Lent
The Circumcision   The Days of Holy Week
The Epiphany   Easter Day and the Day following
The Transfiguration   The Ascension and the Sunday following
Septuagesima   Pentecost and the Day following
Sexagesima   The Festival of the Holy Trinity
Quinquagesima   Reformation

II. When a Lesser Festival falls on a Sunday not noted in Rubric I, the Introit, Collect, Epistle, Gradual, and Gospel for the Festival shall be used, and the Collect for the Sunday shall be said after the Collect for the Day.

Lesser Festivals

All Apostles', Evangelists', and Martyrs' Days
The Presentation, the Visitation, and the Annunciation
St. Michael and All Angels
All Saints' Day

THE THIRTEENTH SUNDAY AFTER TRINITY

With the present Sunday we enter upon what may be regarded as the second half of the Trinity Season. In the first half we have learned the great Christian motive of the love God has to us. We have considered our responsibilities of duty and God's sufficient provision of grace. We now pass to the consideration of the great features of Christian character, of what it is to be a Christian. The Sundays of the second half speak of the various aspects of the Christian life, its aims, its difficulties, its joys, and its final perfection. We may therefore expect even less of a system than in the first half.

The first three Sundays of the second half teach the three great essentials of true religion: love, purity, and singleness of heart. The Introit for the Thirteenth Sunday directs us to the teaching of the day: "Have respect, O Lord, unto Thy covenant." The Epistle speaks of the Old and the New Covenant. The holy Gospel shows the aspects of life under the two. The Collect, inspired by both the Epistle and the holy Gospel, asks for the increase of faith, hope, and charity, and tells us that God's promises are ours through an obedience that is born of an inspiration of love for that which He commands, because we love Him and His.

The Introit. "Have respect, O Lord, unto Thy covenant; oh, let not the oppressed return ashamed! Arise, O God, plead Thine own cause; and forget not the voice of Thine enemies. O God, why hast Thou cast us off forever? Why doth Thine anger smoke against the sheep of Thy pasture?"

The entire Introit is from Psalm 74. We are the sheep of His pasture. Seeing the plight of the Church, beset by enemies, we plead for help, but base our petition for help not on selfish considerations, for our chief concern is God's name, His reputation. The impious must not scoff at a God who claims to be omnipotent but will not deliver the oppressed who are in covenant relation with Him. Through it all runs the note of confidence and trust.

The Collect. "Almighty and everlasting God, give unto us the increase of faith, hope, and charity; and that we may obtain that which Thou dost promise, make us to love that which Thou dost command."

We pray for a truly Christian life, the ministry of the New Covenant, for which the living and life-giving Spirit has equipped us. The increase of faith, hope, and charity is the renewing and increase of baptismal grace. We pray not only for the grace to do the commandments but also to love them. We ask for growth in grace, greater strength for the whole religious life in its three aspects, more faith toward God, more hope in respect to ourselves, and more love towards others, Col. 1:4, 5. We ask also for conformity to the will of God, the perfect conformity in affection and desire, that we may obtain the promises and Kingdom of God.

The Epistle, Galatians 3:15-22. Through pure grace, without any merit on our part, we became children of God. The Galatians, called into the New Covenant, appear to have been forsaking Gospel liberty. The Apostle summarizes the development of the Old Covenant. The inheritance was given to Abraham by promise. The Law was added many years later because of transgression. The Law does not annul a covenant previously ratified, so as to make the promise void, but it does not cure, make alive, it only condemns. Life comes by faith, as a free gift, of grace. The Scriptures consigned all things to sin, and sin brings forth death.

The Gradual. "Have respect, O Lord, unto Thy covenant; oh, let not the oppressed return ashamed! Arise, O God, plead Thine own cause; and forget not the voice of Thine enemies. Alleluia! Alleluia! O Lord God of my salvation, I have cried day and night before Thee. Alleluia!"

The Proper Sentence. "Alleluia! O Lord, deal with Thy servant according unto Thy mercy, and teach me Thy statutes. I am Thy servant, give me understanding, that I may know Thy testimonies. Alleluia!"

Or: "Alleluia! Blessed be the Lord God of our fathers; praise Him, and highly exalt Him forever. Alleluia!"

The Gospel, St. Luke 10:23-37. The lawyer is under the Old Covenant. He asks questions about the Law, putting our Lord to the test. As far as the lawyer was concerned, it was a lifeless Law. To the robbers the Law was as empty as their lives, they were against all right and law. The priest and the Levite were doers of the Law in the strictest sense. Yet they failed in the essential. The Samaritan was outside the Law, yet he served God truly in the self-sacrificing ministry of brotherly love. "Love is the fulfilling of the Law" (Rom. 13:10).

The Proper Preface. "Who with Thine only-begotten Son and the Holy Ghost art one God, one Lord. And in the confession of the only true God we worship the Trinity in Person and the Unity in Substance, of Majesty coequal."

OUTLINE FOR SERMON ON THE EPISTLE

This is the first of three Sundays which teach us the great features of the Christian character, what it is to be a Christian. The three essentials are love, purity, and singleness of heart. In considering the first, we speak today of

Types of Service

A. The Service of Abraham. This was the primitive and original type of service. Its motive was a covenant of unconditional grace. God conferred upon Abraham and his children a special relationship to Himself. He was their God, and they were His people, His children as the children of the faithful Abraham. From this happy relationship proceeded all obligations to service, but of these little mention was made, and duty was left to follow naturally from the inward constraint of love.

B. The Service of Law. This type of service succeeded that of Abraham, but it was not a development but a retrogression rendered necessary by sin. "It was added because of transgression." Special rules of service had become an absolute necessity when the conscience no longer responded to the unwritten laws of duty. But the Law removed God farther away. When the unspoken will of a parent is no longer obeyed and the limits of conduct have to be defined by strict rules, there is a feeling of loss. So it was here. God was no longer a loving friend as He had been to Abraham. "It was ordained by angels through an intermediary," Moses. All this was a falling away from the sacred fellowship of the past and from the simple religion of Abraham, Isaac, and Jacob.

C. Christian Service. Christianity was a reversion to the primitive type of religion. The religion of Abraham was nearer Christianity than the religion of Moses, and St. Paul delights to consider Christians as Abraham's seed and heirs, through Christ, of ancient promises. He sweeps away the centuries of Law as a transitory condition of things, a comparatively modern departure from primitive custom. He is careful to guard the Law from being thought a contradiction. There was nothing wrong about it. It was a stage in growth. It was not an evil, but it was a lower form of good, and yet it is wrong to go back from the higher to the lower. The reign of the Law has long passed away, but the Christian must remember (1) that the baptismal covenant makes each Christian an Isaac, a child of promise, the possessor of a rich inheritance, and the heir of heavenly promises, (2) that this relationship of love must be the motive for true and laudable service, the service of filial devotion, even as Abraham served God and was called the friend of God.

OUTLINE FOR SERMON ON THE HOLY GOSPEL

The Service of Love

A. A Position of Love. This is the blessedness of the Church of Christ and of each Christian, that he sees the love of God. Behind him he sees the Cross, the final revelation of God's love to the world. He sees, but a few years back, a little procession, the chief figure in it a woman bearing in her arms an infant. The infant was he himself, then brought individually to the Cross for pardon. In his very sight he sees the altar and on it God's best gift of love. Here is the altar of his acceptance and his sustenance. Blessed are the eyes that see this sight, which brings the Cross into the life of the present and assures of every blessing. In front of him he sees a hope of quiet rest, when service is done, in the

Paradise of God. On a certain day blessed will be his ears, for they shall hear the voice of the Son of God. Blessed are the eyes that see in Christ the pardon of sins past, the pledge of present grace, and the hope of future glory.

B. The Essentials of Love. These are ever the same. They have never changed, for they were as essential in the days of Abraham, of Moses, of the prophets, as in the days of the Son of Man. They are the love of God with all the heart and the love of man. These two essentials are, in fact, one, for love fulfills the Law, and true and laudable service is love.

C. The Example of Love. The Good Samaritan is our teacher. This is a shrewd hit at all prejudices and all exclusiveness. We may often learn lessons of true service from those whom we most despise. We see in the Samaritan three marks of the true service of love. (1) Love asks no questions. The lawyer had asked a question. He was afraid of loving too widely. The Samaritan did not ask whether the traveler was his neighbor. It was well he did not, for he would have found only one of an opposing nation and of a rival sect, one who regarded his blood as mingled and his creed unsound. But he asked no questions and let forth his mercy freely. (2) Love listens to no objections. He did not parley with fears for safety, with thoughts of business, of comfort, or of his journey's end. Had he entertained these thoughts, he would have gone on, but love said, "Stay," and he stayed. It is better to make too few objections than too many. Selfishness is very wise in reasons, but we may remember that it was Love which left heaven, and it is a question whether selfishness will ever reach that journey's end. The religiously selfish, like the priest and the Levite, are so anxious to save their souls that they will not lose them, and so cannot save them. The way to heaven does not lie "on the other side." (3) Love spares no pains. Having begun a good work, love spares no pains to carry it through at any cost of self-denial. The oil and wine are used not for refreshment but as remedies. The beast bears the sufferer while the master walks. Time and money are spent freely in completing the cure, and arrangements are made for future provision.

THE FOURTEENTH SUNDAY AFTER TRINITY

The first essential of true religion is love, as we heard last Sunday. Today we come to the second of the great essentials of true religion. The second essential of life in the Kingdom of Grace is purity. The Epistle begins: "Walk by the Spirit, and do not gratify the desires of the flesh." This walk by the Spirit has its difficulties. St. Paul pictures the battle between the flesh and the workings of the Spirit. The enemies must be constantly overcome and defeated. In the Introit we address God as our Shield. In the Collect we pray that God would keep and lead us by His help. The holy Gospel illustrates the development, fruit bearing after we have been cleansed from the leprosy of sin.

The Introit. "Behold, O God, our Shield, and look upon the face of Thine anointed! For a day in Thy courts is better than a thousand. How amiable are Thy tabernacles, O Lord of hosts! My soul longeth, yea, even fainteth, for the courts of the Lord."

Realizing what God has done for them, the anointed have looked forward yearningly to communing with Him in His courts. The congregation, the bride, has longed to spend this Lord's Day in the Lord's courts, in His house, in His tents. This is home to the anointed, and now we plead that God, our Shield, look upon the face of His anointed.

The Collect. "Keep, we beseech Thee, O Lord, Thy Church with Thy perpetual mercy; and because the frailty of man without Thee cannot but fall, keep us ever by Thy help from all things hurtful, and lead us to all things profitable to our salvation."

The form is unusual in that the first word voices the petition, without the usual invocation. The Reformers substituted "with Thy perpetual mercy" for "by Thy perpetual atonement," because *propitiatione perpetua* suggested a possible reference to the sacrifice of the Mass. The original "without Thee human mortality falls" seems better, as a warning that danger to the Church constantly rises from the "frailty of man." Note the repetition of "keep." The Church depends wholly on the divine mercy. We cannot depend on ourselves, for the frailty of man cannot but fall. We need grace to protect us from harm, and grace to lead us to all that is good.

The Epistle, Galatians 5:16-24. "Walk by the Spirit" is the second mark in the Church's teaching on what it means to be a Christian. St. Paul shows the great battlefield of the soul, where two kingdoms are constantly battling, the Kingdom of the Spirit and the kingdom of the flesh, the Kingdom of Grace and the ungodly principle of sin. He shows us the works of the flesh, but also the fruit of the Spirit. Every Christian is like a tree planted by the Holy Spirit and bearing precious fruit. We see the opponents. The Christian life is not all pleasure but a battle. "Those who belong to Christ Jesus have crucified the flesh with its passions and desires." In this battle we have a powerful weapon: trust and confidence in God.

The Gradual. "It is a good thing to give thanks unto the Lord and to sing praises unto Thy name, O Most High. To show forth Thy loving-kindness in the morning and Thy faithfulness every night. Alleluia! Alleluia! Praise waiteth for Thee, O God, in Zion; and unto Thee shall the vow be performed. Alleluia!"

The *Common Service Book* and the *Roman Missal* have Ps. 118:8, 9. The Alleluia Verse of the Common Service is Ps. 90:1, and of the *Missal* Ps. 95:1. *The Lutheran Hymnal* uses Ps. 92:1, 2, and the Alleluia Verse is Ps. 65:1.

The Proper Sentence. "Alleluia! O Lord, deal with Thy servant according unto Thy mercy, and teach me Thy statutes. I am Thy servant, give me understanding, that I may know Thy testimonies. Alleluia!"

Or: "Alleluia! Blessed be the Lord God of our fathers; praise Him and highly exalt Him forever. Alleluia!"

The Gospel, St. Luke 17:11-19. Last Sunday's holy Gospel spoke of the merciful Samaritan, this Sunday's shows us the thankful Samaritan. Leprosy is a type of sin. On the Third Sunday after the Epiphany, the holy Gospel told us of a leper whom our Lord healed. This illustrated the divine mercy. The healing of the ten lepers is here to teach the cleansing power of Christ. "One of them, when he saw that he was healed, turned back, praising God with a loud voice; and he fell on his face at Jesus' feet, giving Him thanks." The Greek word used for giving thanks is the same we use in Eucharist. This Samaritan brought forth "the fruit of the Spirit." The other nine gratified the desires of the flesh. The Eucharist is giving of thanks by those who have been healed of the leprosy of sin. Sunday is the day when we are to praise and thank God with a loud voice, a day of thanksgiving for the grace of Holy Baptism. Sunday is a commemoration of Easter, the day of Baptism. The Eucharist is thanksgiving for our conversion. In the ancient Church the adults were baptized on Easter Eve and cleansed of the leprosy of sin. Every Sunday is a renewal of baptismal grace. The Holy Eucharist is the continuation and completion of that grace.

The Proper Preface. "Who with Thine only-begotten Son and the Holy Ghost art one God, one Lord. And in the confession of the only true God we worship the Trinity in Person and the Unity in Substance, of Majesty coequal."

OUTLINE FOR SERMON ON THE EPISTLE

The evil of impurity is here contrasted with the blessed results which follow the holy workings of the Holy Spirit.

The Service of Purity

A. The Works of the Flesh. The evil of these is shown by its wholesale destructiveness. It spoils all that it touches and is the parent of confusion and of every evil work. Inwardly evil in itself, its results are manifest. It brings: (1) Inward schism. Where "the desires of the flesh are against the Spirit, and the desires of the Spirit are against the flesh," all is confusion in the human heart. It is the battlefield on which opposing forces are engaged. The workings of the Spirit disable us for the pleasures of sin, and the workings of evil for the joys of holiness. Though the old nature is checked by the new, yet the new is still hindered and thwarted by the old. This state of struggle can be ended rightly only by our taking even more decidedly the side of the Spirit. (2) Antagonism against God. When we yield to sin, we come at once "under the law." We are placed in a wrong attitude toward God. We are out of sympathy with His laws, in which we read our own condemnation and which are then felt to be a burden, a restraint, and a bondage. Only by following the Spirit can we find pleasure in doing the will of God and feel it no longer a burden placed on us but a principle within us. (3) Confusion in every sphere of life. It ruins the life of home, breaking the marriage tie on which the home depends, by "immorality, impurity, licentiousness," or the shameless pursuit of gross sin. It darkens religion, for if there is no true religion in them, men will turn to superstition. Men must have a religion, and the last refuge of atheism is superstition, the modern equivalent of "idolatry, sorcery." It breaks up all society. Hatred breeds every act and form of disunion, "enmity, strife, jealousy, anger," and these crystallize into "dissension, party spirit," for the words are wider than the King James Version translates — seditions, heresies. It is not the Church alone that is rent by sin. Sin rends the world and leads to wholesale anarchy. Evil passions no longer held in check break loose in "envy, murders, drunkenness, carousing, and the like." This is the last end of the sins of the flesh. If we have not realized their inherent evil, we can estimate it by these results, for "the works of the flesh are plain."

B. The Fruit of the Spirit. Let the same test be applied to the fruit of the Spirit. This also is plain. The nine graces of the Spirit may be divided into three divisions: (1) "Love, joy, peace." These are for a man's own heart. Love is the restoration of correspondence with God, joy and peace are its constant realization. At peace with God, man is at peace with himself. (2) "Patience, kindness, goodness." These are for a man's home and for the circle of friends and neighbors. In patience he accepts the evil; in kindness he bears himself so as to give to others the least possible need for forbearance; in goodness he overcomes evil with good. (3) "Faithfulness, gentleness, self-control." These are for a man's work in the world. By faithfulness a man makes it easy for others to work with him. By gentleness he is enabled to work with others. By self-control, which is the power within oneself to rule oneself, to abstain from things forbidden, and to refrain from excess even in things allowed, a man may gain higher attainment for himself or benefit to others. "Against such there is no law," for Law exists to restrain, but in the fruit of the Spirit there is nothing to restrain. Such graces are eminently Christian virtues and part of our baptismal duty as Christians, for "those that belong to Christ Jesus have crucified [at Baptism] the flesh with its passions and desires." These virtues are universally needed, the world demands them, but Christ alone supplies them.

OUTLINE FOR SERMON ON THE HOLY GOSPEL

The Cleansing Power of Christ

A. The Leprosy of Sin. The ten lepers are a picture of moral defilement. Leprosy, the disease of the flesh, is the natural type and no doubt often also the punishment of fleshly sin. As unclean they "stood at a distance"; as banished from society they were driven to consort together.

B. The Miracle of Cleansing. The extremity of their misery drove them to Christ, who alone could deliver them from the body of this death. Conscious of defilement, they "lifted up their voices," unwilling to approach. They came earnest, entreating, reverent. To know our sin is the first step toward knowing our Savior. Christ has ever demanded faith. Still in their leprosy, they are to go to announce their cure. No more trying evidence of faith could have been required, but "as they went, they were cleansed." The path of obedience is the way to spiritual health. To believe that prayer has been granted is to receive. See Mark 11:24.

C. Fellowship with Christ. What happens after cleansing is as important as what has gone before. When misery has led us to Christ, gratitude must send us back to Him. The restoration from deadly sin must be followed by fellowship with Christ, and those once blessed must ever return for fuller blessing. Our praises must be as loud and as earnest as our prayers. It is very remarkable, and hardly without intention, that the Church on two successive Sundays teaches true and laudable service by the example of a Samaritan. Religiously they worshiped they knew not what, yet in conduct and character they surpassed many of the chosen people. True and laudable service may be offered by many whom we despise. They may be the grateful, and we the careless.

THE FIFTEENTH SUNDAY AFTER TRINITY

On the past two Sundays we learned that the Christian's service, to be true and laudable, must be the service of love and of purity. Today we learn that it must be marked also by singleness of heart, of aim and purpose. A double or divided service is impossible. The holy Gospel declares: "No one can serve two masters. You cannot serve God and mammon." The Epistle tells us that to walk by the Spirit we must fulfill the law of Christ and so serve God in serving one another. Many things hinder the fulfillment of Christ's law. In the Collect we pray to be cleansed from and defended against them. The Gradual speaks of trusting God and putting all our confidence in Him. Only then will we seek first His Kingdom and His righteousness.

The Introit. "Bow down Thine ear, O Lord, hear me. O Thou, my God, save Thy servant that trusteth in Thee. Be merciful to me, O Lord, for I cry unto Thee daily. Rejoice the soul of Thy servant, for unto Thee, O Lord, do I lift up my soul."

Gathered before the Lord in His house is not a joyous congregation with faces shining but servants of God oppressed by the week's battle. We come seeking rejoicing and uplifting of the soul. "Incline Thy ear, O Lord, and answer me. Save Thy servant who trusts in Thee. Be gracious to me, O Lord, for to Thee do I cry all the day. Gladden the soul of Thy servant, for to Thee, O Lord, do I lift my soul."

The Collect. "O Lord, we beseech Thee, let Thy continual pity cleanse and defend Thy Church; and because it cannot continue in safety without Thy succor, preserve it evermore by Thy help and goodness."

Very humble are the views of the Church about herself, needing "continual pity," as last Sunday she asked "perpetual mercy." We ask not merely for the compassionate feeling, but for the acts of pity: (1) Cleansing. This implies the pollution of inward sin. He who has cleansed the Church by one Baptism for the remission of sins must continually cleanse her by His Spirit from error, inconsistency, and all abuses. The Church of God needs continual reformation, not one in the sixteenth century only. (2) Defense. The best defense for the Church is her cleansing, but beyond this she needs defense against those who desire not her reformation but her destruction and attack her doctrines and rightful liberties. (3) Preservation. Dangers threaten from within and from without. The very existence of the Church depends upon Christ's pity and power, without which she would have been swept from the earth long ago (Psalm 124). The Church needs help to defend and goodness to bless.

The Epistle, Galatians 5:25—6:10. Giving undivided service to God implies that we fulfill the law of Christ by walking by the Spirit, in all gentleness and meekness. The Epistle follows that of last Sunday. St. Paul spoke of the walk by the Spirit in contrast to fulfilling the lust of the flesh. Today the Apostle gives a number of practical hints as to the walk by the Spirit. No self-conceit, no envy. Gentleness and sympathy for the brethren overtaken in a trespass. "Bear one another's burdens, and so fulfill the law of Christ." Honor to the teachers of the Word. Do good especially to those who are of the household of faith. A church united in love is the ideal.

The Gradual. "It is better to trust in the Lord than to put confidence in man. It is better to trust in the Lord than to put confidence in princes. Alleluia! Alleluia! O God, my heart is fixed! I will sing and give praise, even with my glory. Alleluia!"

Leading over to the holy Gospel, the Gradual declares that it is better to take refuge in the Lord than to put confidence in man and princes (Ps. 118:8, 9). The Revised Standard Version translates: "My heart is ready, O God! I will sing, I will sing praises! Awake, my soul!" The American Standard Version reads: "My heart is fixed, O God; I will sing praises, even with my glory" (Ps. 108:1). The King James Version has a marginal reference to Psalm 57, where we read: "I will sing and give praise. Awake up, my glory."

The Proper Sentence. "Alleluia! O Lord, deal with Thy servant according unto Thy mercy, and teach me Thy statutes. I am Thy servant, give me understanding that I may know Thy testimonies. Alleluia!"

Or: "Alleluia! Blessed be the Lord God of our fathers; praise Him, and highly exalt Him forever. Alleluia!"

The Gospel, St. Matthew 6:24-34. The Christian may make no compromises with the world, may not serve God a little and nibble at worldly things. "He who sows to his own flesh," as the Epistle puts it, is a man who constantly asks: What shall I eat, what shall I drink, what shall I wear? Our Lord demands a deep confidence in the heavenly Father's love and mercy. The Gospel of the birds for which God provides, of the lilies which the Lord arrays like Solomon in his glory, has given much comfort to destitute humanity. Through this entire portion of the Sermon on the Mount we may trace God's intimate relation to us, that of Father and children. May we ever be conscious that we are a holy congregation, faithfully guarded by God's angels. The world and hell cannot touch us. This is a Gospel of carefreeness, of contentedness. The many evidences of God's loving care, which we see all about us and experience constantly, teach us that our Father not only cares for us but is bearing our burdens.

The Proper Preface. "Who with Thine only-begotten Son and the Holy Ghost art one God, one Lord. And in the confession of the only true God we worship the Trinity in Person and the Unity in Substance, of Majestly coequal."

OUTLINE FOR SERMON ON THE EPISTLE

This is the third of the Sundays that teach the great essentials of true religion: love, purity, and singleness of heart.

Walking by the Spirit

A. Bearing One Another's Burdens. "If a man is overtaken in any trespass, you who are spiritual should restore him in a spirit of gentleness." The Apostle is speaking of a Christian brother who is one with us in faith, confession, and hope. He is not to be treated as a godless man because he was overtaken in a trespass, against his will has committed an apparent sin. His sinful flesh may have caused him to lose his temper and to speak offensively, insultingly. Or the world may have outwitted him, so that he became confused regarding divine truth and spoke like an unbeliever. Such a brother is to be restored gently. We are to regard him not as a non-Christian but as a brother in need of loving help. If he is not freed from his trespass, he may fall from faith and be lost. Therefore we desire that he recognize his sin, regret it, and return wholly to his Savior. He must be made to feel that we consider him a brother and wish to help him and that only for this reason we correct him and plead with him to repent. At times we hesitate because it may prove embarrassing if the brother should not receive our attempt at restoration in the spirit it is meant. We tell ourselves that we may expect only unpleasantness. We have our hands full with our own weakness. So we incline to ignore our brother's sin and say nothing to him, but air our disapproval to others. The Apostle reminds us that we as Christians are not to deal with our brother as is agreeable and pleasant. "Bear one another's burdens, and so fulfill the law of Christ." Also for the brother it is a great burden that he has been overtaken in a trespass. Perhaps he has realized this long since and is ashamed. He needs to be comforted and encouraged. If this should not be true of him, his soul is in great danger. If, then, we are Christians, with love and gentleness in our heart, we must be moved to be patient and forbearing, speak to him in a friendly manner and help him in his hour of weakness. Even though it may be difficult like carrying a burden, the salvation of our brother's soul is worth all. Self-conceit keeps us from showing this love to a brother. "Let us have no self-conceit." "If anyone thinks he is something, when he is nothing, he deceives himself." The erring brother has insulted us, cast reflections on our honor, so we are resentful, deny his Christianity, and demand satisfaction. Vindication of our honor means more to us than the salvation of the brother. We draw comparisons: "I would never have done that. Whoever does anything like that is not a Christian." Thereby we deceive ourselves. What good is it that we can say we would never have done this or that? Before God we can have only one honor: that we have no sin whatever. "Let each one test his own work." God will judge each by that and not by what others have done. Such a testing will reveal that we, too, have many faults and sins, that God has had and still has endless patience with us if we are not to be cast away. This realization will drive all self-conceit from our heart and make room for love and gentleness, so that we do not despise and condemn the erring brother but be patient and bear his burden.

B. Sharing with Him Who Teaches. If the preacher were to follow his own inclination and wish, he would refrain from speaking on this subject. But the words of the text were not written to be passed over, but to be preached and explained. "Let him who is taught the Word share all good things with him who teaches." When our Lord sent out His disciples to preach the Gospel, He said: "Eating and drinking what they provide, for the laborer deserves his wages" (Luke 10:7). Preachers and teachers are not to be without wages but are to receive the compensation due them. Who are to give these wages? They who are taught the Word. This is said to all Christians, young and old, male and female, all who are served with Word and Sacrament and who possess good things. It is most significant that in this connection the solemn words are written: "Do not be deceived, God is not mocked; for whatever a man sows, that he will also reap. For he who sows to his own flesh will from the flesh reap corruption; but he who sows to the Spirit will from the Spirit reap eternal life." Many imagine that sharing all good things with him who teaches is left to their own free will and choice. Others share, not because they recognize it as a duty, but because they are persuaded and urged. But God regards it as a chief part of walking by the Spirit. He esteems it a supreme grace that He has the Gospel taught. It is His greatest gift. When a man refuses to recognize and acknowledge this, considers it not worth giving something of his earthly possessions for it, God regards this as mockery of Himself. God is not mocked! The unappreciative and ingrateful person sows to his own flesh, allies himself with his sinful heart against God. This is like sowing weeds in a field. What will he reap but weeds? If a man regards being taught the Word of so little value, he is responsible for the teaching remaining without results and fruits. God withholds His blessing. Refusal to share will be lamented in all eternity. Sharing is a part of walking by the Spirit.

C. Doing Good to Others. "Let us not grow weary in well-doing, for in due season we shall reap if we do not lose heart. So, then, as we have opportunity, let us do good to all men, and especially to those who are of the household of faith." Here the Apostle speaks of a part of the walk by the Spirit which is highly regarded also by the world. Unbelievers declare: "Do good to others, that is true religion, better than praying and going to church." But when God says, "Let us do good," He is thinking only of the Christian, for He desires the good that comes from the heart and is done out of love for Him and the neighbor. Such good is possible only for the believer. The unbeliever does good because he derives satisfaction, and only to those toward whom he is well disposed, or who have done good to him, or seem worthy. This is not love of the neighbor but love of self, at best. Love seeks not its own, does good to others whenever needed. We are to do good to all men, also to those who are not worthy and not deserving. There is only one limitation: "Especially to those who are of the household of faith." Fellow believers come first. If two need help, a Christian and a non-Christian, and our ability limits us to one, the fellow believer has priority. "Let us not grow weary in welldoing." The Holy Spirit knows how necessary is this admonition. We are to help not once or twice, not once each year, not as long as we are young, have an income, not when we are older and have provided for ourselves, but "as we have opportunity." Now is the time of opportunity, here in this life. We are living not merely to provide for ourselves but to serve and to do good to others, not with what we have not but with what we have, with what God has given us. This we must not forget, lest we grow weary. If demands on us are frequent, we are apt to think too much is expected. Since God knows this, He has the Apostle call to us: "Let us not grow weary in welldoing." Are we no longer living by the Spirit, in faith and gratefulness? Do we no longer remember that God gave His own Son for us and that He gives to us day after day and does not grow weary? We know that if He were to grow weary, we should soon have nothing to give and have nothing even for ourselves. So we shall continue to do good and not grow weary. "For in due season we shall reap if we do not lose heart." It is our flesh that fears we might lose by giving. The spirit is always willing. To strengthen the spirit against the flesh this promise is given. We must indeed admit that we have received the reward beforehand, for we have all from God, who blesses and rewards daily. But to encourage us, that we no longer fear giving too much and doing too much good, He assures us that in due season, when we are with Him in heaven, we shall reap without end. For our Christian life, our walk by the Spirit, is merely sowing. In the eternal harvest we shall reap bountifully.

OUTLINE FOR SERMON ON THE HOLY GOSPEL

This is the Sunday of undivided service. The keynote is struck by the first sentence of the holy Gospel: "No one can serve two masters." The secret of undivided service is:

Undivided Trust

A. The Necessity of Trust. We cannot trust unless we serve, and we cannot serve unless we trust. Man has only one heart, and if he fills it with worldly cares, he will leave in it no room for God. Faith and anxiety cannot live together, for if faith does not cast out anxiety, anxiety will cast out faith. Either God is to be depended upon, or He is not. If He is, there is no room for anxiety; and if He is not, there is no room for faith.

B. The Reasonableness of Trust. God is to be trusted (1) for His power. He who has given the greater gift has power to bestow that which is less. He who has given life must be able to supply the means of living, and He who has given us our bodies, so fearfully and wonderfully made, must be able to give us the wherewithal to clothe them. Man's helplessness proves that he was intended to trust in God. Care is condemned by its uselessness. (2) For His love. The birds trust God for food, for "they neither sow nor reap nor gather into barns." They can make no provision for the future, yet they are quite happy about it, and God never forgets them. God has a closer relation to us, for He is our heavenly Father, and we are more precious in His sight than they.

God clothes the grass of the field, so transient in its existence, and clothes it so richly. Will He not much more clothe us? To doubt this is to be like the heathen who do not know God or His relation to them. We know our heavenly Father, and what is still better, He knows us and what we need. (3) For His promise. God has given us a sure charter against care. The agreement into which He enters and by which He is pledged to act is this: If we will attend to the needs of the soul, He will attend to the needs of the body. If we give the first of our affections, energies, and time to things eternal, He will provide for things temporal. Those who make God their one care shall have no other.

THE SIXTEENTH SUNDAY AFTER TRINITY

Last Sunday we learned that we are to serve God with undivided trust. The cares and worries of life, the lack of complete trust in the Father's love, will gradually grow into a deliberate sowing to the flesh and utterly wreck our allegiance to God. The cure of anxiety and the inspiration to rise above it is in the blessed assurance that the Father cares for us if we but trustingly serve Him with all our heart and life. This Sunday's teaching is that we are to seek God's comfort and consolation in our troubles, in persecution, and in the inner battles. In the Introit we declare that we cry unto God daily, for He is good, plenteous in mercy, and ready to forgive. The Epistle speaks of St. Paul's suffering, which was wholly due to his allegiance to God, to his service of God. The Apostle bows his knees before the Father, whose children we are, whose name we bear. The Gradual brings a vision of our Lord's Second Coming, when the Church, now persecuted, is built anew, clothed like a bride, and the Savior is seen in glorious majesty. Then the full, jubilant Easter joy will reign, and the Church will sing the new song of salvation, the Alleluia. The holy Gospel leads us to consider the agonies of the human heart caused by sorrow, separation, loss, which may cause doubts and rebellion, weariness and loss of faith. The lesson of the day may be summarized: Patience in Tribulation.

The Introit. "Be merciful unto me, O Lord, for I cry unto Thee daily. For Thou, Lord, art good and ready to forgive and plenteous in mercy unto all them that call upon Thee. Bow down Thine ear, O Lord, hear me, for I am poor and needy."

The Revised Version has: "To Thee I cry all the day." We cry in every need, at every hour. "I am poor and needy." We think of the suffering and persecutions and sorrows of life, of St. Paul, and the widow of Nain.

The Collect. "Lord, we pray Thee that Thy grace may always go before and follow after us and make us continually to be given to all good works."

The soul is poor and needy. Great grace is required to prepare our walk by the Spirit, as the star went before the Magi, and to accompany us on our way through life. Only by and through this grace shall we be able to do good works.

The Epistle, Ephesians 3:13-21. The Apostle pours out his heart in a tender prayer for his beloved Ephesians. We are reminded of last Sunday's Epistle, in which he spoke of bearing one another's burdens. "What I am suffering for you." He seems to be at a loss for words adequately to express God's love and grace. He prays that the Ephesians may have power "to know the love of Christ, which surpasses knowledge, that you may be filled with all the fullness of God."

The Gradual. "The heathen shall fear the name of the Lord, and all the kings of the earth Thy glory. When the Lord shall build up Zion, He shall appear in His glory. Alleluia! Alleluia! Ye that fear the Lord, trust in the Lord! He is their Help and their Shield. Alleluia!"

Instead of Ps. 115:11 the *Roman Missal* and the *Common Service Book* have Ps. 98:1: "Oh, sing unto the Lord a new song, for He hath done marvelous things." On this Sunday the Propers are the reflections of a soul in the shadows and persecution. However, in the Gradual the sun bursts through the clouds, and we have the motif of the Second Coming which becomes more and more pronounced on the following Sundays. The Epistle closes with: "To Him be glory in the Church and in Christ Jesus." Now the Gradual presents a vision of the Second Coming, when Christ will gather all kings about Him and will be seen in His glorious majesty.

The Proper Sentence. "Alleluia! O Lord, deal with Thy servant according unto Thy mercy, and teach me Thy statutes. I am Thy servant, give me understanding, that I may know Thy testimonies. Alleluia!"

Or: "Alleluia! Blessed be the Lord God of our fathers; praise Him, and highly exalt Him forever. Alleluia!"

The Gospel, St. Luke 7:11-17. The Epistle speaks of experiences which bring suffering that is due entirely to our allegiance to God, to our being His children. The holy Gospel opens another field of suffering, the agonies of the human heart that come to all men, believers and unbelievers. It teaches us "to know the love of Christ, which surpasses knowledge." He is good, He hears our every sigh, He feels our every sorrow. When the Lord saw the widow of Nain, He had compassion on her and said to her: "Do not weep." To the dead man He said: "Young man, I say to you, Arise!" "And He gave him to his mother." He knows, He feels, He comforts, He helps. If we know and believe this, His grace will always go before and follow after us, as we pray in the Collect.

The Proper Preface. "Who with Thine only-begotten Son and the Holy Ghost art one God, one Lord. And in the confession of the only true God we worship the Trinity in Person and the Unity in Substance, of Majesty coequal."

OUTLINE FOR SERMON ON THE EPISTLE

The evident teaching of this Sunday is that we are to seek God's comfort and consolation in our troubles. As last Sunday was the Sunday of the anxious, today is the Sunday of the sad.

The God of Comfort

St. Paul is anxious not to discourage the Ephesians by dwelling on his many sufferings, and he bids them not to lose heart, as though the Christian life were beyond their attainment. He offers a prayer, not that they may escape troubles but rise above them into the peace of God. He teaches us that God is our very present Help in trouble and that He is a Trinity of Comfort.

A. The Love of the Father. St. Paul bows his knees to the Father, who is the Source of all comfort, by His very name of Father, by the tenderness of His love, by the constancy of His care, by the certainty of His guidance home. God is a Father, or, more accurately, the Father, not because He is like earthly fathers. Rather, earthly fathers are so named because of their likeness to Him. He is the Fount of fatherhood, and "every family" of men or angels is a type and far-off resemblance of that great family whose Father is God. It was well said, "No father was ever so fatherly."

B. The Fellowship of the Spirit. This is the second help in trouble to be sought also from the Father, who gives the Holy Spirit to them who ask Him. Here is the remedy for the faintness of the Ephesians and ours, "to be strengthened with might through His Spirit in the inner man," and that not in a niggardly way but according to the riches of infinite power and infinite love. Enabled by such grace, we shall find the yoke easy and the burden light.

C. The Grace of Our Lord Jesus Christ. As we are to seek the Spirit from the Father, so are we to gain the indwelling presence of Christ through the Spirit. Through this alone can we realize our position in the temple of grace, the breadth of its liberty, the depth of its security, the length of its continuance, and the height of its glory. Only through Christ's personal presence can we realize the love that surpasses realization. Our earthly position, with all its mental and spiritual difficulties, its many sorrows and its awful outlook into the critical future, has much need of comfort; but in God we have a holy mystery of comfort. The Savior is one Comforter, the Spirit is another Comforter, and both proceed from the Father (John 14:16, 17), who is Himself the Source of all comfort. Only as we realize this can we rise to St. Paul's doxology of adoration to Him whose grace is not limited by human prayers or conceptions and whose power can enable our human weakness.

OUTLINE FOR SERMON ON THE HOLY GOSPEL

Christ came to reveal all the attributes of God, and especially those attributes of tenderness which might have seemed inconsistent with the glory of Godhead. The miracle of comfort recorded in the holy Gospel is a touching instance of Christ's continual pity, from which His Church may gain patience in tribulation.

The Compassion of Christ

A. Christ Knows Our Sorrows. It was not by chance that our Lord "went to a city called Nain" and so timed His visit as to meet the funeral procession. He arranges both His path and ours, and arranges them so that they meet. He is never too soon or too late. He knows not only when our troubles come but how heavy they are, and He is at hand to make the burden light. There is no such thing as accident, all is arrangement.

B. Christ Feels Our Sorrows. The Lord sees. That is good. He has compassion. That is better. But best of all is that we can hear His comfortable words "Do not weep." He has a heart to love, to sympathize, and to beat with ours. Learn to believe in the heart of the Lord Jesus, and if you have not met Him, seek Him, for "he who seeks finds." Never was a greater sorrow, never a kinder Comforter. His pity is continual. His compassion fails not.

C. Christ Removes Our Sorrows. How different was Christ's "Do not weep" from that of human comforters! When He commands, He sends forth power with the command enabling us to obey. This miracle gives special comfort for mourners, for the dead are not beyond hearing Christ's voice. Three times He spoke, once to the newly dead, "Child, arise"; once to the young man borne to burial, "Young man, I say to you, arise"; once to the actually buried, "Lazarus, come out." It matters not how long death has held us, nor what our age at death, for all will hear His voice. His call will be a call not only into His presence, but into the presence and recognition of one another, and He will deliver all the separated to their beloved. He will restore the dead to the living and the living to the dead, and will wipe away all tears in the final consummation of pity. Christ's sympathy, as taught in the Epistle, is far more abundant than all we ask or think, and the power at work within us will give life to our mortal bodies through His Spirit, who dwells in us (Rom. 8:11).

THE SEVENTEENTH SUNDAY AFTER TRINITY

The first half of the Trinity Season brought before us the fundamental motives of the Christian life and the grace needed for its realization. The second half presents in detail the various aspects of the Christian character. It teaches first those passive graces that form the only solid foundation for future activity and usefulness. The Church's teaching is most obviously parallel with the Beatitudes and in harmony with the Sermon on the Mount. First she insists on love as the great essential of "true and laudable service." Next she brings before us the silent graces of purity on the Fourteenth Sunday, singleness of heart on the Fifteenth, patience in tribulation on the Sixteenth, and humility on the present Sunday. The insistence on humility is a very marked feature. Many of the Collects emphasize this Christian virtue. It is the theme of Sexagesima, Palm Sunday, and the Eleventh Sunday after Trinity. This last treats of humility towards God as seen in St. Paul's character and in the Publican's prayer. Today we are to learn the still harder lesson of humility in our dealings with men. Poverty of spirit toward God is needed for the Kingdom of Heaven. Meekness alone can inherit the earth. Notice that both Gospels, this day's and that for Trinity XI, end with the same words: "Everyone who exalts himself will be humbled, and (but) he who humbles himself will be exalted."

The Introit. "Righteous art Thou, O Lord, and upright are Thy judgments. Deal with Thy servant according to Thy mercy. Blessed are the undefiled in the way, who walk in the Law of the Lord."

The words "way" and "walk" suggest that the Christian life is a journey, a pilgrimage of exiles through a strange land toward home. All visitations are right and upright, for God is righteous. For this reason we pray that the Lord deal with His servant according to His steadfast love, His mercy. Our concern is that we walk blamelessly in the Law of the Lord to the end.

The Collect. "Lord, we beseech Thee, grant Thy people grace to withstand the temptations of the devil and with pure hearts and minds to follow Thee, the only God."

An allusion to the life of the Christian as a journey is again brought in the word "follow." We pray that God would give us grace to withstand the temptations of the devil as we walk through this earthly life. The *Missal* translates, "To avoid every contact with the devil." We ask for the equipment of grace that will enable us to conquer all temptations of our great enemy and for such devotion to God as Christ demands when He bids us to love God with all our heart, soul, and mind. The "only," the undivided God demands an undivided service in faith, purpose, and life.

The Epistle, Ephesians 4:1-6. Humility, lowliness, and meekness is demanded not only by the calling to which we have been called but also by the unity of Christ's mystical body. He who has called us to follow Him said: "I am meek [gentle] and lowly in heart." We must follow His example. We are members of His body. The individual and his aims must be merged entirely with his fellow believers, sacrificing and dedicating self for the common love and peace. The Apostle gives seven bases of and for this unity. One body, one Spirit, one hope, one Lord, one faith, one Baptism, one God and Father of us all.

The Gradual. "Blessed is the nation whose God is the Lord, and the people whom He hath chosen for His own inheritance. By the word of the Lord were the heavens made, and all the host of them by the breath of His mouth. Alleluia! Alleluia! The right hand of the Lord is exalted, the right hand of the Lord doeth valiantly. Alleluia!"

The *Common Service Book* has Ps. 116:1 instead of Ps. 118: 15, 16 as the final verse. The Gradual may be closely related to the Epistle, for if we reflect the Lord Jesus and the unity of Christ's body in our lives, we shall be a blessed nation, chosen by God for His inheritance. Especially uplifting is the concluding note of Easter victory. The entire verse of Psalm 118 reads: "Hark, glad songs of victory in the tents of the righteous: 'The right hand of the Lord does valiantly!'" The following verses sing: "I shall not die, but I shall live and recount the deeds of the Lord. The Lord has chastened me sorely, but He has not given me over to death." The last words echo the thoughts of the Introit.

The Proper Sentence. "Alleluia! O Lord, deal with Thy servant according unto Thy mercy, and teach me Thy statutes. I am Thy servant, give me understanding, that I may know Thy testimonies. Alleluia!"

Or: "Alleluia! Blessed be the Lord God of our fathers; praise Him and highly exalt Him forever. Alleluia!"

The Gospel, St. Luke 14:1-11. We have here a lesson against pride. The attitude of the lawyers and Pharisees to our Lord and the man with the dropsy reveals an utter lack of fellow feeling, of sympathy, patience. It reveals nothing but envy, jealousy, and enmity. After healing the sick man, our Lord told the parable of humility, teaching the proud, conceited, contemptuous, who chose the places of honor, the law of humility. Their relationship with others was purely individualistic.

The Proper Preface. "Who with Thine only-begotten Son and the Holy Ghost art one God, one Lord. And in the confession of the only true God we worship the Trinity in Person and the Unity in Substance, of Majesty coequal."

OUTLINE FOR SERMON ON THE EPISTLE

The Epistle teaches that humility is a great Christian duty and enforces this by two cogent reasons.

The Necessity of Humility

A. Our Vocation as Christians Demands It. Our highest duty is to "lead a life worthy of the calling to which you have been called," and this high calling must keep us humble. We can be worthy of the grace of God as seen in our baptismal standing. God took us as we were, and we cannot be otherwise than humble. Lowly in himself, the Christian will be meek toward others. He will show patience and forbearance when the offense seems against himself. Any pride or harshness is absolutely unchristian.

B. The Unity of the Church Demands It. The unity of the Church is a fact. St. Paul does not say that there ought to be one body but that there is one body. To cut that body asunder is not to make two bodies any more than the sword of Solomon could make two children out of one. But the unity of the Church can be realized only in the bond of peace, just as the unity of husband and wife or the unity of a family can be realized only by forbearance and mutual love. The unity is there, but it must be felt. Individual aims and opinions must be willingly sacrificed. The things that unite must be preferred to the things that separate. St. Paul gives seven claims of unity: one body, one Spirit, one hope, one Lord, one faith, one Baptism, one God and Father, above all in His dignity, through all by His providence, in all by His grace. These great unities, once realized, will make easy any degree of needful mutual subordination in the interest of unity, for whatever testifies to the one must be an argument for the other. As we are all members of one mystical body and have one divine Spirit in us; as we all have one hope of our common home, one Lord and Master, whom we serve, one saving truth on which to feed and live; as we all had the same baptismal water poured on us, and the same cross impressed upon our brows; as we all are children of one Father, who is watching over us all, ever mingling with us all, and in us all by His Spirit, we must of necessity cultivate every grace of humility toward those who are so united with us in God.

OUTLINE FOR SERMON ON THE HOLY GOSPEL

The part of the holy Gospel which is most nearly connected with this Sunday's subject of humility is towards the close, but it was the behavior of the Pharisees in the earlier portion that gave rise to our Lord's teaching on humility.

Humility as the Command of Christ

A. An Example and a Warning. Christ would not refuse the invitation of a Pharisee, even if it were given with hostile intent. He answered objections by an appeal to conscience rather than by denunciation, with all meekness and forbearance. In the Pharisee we see the unreasonableness of pride, how it is ready to condemn, slow to receive correction and to acknowledge error. All bigotry is rooted and grounded in pride, and is in danger of the unpardonable sin, for it refuses to repent and is therefore incapable of forgiveness.

B. A Parable of Humility. The aim of this parable, or illustration, is to show that pride defeats its own ends. He who claims the place of honor will always find it claimed by others, and probably with greater justice. Pride is doomed to fall, if only because it must encounter the pride of others. It is hard to believe that the lowest place is nearest the front, but it is a fact of experience.

C. The Law of Humility. Our Lord shows humility to be not only our wisdom but also our duty, for it is His law that everyone who exalts himself will be humbled. These words are not to be understood to forbid: (1) The desire of approval. We do ill indeed if we merit contempt; rather, by our attainments, the management of our affairs, our soundness of judgment, our weight of character and depth of principle, we should seek to hold anything but a low place in the estimate of men who know how to estimate, and in God's estimate. (2) The claims of self-respect. There is a certain conscious dignity not inconsistent with humility. There is no man who does not owe something to himself, and Christianity calls upon no one to cease to be a man. But this being granted, humility must be seen in the whole spirit and feeling of our natures. It must be based on the sense of our unworthiness before God, on our knowledge of ourselves, on the comparison of ourselves with others, of whom many surpass us in everything and all in something, on the fact that such lowliness is the invariable characteristic of true worth, and that by it alone can we render ourselves endurable to persons whose regard and confidence are worth the having. We must also remember that we can only rise by humility and only sink by pride, for humility, comparing itself only with that which is above itself, must tend to rise, while pride, comparing itself with what is mean and low, is too satisfied to see the need of improvement. This is our Lord's justification of the virtue which men call a vice but which is rather that which makes all virtue possible.

SAINT MATTHEW, APOSTLE AND EVANGELIST

September 21

This is another feast of Eastern origin. Little is known of St. Matthew apart from his Gospel. He is the same as Levi the Publican, the son of a certain Alphaeus. St. Mark and St. Luke relate his call to be an Apostle and speak of him as Levi. In his own account, the appointed Gospel for this day, the author speaks of himself as Matthew. St. Luke tells us that he made a great feast in his house before he left to follow the Lord and invited a large company of his own calling to meet the Great Prophet and to hear His words. In giving the names of the Twelve in Chapter 10 of his Gospel he does not omit his title "Matthew the tax collector." The publicans were regarded as traitors and apostates, defiled by their frequent association with the heathen. In Galilee they consisted probably of the least reputable portion of the fishermen and peasant class. They were classed with sinners, harlots, and heathen. In all likelihood our Lord was not a complete stranger to St. Matthew when He called him, as he had learned to know Him as a disciple of the Baptist. It is said that, like the other Apostles, St. Matthew went to foreign countries. Legend speaks of Persia and Asiatic Ethiopia. Heracleon in the second century, Clement, Origen, Tertullian, and other trustworthy authorities say that he died a natural death. The story of his martyrdom originated much later.

The Introit. "The Lord God said unto me: Write all the words that I have spoken unto thee into a book for a memorial. His name shall endure forever, His name shall be continued as long as the sun."

The Collect. "O almighty God, who by Thy blessed Son didst call Saint Matthew from the receipt of custom to be an Apostle and Evangelist, grant us grace to forsake all covetous desires and inordinate love of riches and to follow the same, Jesus Christ, Thy Son, our Lord."

The Epistle, Ephesians 4:7-14. This lesson is the same as the Epistle appointed for Saint Mark the Evangelist's Day but for the elimination of verses 15 and 16. It is also the continuation of the Epistle for the Seventeenth Sunday after Trinity, which ends with a description of the Una Sancta. The Christians are one body, but this body is not yet fully grown, the building of the Church is not yet completed. That this may be accomplished, Christ, the Head, gives His body, His mystical body, gifts and offices and competent members to administer these offices. St. Paul names the foremost gifts: apostles, prophets, evangelists, pastors, and teachers. The eighth verse presents a difficulty for which almost countless solutions have been offered. "Therefore it is [God] said, When He ascended on high, He led a host of captives, and He gave gifts to men." This is a quotation from Ps. 68:18. But the Psalm says: "Thou didst ascend the high mount, leading captives in Thy train and receiving gifts among men." St. Paul writes that Christ gave gifts, the Psalm says that He received gifts, took gifts. It will not do to dismiss the difficulty by saying that the Apostle misquoted or adapted, for divine inspiration is involved. Nor can it be said that Christ's taking from His conquered enemies was followed by His giving, that He took gifts and then gave them to His Church. It seems that the best solution is to limit the quotation to "When He ascended on high, He led a host of captives" and to regard "and He gave gifts to men" as an addition by St. Paul. Grace was given to each of us according to the measure of Christ's gift. Therefore, to make this possible, Christ, as God said in the Psalm, ascended on high and led a host of captives. Note that the words in parentheses (vv. 9, 10) refer only to the ascension on high and the descent into parts deeper than the surface of the earth.

The Gradual. "How beautiful are the good tidings of him that publisheth peace, that saith unto Zion, Thy God reigneth! The Lord hath made bare His holy arm in the eyes of all nations, and all the ends of the earth shall see the salvation of our God. Alleluia! Alleluia! The Word of the Lord endureth forever. This is the Word which by the Gospel is preached unto you. Alleluia!"

The Gospel, St. Matthew 9:9-13.

The Proper Preface. "Because Thou didst mightily govern and protect Thy holy Church, which the blessed Apostles and Evangelists instructed in Thy divine and saving truth."

THOUGHTS FOR SERMON ON THE EPISTLE

From a sermon by Joseph A. Seiss

1. The Wonderful Savior. — On this day we commemorate St. Matthew the Apostle and Evangelist, whom the Head of the Church gave for the equipment of the saints, for building up the body of Christ. We observe days of commemoration not to glorify the individual saint but to thank and praise Christ for giving His Church great men, to glorify the Savior. There have been many great men in the history of God's people. In ancient times there were Adam, Seth, Enoch, Noah, Abraham, Moses, Joshua, Samuel, David. Some were also distinguished saviors, types of the greater Savior to come. But there was none to rank with the Second Adam, the Son of David, who rebuilt David's throne and was in truth David's Lord. An overruling Providence endowed and placed also other men so that they impressed the world, turned the course of history, imparted a new spirit to humanity. We think of St. Paul, that marvelous man. He was stripped of his early prestige, of friends, and of earthly possessions. He was forced into battle with universal superstition, threatened with perils at every turn. Yet he pressed his way over mountains of difficulty and through seas of suffering, until he gave nations and continents a new commonwealth and King. We think of Luther, the miner's son, the teacher in a newly founded university, his only title that of a doctor of the Church, without power or authority except in the convictions and qualities of his own soul, and with no other implements than his Bible, tongue, and pen. Yet he aroused the Old World to a new consciousness and led a movement by which the ages were divided and human history took a new departure.

But all these men owed all to Christ and cannot be thought of in comparison with Him. There is no one to stand beside Him. He is forever alone among men in uniqueness, in the greatness of His power, character, and achievements. He is in a class by Himself and to Himself, unapproached and unapproachable in His transcendent superiority. He has proved Himself the most powerful personality in the world's history, the center of the mightiest and divinest forces that ever penetrated the spirit or ruled the thinking and activities of man, the potential source of the grandest moral and beneficent influences that ever affected the condition and career of our race.

Think of the glory He had with the Father before the world was and of the depth of His voluntary condescension to be born into our world as a man, to endure the toil, persecution, and poverty that marked His earthly life, to die the deepest death that mortal ever died, and to go down even into the hell of God-forsakenness, that He might conquer man's enemies and procure for sinful men deliverance from sin, death, and the devil. Think of the victory He has achieved, of the foes of our peace He has chained to His triumphal chariot, of the grandeur of His resurrection and ascension, of the sublime heights to which He has been raised, of the invincible dominion assigned Him over all created things, and how it is ordained for every knee to bow and every tongue to confess that He is Lord to the glory of God the Father. When we think of all this and learn to take in the wonderfulness of the facts, we cannot but feel that here is a history without a parallel in the universe and a Being before whom we may well bow down in deepest reverence and sing as we do in the Te Deum Laudamus: "Thou art the King of Glory, O Christ! Thou art the everlasting Son of the Father!"

2. His Wonderful Purpose. — This was nothing less than the unification of mankind in one common brotherhood of life and salvation. When He came, there was no common bond of union among men. The populations of the earth were widely separated and estranged by endless differences of race, nationality, interest, and civilization. Though sometimes forced together by grasping despotic power, their alienations, antagonisms, and hatreds of one another could not be overcome. Each nationality and almost every city had its own gods, its own religion, and its own cherished worship as against all others. The professed teachers of mankind were in hopeless conflict, each claiming to have the only truth, while there existed no common tribunal of appeal. The world was

a babel of notions, beliefs, and unbeliefs, and all attempts to reach any settled truth had proved so futile that many only sneered at talk about it and contemptuously asked, "What is truth?" Even those who thought it of sufficient worth to merit their attention were like children, turned hither and thither by every new breeze of doctrine or conceit as a ship without a rudder is driven by the veering winds.

But when Christ came as the embodied truth of God and set Himself to work among men, it was to lay a sure foundation for all humanity to rest on and to create a common center of unity for the whole race. "One Lord, one faith, one Baptism, one God and Father of us all, who is above all and through all and in all," were the principles He enunciated for the acceptance of all the children of men and which, in all reason and conscience, should command every heart. By the acceptance of these immutable truths He meant to create a bond of common interest, fellowship, and hope between Jew and Greek, bond and free, male and female, uniting all nationalities, races, and classes in one grand commonwealth with one Head and one Spirit.

Never before was anything of the kind heard of or propounded. It looked to the formation of a state far more sublime and commanding than Plato ever imagined or Solon ever dreamed. It contemplated more splendid conquests than ever dawned upon the soul of Xerxes, Alexander, or Caesar. It started out for the building of a city transcendentally nobler in ideal and incomparably grander than Babylon, Jerusalem, Athens, or Rome. It meant the casting out of all heathen gods from their heavens and the establishment of a new universal worship for a new universal humanity.

To the eye of man there perhaps never was an undertaking so unlikely to succeed. Even after one century, Celsus pronounced it absurd to think that such a cause could possibly amount to anything of consequence. Yet it has succeeded, and is succeeding, beyond any cause on earth. It has shown a greater power to influence and command the human soul, to submerge the barriers of separation between men, and to unite the most diverse peoples, kindreds, tribes, and tongues, than anything else that has ever found place on earth.

The whole world has not been brought into this vast and wonderful corporation as yet. Nor have all who take the name of Christendom come to thorough agreement and accord. But there has been a growing approximation toward the sublime ideal, and everything in the Word and arrangements of our Lord looks onward to a consummation when all the inhabitants of the earth will "attain to the unity of faith and of the knowledge of the Son of God" and when the body corporate of His redeemed will have attained "to mature manhood and to the measure of the stature of the fullness of Christ." A perfect consummation will never be reached in the present order of things. The human heart is so perverse, the minds of men so full of darkness, the pride of opinion so strong, the devil so active with his subtle deceivings, and the Christianity of many who profess it so defective and unsound, that the complete realization will come only at the restoration of all things on the Day of Judgment. But the ultimate result is as certain as the triumph and heavenly enthronement of our Lord. It was in His purpose when He undertook the world's redemption, and He has the power to carry it into effect.

3. The Gifts Vouchsafed to This End. — There was to be a body formed and an ever-growing spiritual temple built, the materials for which needed to be gathered, fitted for their places, and joined together in the mystic structure. Sinners had to be transformed into saints and disciplined for their spheres. Truth had to be voiced, and arrangements instituted for its maintenance, dissemination, and conveyance to the attention, hearts, and minds of those who were to be influenced by it. Organization and distribution of labor had to be established, and a variety of agencies and offices brought into activity, in order that the building which was to personate Christ and embody His living presence and saving power might go on. For all this our Lord provided when He ascended up on high, giving unto everyone a certain measure of grace and furnishing to His Church such offices and officers as might serve it.

Christ's greatest gift, next to Himself, was the gift of Apostles. These were the men whom He Himself had selected, trained, ordained, endowed with power from on high, and sent forth into the world as witnesses for Him, heralds of His Gospel, planters and organizers of His Church, and the princes of His Kingdom. They were kept with Him for years that they might hear His teachings, see His miracles, and know the manner of His life, so as to be able to testify to the facts of His history. To these He gave His special instruction and committed the establishment of His cause, having bestowed upon them the illumination and energizing power of the Holy Spirit. Their office was to extend and preside over His household, to set in order its affairs according to His Word and the inspiration of His Spirit. They were the Church's supreme officers and teachers under Christ, and their Word was to be the rule and law of faith and life then and for all succeeding ages. Others might teach the truth and effectually witness for Christ, but never otherwise than the Apostles taught and testified. Other important officers and servants of the Church were necessary even while the Apostles lived, and especially after they were gone, but they could not be and act for Christ in any matter in conflict with apostolic teachings and directions. There can never be, by divine right, any agency, doctrine, office, or membership in the Church except as it is "built upon the foundation of the apostles and prophets, Christ Jesus Himself being the chief cornerstone" (Eph. 2:20). The office is perpetual but not transmissible from man to man. The Apostles Christ made are and remain the only officers of their class in all time. The Church is still obligated to defer to them and obey them now as when they were living. Next to Himself they are the first and highest gift of the ascended Lord to His Church on earth. Other offices, agencies, and instrumentalities have been given, but all in subordination to the Apostles.

Another gift are prophets. Not the prophets of the Old Testament are meant, but believers who were occasionally moved by the Holy Spirit to give notice of coming events or to deliver some special indications from God. "One of them [prophets] named Agabus stood up and foretold by the Spirit that there would be great famine over all the world; and this took place in the days of Claudius" (Acts 11:28).

Evangelists are another gift. They preached the Gospel as missionaries, spread the apostolic word where the Apostles did not come. Their office may be compared with the ministry of

missionaries today. Philip in Caesarea was such an evangelist
(Acts 21:8). Others were Mark, Luke, Stephen, Timothy, and
Titus, all of whom were associated with the Apostles and served
as their messengers and commissioners.

"Pastors and teachers" also are a gift. The regular ministry
of the Word is meant. "Teachers" refers particularly to the public
teaching of preachers; "pastors, or shepherds" to the care of individual souls, the application of the Word to individual members.
They are appointed and ordained to preside over the local assemblies of believers. They were to live with their flocks and to go
in and out before them as instructors and leaders, to feed them
with sound doctrine, to teach and baptize and administer the Lord's
Supper, to admonish and exhort to fidelity in faith and duty, and
to see that proper discipline was exercised upon those who walked
disorderly. Such pastors and teachers all local congregations were
to have and maintain, so that "the whole body, joined and knit
together by every joint with which it is supplied, when each part
is working properly, makes bodily growth and upbuilds itself
in love."

These gifts are very wonderful, both as to their simplicity
and their efficiency, and amazing results have been achieved
through them. The cause of the crucified and hated Nazarene
prospered and grew. It required only a few centuries until the
whole Roman Empire and the whole world was moved and thrilled
by its story. By that same power, against all hindrances from
without and many terrible defections from within, it has since
lived through all revolutions of empire, survived many generations,
and today holds the most living and most potent sway among the
nations. Our Lord said from the beginning that the gates of hell
should never prevail against His Church. So it has been through
the centuries, and so it will be to the last, for His gifts to His
Church cannot fail in their purpose.

4. Our Duty Regarding These Things. So sublime a Savior
ought to command our confidence and most reverent regard.
Having learned to know of Him, we should accept Him as our
Savior and confide in Him to bring us to His glory. There could
be no more burning shame or guiltier ingratitude than to treat

Him and His work and purpose with unconcern or to turn away from the Son of God as if He deserved nothing from us.

Such grand and beneficent aims and purposes ought likewise to command our holiest sympathy and devoutest co-operation. What greater or more blessed good fortune can a soul have than to be built into Christ as a member and part of His body and His Kingdom? What cause under the sun is of more importance and value to all the personal, social, and political interests of man than the cause of Christ and His Church? On what has the best and widest-reaching good of the world most depended, on what does it most hang at this hour, and on what does it most rest for all years to come, but on this selfsame cause of evangelic light, faith, hope, and love, of which the Church is the conservatory and stay? If it is at all in man to consider the welfare of his fellow man, the preservation of society, the maintenance of righteous law and order, the good of his family, his country, and the world, to say nothing of his own soul, what should be to him a greater privilege or higher joy than to employ all his means, powers, prayers, and influence to sustain and advance the Christian religion and Church, freighted as it is with the salvation of the world? For this very purpose we have our gifts. We are here that we may co-operate with Christ and His people for the world's peace and salvation, and we are recreant to all the highest interests of humanity and our own souls if we do not set ourselves to it as the chief work of our lives.

With all the merciful favors given us in and through the Gospel, it becomes us to anchor firmly on its teachings and to be no longer children like the heathen, "tossed to and fro and carried about with every wind of doctrine, by the cunning of men, by their craftiness in deceitful wiles." "See to it that no one makes a prey of you by philosophy and empty deceit" (Col. 2:8). "Follow the pattern of the sound words which you have heard from me," writes the Apostle Paul (2 Tim. 1:13). "Let us hold fast the confession of our hope without wavering" (Heb. 10:23). "Therefore, my beloved brethren, be steadfast, immovable, always abounding in the work of the Lord, knowing that in the Lord your labor is not in vain" (1 Cor. 15:58).

SERMON ON THE HOLY GOSPEL

On this day the Christian Church observes the Feast of Saint Matthew the Apostle and Evangelist. It is altogether fitting that we should set aside days for the remembering of the great heroes of faith. In secular history there are altogether too many names we remember because of the evil done by these men. We do well to preserve the memory of good lives, especially of those which glorified the name of Jesus Christ. The Church commemorates great men of faith in order to set their lives before the faithful that they might imitate and follow them. The fact that they held firmly to the Christian faith amid trials and persecutions is to give us encouragement. We are to trust in the same Lord and Savior as they. He gave them strength and courage, and He stands ready to supply all our needs. The holy Gospel appointed for this day tells us how Saint Matthew became an Apostle. We consider then:

Saint Matthew's Call into the Lord's Service

The text brings three scenes before us:

I. *The Call of the Master*
II. *The Feast of the Sinners*
III. *The Criticism of the Pharisees*

I

"As Jesus passed on from there, He saw a man called Matthew sitting at the tax office; and He said to him, 'Follow Me.' And he rose and followed Him." Our Lord had just healed a paralytic to prove that He had authority to forgive sins. As He passed on from there, He saw a man called Matthew sitting at the tax office. This man was a Galilean, and his occupation was that of tax or customs collector at Capernaum, in the territory of Herod Antipas. Tax collectors were roundly hated by their fellow Jews. That a Jew should work for the hated Romans and help to collect their unjust taxes made him a traitor in the eyes of his own people. The Roman system offered many opportunities for thievery and dishonesty, and it was taken for granted that all collectors were grafters, and they were despised and classified with public sinners.

No self-respecting person would have any contact with them. They were social lepers and outcasts. We are not told that Matthew was dishonest like the chief tax collector Zacchaeus of Jericho, who confessed to our Lord that he had defrauded. But very likely Matthew also was unable to resist the temptations of his profession, associations, and environment. Whether honest or dishonest, the mere fact that he was a publican was enough to include him in the classification of traitor and sinner.

We need not suppose that the meeting at the tax booth at Capernaum was the first time that Matthew had seen and heard our Lord. His conversion was not the result of some sudden, miraculous summons he could not resist. Christ never compels anyone to follow Him. Although He has all power, He will not use it to force acceptance of Him. He calls, He lets us know that He wants us and loves us, but the decision is ours to make. The choice must be voluntary on our part. Matthew, no doubt, had heard of our Lord long before. He had perhaps seen the mighty works He did, and had been moved by the mightier words He spoke, and the whole soul of the man had gone out after this Man and the higher life He offered. Matthew had come to loathe the life he lived, to hate the tricks of his trade. He had caught sight of a higher and nobler life, and that vision had created in him disgust with himself. Had he heard that our Lord had brought forgiveness to the paralytic? Perhaps, on his way to work that morning, he uttered the prayer: "O God, take me out of this! Open up some way that I may be rid of this sinful life."

If he hesitated to make the break, it was for reasons we can well understand. Consider what he had to give up. He had to give up his business and livelihood. Probably he had a wife and children. What was to become of them if he gave up his livelihood? Who would employ a former publican?

As Matthew sat there at the tax office, our Lord passed. "He saw a man called Matthew." When our Lord sees a man, this means something more than when you or I see anyone. We see only the outside, the face, the clothes, the expression, and we judge a man from what we see. But when Jesus sees a man, He sees infinitely more. He sees down into the very heart. He saw the tax collector. His eyes pierced right down into the man's struggling soul, and He said: "Follow Me. I have come to save you from it all. Follow Me, and I will make you, publican that you are, despised as you are, I will make you right with God, the man God wants you to be."

This was the turning point in Matthew's life. His whole soul rose up at that appeal. "It is now or never," he said, and immediately he rose and followed Him, rose from the publican's desk, went forth and left it all. "He rose and followed Him." There is no better way of putting what conversion means. To follow Christ means to lay aside the old life and to go with Him into the new life in God. Conversion is simply doing what Matthew did, leaving all to follow Christ. He steadfastly followed Him from that day and accompanied the Savior up to the time of the Crucifixion. He was one of the witnesses of the Resurrection, and among the chosen ones who were present at the Ascension and who afterwards retired to the Upper Room in Jerusalem, where they all with one accord prayed and waited for the outpouring of the Holy Spirit.

II

We pass on to the second scene in the holy Gospel, the feast of the sinners. The severity of the struggle in Matthew's mind before he broke away from his sordid old life may be measured by the joy that filled it when once he did. His joy at finding Christ he demonstrated by making a great feast. Any glad event is usually signalized in this fashion. Like the father of the lost son, we say: "Rejoice with me, for great happiness has come into my life, and I want to share it." So it was with Matthew. This was the wedding feast of his spiritual life. The breaking with the sordid past and the pledging of faithfulness to the new life was the marriage of his soul.

But a difficulty arose at this point. Whom will he invite to the feast? Whom will he ask to come in honor of the Savior? His old friends? But these were sinners as bad as he. Would the Lord care to dine with sinners? He felt instinctively that his old associates were not worthy to sit at the same table. Yet he felt he would like to have them there. It would be a splendid opportunity for bringing them and Christ together. Who could tell what might happen if they saw Jesus as he himself saw Him? More than that, it would be an act of confession before the world, a testimony to the very class among whom his past life had been lived. It would be a confession of a publican to publicans, like a soldier confessing Christ in the barracks, a workman in the factory, a merchant in the office, a sailor on the ship. It was Matthew's way of saying: "Old friends and companions, I have resolved to give up my old life and follow Christ. If you will come with me, it will be good for you. This is the gladdest day of my life. But if you will not follow Him, we must now say farewell."

So our Lord was invited to the feast of sinners. It was not in Him to refuse an invitation like that. "Will I come?" we hear Him say. "Why, of course I will come. Bring every sinner in the city to meet Me, if you like. I love to be where sinners are." So He came. It was a daring thing to do. It was not like inviting thieves and harlots to a Christmas dinner in some rented hall. It was like making these people your friends, sitting down with them as your equals. "Many tax collectors and sinners came and sat down with Jesus and His disciples."

III

Finally, we look at the third scene, the criticism of the Pharisees. They saw this and said to His disciples: "Why does your Teacher eat with tax collectors and sinners?" He is gone to be guest with a man that is a sinner. Even worse, He is dining with publicans and sinners. Knowing them, we well imagine that they implied: "Birds of a feather flock together." This Prophet claims to be sinless, yet He associates with this kind of people. He must feel at home with them, for He is like them. How outrageous for a rabbi, a teacher of God's law, to mingle with the scum of the town!

Our Lord's defense of His conduct on this occasion is full of pathos and beauty. There is also a touch of irony in it, showing He sized up His critics for what they were, loveless fanatics, if not hypocrites, who in spite of all their religiosity had not one spark of the love of God in their hearts. "Those who are well have no need of a physician, but those who are sick." I have come to be the Physician of sinners. Where would you expect to find a doctor but among his patients? Only among those who realize and know their need for healing could He perform His wonders. Among the self-righteous, who do not acknowledge their sinful condition, our Lord cannot come as a Savior from sin.

Then our Lord adds, quoting from Hos. 6:6: "Go and learn what this means, I desire mercy and not sacrifice. For I came not to call the righteous but sinners." You are great and meticulous in your external observances of religion. You keep the outward rules. But you know nothing of mercy and love, which are the first requisites of religion and without which all outward observances are not acceptable.

Have we learned anything from this day's holy Gospel? Have we heard our Lord's call to follow Him, and have we responded? Are we willing to give up the things of the old life? Have we shown any joy that we belong to Christ? Have we asked our friends and acquaintances to rejoice with us because we have found Christ? Or have we judged people from the outside? Have we hesitated to invite certain people to meet the Lord? Have we resented the presence of people who we feel are not good enough? Have we ourselves refused the ministrations of the Great Physician?

In conclusion we remind ourselves how grandly Christ compensated the publican for the sacrifices he made. When Matthew rose from his tax office that day, he well knew that he was making the sacrifice of his subsistence, of his very all. But Christ made it up to him, even from a worldly point of view. What would Matthew have been if he had remained in his countinghouse and said, "Lord, I cannot follow You now. First let me make a little more money, lay something aside for a rainy day and old age"? If he had said that, he would have remained unknown or known only like the rich young ruler who made the great refusal and went away sorrowful.

Where is Capernaum or its customhouse today? Gone forever! You cannot even trace its ruins on the deserted shore of Galilee's lake. But from the midst of its dust there rises one monument which time can never efface. It is the first Gospel of our New Testament, the Gospel written by St. Matthew, once a publican, now an Apostle and saint.

Do not think that in following Christ you are narrowing your life. Just as well might the little stream think it is narrowing its waters when it pours out into the Amazon or the Mississippi. Do not think that in accepting Christ you are entering on a gloomy service that will make of all your life a doleful dirge. Just as well might Matthew's publican friends have pitied him when he sat at his feast and smiled happily as he looked on the face of Jesus. In following Christ, Matthew received even here a hundredfold; but in the life to come — who can tell his story?

SAINT MICHAEL AND ALL ANGELS

September 29

Feasts in honor of angels developed particularly in the East. After the time of Constantine many churches were dedicated in honor of Michael, the only archangel mentioned by name in Scripture (Jude 9), although in the ordinary traditions, Jewish and Christian, Gabriel is also one of the archangels. St. Michael is called one of the chief princes, a prince, one of the great princes (Dan. 10:13, 21; 12:1). In the fifth century a small basilica six miles from Rome was dedicated in his honor on September 29. The feast which commemorates this event was eventually observed in honor of Michael as the representative of all angels and gradually spread through the West. The term "All Angels" is an Anglican addition at the time of the Reformation. Evidently this feast is largely ignored in modern Lutheran circles, with the result that the faithful are rarely taught the doctrine of the angels.

Dionysius the Areopagite arranged the angels in the following celestial hierarchy. A. Universal Providence: 1. Seraphim, 2. Cherubim, 3. Thrones. B. General Providence: 4. Dominations, 5. Virtues, 6. Powers. C. Particular Providence: 7. Principalities, 8. Archangels, 9. Angels. The first order is engaged in God's immediate Presence, in the act of constant adoration; the second in the struggle constantly going on with evil; the third in the care of creation. Each of these choirs has its appointed office. All unite in ministering to man, for every angel is a ministering spirit. A seraph was sent to Isaiah (6:6); a cherub to guard Paradise (Gen. 3:24); Michael, the Prince of the Order of Principalities, was dispatched by God to Daniel; Gabriel, who stood in the Presence of God, was sent to Zacharias and Mary. All, in their ministry to God, minister to us men. Angels have the power and guardianship over nations. In Daniel 10 we read that Michael, the

Prince of the Jewish nation, fought the prince, or king, of Persia and contended with the prince of Greece. Angels fight for us against Satan and his evil angels, as Michael fought with the dragon. They guard us in peril. The angel of God stopped the mouths of the lions when Daniel was cast into their den. St. Peter was delivered from the cruelty of Herod by an angel. Angels provide for man's necessities. An angel showed Hagar a fountain where she and her son might drink. An angel provided bread and water for Elijah under the broom tree.

The Introit. "Bless the Lord, ye His angels, that excel in strength, that do His commandments, hearkening unto the voice of His Word. Bless ye the Lord, all ye His hosts, ye ministers of His that do His pleasure. Bless the Lord, O my soul, and all that is within me, bless His holy name."

We call upon all angels to praise God and at the same time emphasize that they thereby fulfill His will. We encourage our own soul to imitate the holy angels by giving inmost praise to God and His name.

The Collect. O everlasting God, who hast ordained and constituted the services of angels and men in a wonderful order, mercifully grant that, as Thy holy angels always do Thee service in heaven, so by Thy appointment they may succor and defend us on earth."

As in the Introit, we have in mind all angels but particularly those whose special work it is to succor and defend men. This Collect is a Gregorian original, translated in 1549, slightly altered in 1662.

The Epistle, Revelation 12:7-12. The Book of Revelation is a book of angels, for no other book of the Holy Scriptures speaks as much of angels. The Epistle shows the holy angels in action to keep the divine work of salvation from having been done in vain and fighting against the hellish foe. War arose in heaven. The dragon and his angels fought against Michael and his angels. The name Michael means "Who is as God?" The holy angels, with Michael at their head, defeated and were victorious over the ancient serpent, and the devil, Satan. The deceiver was expelled from heaven and thrown down to earth with his angels. The victory was won by the blood of the Lamb and by the word of testimony. Satan must have been a powerful prince in heaven, for he made himself prince of this world. He came down to earth in great wrath because he knows that his time is short.

The Gradual. "God hath given His angels charge over thee to keep thee in all thy ways. Bless the Lord, O my soul, and all that is within me, bless His holy name. Alleluia! Alleluia! And one cried unto another and said, Holy, holy, holy, is the Lord of hosts, the whole earth is full of His glory. Alleluia!"

The *Common Service Book* adds at the beginning: "Bless the Lord, ye His angels, that excel in strength, that do His commandments, hearkening unto the voice of His Word."

The Gospel, St. Matthew 18:1-11. In the light of the liturgical texts it appears that this portion was appointed and chosen merely because of the last verse. The disciples asked: "Who is the greatest in the Kingdom of Heaven?" Our Lord answered that unless they turn and become like children, they will never enter the Kingdom of Heaven. Whoever humbles himself like this child, he is the greatest. The followers of Jesus Christ should be humble and trusting, with an abounding faith and with a simple love that is without fear. See that you do not despise one of these little ones who believe in Me, not only the little ones of tender age but also the little, the new, the weak believers, who are like children. "For I tell you that in heaven their angels always behold the face of My Father who is in heaven." Littleness is greatness.

The Common Preface.

Outline for Sermon on the Epistle

The Epistle speaks of a war that is really a world war. Every other war is only a shadow and a phase of this war of spirits. It has raged from the beginning of the world and will end only at the end of time. We may distinguish four stages.

A. The first stage or phase is enacted in heaven (vv. 7-9). It is not stated what was the original cause or reason. Probably one of the highest spirits rebelled against God. Some have applied the fall of the Assyrian king to this revolt, Is. 14:12-14. The war of the text ended with the victory of the archangel Michael. Pertinent passages are Jude 9; 2 Peter 2:4.

B. The second stage of this war is enacted on earth. The devil was permitted to retain a certain power over the earth. He now transferred the battle to the earth when he deceived Eve and, with her, Adam. Hereby evil triumphantly entered the world, and Satan became the prince of this world. Our Lord describes his power in the parable of the strong man and one stronger than he (Luke 11:21, 22). Satan extended his rule over the whole of humanity. Heathenism with its idolatry, cruelty, and sensuality became his domain. Then came the Stronger One, Christ. The battle was fought on Golgotha, and Satan was vanquished. Before His Passion, Christ distinctly declared: "Now is the judgment of this world, now shall the ruler of this world be cast out" (John 12:31). Also this second phase ended with the defeat of the devil.

C. The third phase is the warfare of the devil against the church. This war will rage until the end of time. Of this world war in the true sense of the term the Apocalypse tells us many things. The entire book is really the history of this war (Rev. 12:1-4, 17). This warfare continues with all violence throughout all ages. The devil employs men also. In his service are worldly power and intellectual strength. Toward the end the devil will increase his fury and fight with increased strength.

This third phase of the war has its counterpart in our hearts. This war must be fought in every human soul. The front runs through the center of our hearts. Here the devil, there Michael and his angels. Child of man, fight the good fight, that you may gain the crown of victory! You are not left to yourself, God is with you. You are on a battlefield, as Psalm 91 pictures it: "A thousand may fall at your side, ten thousand at your right hand." You must pass through. "For He will give His angels charge of you. . . . On their hands they will bear you up, lest you dash your foot against a stone." Your eternal happiness depends on the outcome of the battle. The devil is like a dog fettered with a chain. He bites only him who comes near him. Otherwise he is powerless.

D. The fourth stage is the final battle. It ends with the complete overthrow of the devil and his accomplices. "The devil, who had deceived them, was thrown into the lake of fire and brimstone, where the beast and the false prophet were, and they will be tormented day and night forever and ever" (Rev. 20:10). "Depart from Me, you cursed, into the eternal fire prepared for the devil and his angels" (Matt. 25:41). Also in this final battle the holy Michael will be the leader. This is the end of the great and only world war in which the opponents are God and the devil.

Sermon on the Holy Gospel

According to Johann Gerhard (with omissions)

"Beloved, we are God's children now" (1 John 3:2). By grace we now belong to the little ones, for whom our Lord expresses deep concern in the holy Gospel. "Whoever causes one of these little ones who believe in Me to sin, it would be better for him to have a great millstone fastened round his neck and to be drowned in the depth of the sea," and "See that you do not despise one of these little ones." Although it would have been a very simple matter to shield and protect His beloved children against all danger directly and immediately, it pleased His wisdom to entrust this service chiefly to the holy angels. "Are they not all ministering spirits sent forth to serve, for the sake of those who are to obtain salvation?" (Heb. 1:14.) We may rest assured that God did this to increase our faith and trust in the divine mercy, for we hear not only that "the Lord God is a sun and shield" (Ps. 84:11), but also that He sends His noble servants, His mighty heroes and princes of heaven, the holy angels, to protect and guard us. Of this we shall speak.

I. *The Angels' Attitude Toward God and Us, and*

II. *Our Attitude in Response to Their Services*

I

Our Lord says in the text: "I tell you that in heaven their angels always behold the face of My Father who is in heaven." This beholding is not the end, but it calls forth a lofty, inexpressible joy. For God is the highest good, and in Him all is good. Therefore this beholding of God must result in a great, incomprehensible joy. The nobler and higher the good is, the more it communicates its good. Since God is the highest Good, He communicates His goodness, His loveliness, His joy, to the holy angels by this beholding. That we shall someday behold God face to face in the life eternal (1 Cor. 13:12) is the highest joy we may expect, the greatest promise given us. The holy angels have even now what we still hope to have. This blissful beholding of God and this immeasurable joy was given the holy angels as a reward for remaining faithful and not turning from God. For though all angels were good in the beginning and were created after the likeness of God in true righteousness and holiness (Eph. 4:24), many of them did not keep their own position but left their proper dwelling (Jude 6) and have nothing to do with the truth (John 8:44). Therefore only the good angels attained to this great, inexpressible joy and glory, that they behold the face of God. The fallen angels were cast out and committed to pits of nether gloom to be kept until the Judgment (2 Peter 2:4) and no longer share in the inheritance of the saints in light (Col. 1:12).

Again, this beholding of God results in heartfelt praise of God. For from the full knowledge of the highest good must flow the love of it. Since it is the highest Good the angels behold, they love it in the highest degree. So in the life eternal the love of God will be full in the elect because the knowledge and the beholding will be full. Upon this love follows the praise of God, for what one loves, that one also praises. For this reason it is said that the morning stars and the sons of God shouted for joy even before man was created (Job 38:7). The prophet Isaiah saw the Lord sitting upon a throne, high and lifted up, and he heard the seraphim calling one to another, "Holy, holy, holy, is the Lord of hosts," holy is the Father, holy is the Son, holy is the Holy Spirit (Is. 6:3). Because this divine Majesty is to be feared and honored, the angels covered their faces, as is written Heb. 1:6, that all God's angels desire to worship the First-born, the Son of God.

This beholding also results in the knowledge of divine mysteries. How could it be otherwise? Beholding includes knowledge of God, of His will. Whoever knows God's will knows divine mysteries. St. Peter tells us that the angels long to look into the things that are announced in the good news (1 Peter 1:12), and

St. Paul writes that "the manifold wisdom of God might now be made known to the principalities and powers in the heavenly places . . . according to the eternal purpose which He has realized in Christ Jesus, our Lord" (Eph. 3:10, 11).

Furthermore, because the angels now behold God, they need not fear that this their joy be taken from them, just as the elect need not fear that, once having attained to this beholding, they could again depart from it. St. Paul speaks of "the elect angels" (1 Tim. 5:21). As the cursed devils can never attain to God's grace because they are kept in eternal chains (Jude 6), so the holy angels can never fall from grace into sin, but they are confirmed in their bliss. Therefore they are called "morning stars" (Job 38:7), not only because of their brightness and beauty but also because they remain unchangeable in their order as the stars in the heavens.

Finally, beholding God's face includes also that the angels stand before His throne, serve Him, and carry out His commands. The prophet Daniel sees that a thousand thousand serve Him and ten thousand times ten thousand stand before Him (Dan. 7:10). We must not think of them as ordinary, powerless servants, but they are mighty ones and hosts (Ps. 103:20, 21). They are divided into orders, for there are Seraphim, Cherubim, Thrones, Dominions, Virtues, Powers, Principalities, Archangels, Angels. What their order and the difference is He alone knows who has created and ordered them. We shall see when in the eternal life we are equal to them (Luke 20:36).

This is the angels' attitude toward God. What is their attitude toward men? This the Lord Christ reveals with one word when He calls them "their angels," that is, the angels of the little ones, the servants of the children and all believers. Here is real comfort for us, to know that the angels not only stand before God's throne and behold the face of the heavenly Father but also are sent forth to serve for the sake of those who are to obtain salvation (Heb. 1:14). They render this service to every Christian in manifold ways. While we are children, God assigns our angels to us, as Christ tells us in the holy Gospel. When we grow older and go our own way, that is, walk in the ways of our calling, God also assigns angels to us (Ps. 91:11, 12). When we sleep, the angels watch and protect us against the devil. When we die, they carry our soul to Abraham's bosom (Luke 16:22). Their protection is ours throughout life.

This protection and help extends both to body and to soul. Whatever was done by angels in the Old and New Testaments in visible, assumed form is still done daily, although we do not see it with our eyes. God has made this a matter of faith. The angels have not flesh and blood as we have, that they can be seen where they are present, but they are spirits. That they appeared in human form, as a young man, or in the form of fire, lightning, and the like, was done that in an outward image they might prove their presence to men.

We marvel that God sent an angel who commanded Hagar, when she had fled from her master Abraham, to return to him (Gen. 16:7 ff.). Yet this happens daily. When we have departed from God's service by sinning, God's angel often gives us a deepfelt good thought to repent. For if the devil can instill evil thoughts, a good angel can give us good thoughts.

We marvel that angels led Lot out of Sodom when fire from heaven was about to consume the city (Gen. 19:15-17). This happens daily. For what is the world with its lust of the eyes and flesh and pride of life but a spiritual Sodom that will someday be burned with fire? Then the holy angels will gather the elect and bring them security and rest.

We marvel that the Lord sent an angel to show Hagar a fountain in the desert when her child was dying of thirst (Gen. 21: 17-19). Yet this occurs daily. For often when we are weak and powerless in temptation of the soul, God sends His angel to comfort and strengthen us, as an angel strengthened Christ in His agony of soul (Luke 22:43).

We marvel that the angels appeared to the patriarch Jacob in the form of an army when he was on his way home (Gen. 32:1, 2). Yet the angel of the Lord daily encamps around those who fear Him (Ps. 34:7).

We marvel that a man with a drawn sword appeared to Joshua and said, "As commander of the army of the Lord I have now come" (Joshua 5:14). To this day the angels fight against the world for the spiritual army of the Christian Church, especially in these last times, when, according to Dan. 12:1, Michael, the great prince, who has charge of Daniel's army, has arisen.

We marvel that an angel came to Elijah and brought him a cake baked on hot stones and a jar of water, also awakened him and instructed him to travel to Horeb, the mount of God (1 Kings 19:5-8). This occurs daily when we are wearied and powerless and discouraged to walk the ways of God's commandments and inward thoughts of God's angels encourage us.

We wonder that Elisha's servant saw the mountain full of horses and chariots of fire which protected the city against the army of the Syrians (2 Kings 6:17). This happens daily, for to this day God is a wall of fire round about us by means of the angels' protection. (Zech. 2:5)

We marvel that God sent His angel to shut the lions' mouths to keep them from hurting Daniel (Dan. 6:22). This is a daily occurrence, for the devil truly is the roaring lion who prowls around seeking someone to devour (1 Peter 5:8). That he can do us no harm is due to the angels' protection.

We marvel that the Lord sent an angel to rescue St. Peter from prison (Acts 12:7). This happens daily. When our soul is led out of the prison of the body, God sends His angel to bring us to the heavenly Paradise.

St. John saw an angel who "stood at the altar with a golden censer; and he [the angel] was given much incense to mingle with the prayers of all the saints upon the golden altar before the throne" (Rev. 8:3). This indicates that the angel mingled his prayers with those of the saints, that the angels pray for us (Zech. 1:12). In this passage the angel of the Lord prays to God: "O Lord of hosts, how long wilt Thou have no mercy on Jerusalem and the cities of Judah?" In short, it is impossible to recount all the kindnesses God shows us through the angels, in body and soul, throughout the whole of life.

Why is it that the angels readily serve the believers though they are much nobler and higher than we? (1) Because they are confirmed in the good and therefore gladly and fully obey God's will. God's will and order is that they serve us (Heb. 1:14). The army of the heavens — sun, moon, and stars — maintain their order given them by God for man's sake. All the more will the heavenly army of holy angels maintain its order. (2) Because our nature is raised in Christ above all angels and archangels (Eph. 1:20, 21; Heb. 1:4). Therefore the angels do not refuse to serve us men, in honor of the human nature assumed by Christ. As an entire race is brought to honor by a marriage, so the marriage of the Son of God with humanity has restored the human race to honor (Matt. 22:2). What wonder, then, that the angels serve us, since the Son of God, the Lord of the angels, came to earth that He might serve us? (3) Because love is pure and perfect in them, the angels joyfully serve us, as does the Lord, who Himself is Love (1 John 4:8), in whose image the angels were created, and who declared: "I will rejoice in doing them good" (Jer. 32:41). (4) Finally, because we shall someday be with them in heaven and join their choir in praising God, the angels are happy to serve us here on earth.

II

What, then, is to be our attitude? How are we to comport ourselves? First, since they are our angels, assigned to serve us, we should recognize God's great love for us poor men, that these noblest creatures, the purest spirits, are sent to us, who are so saturated with the impurity of sin that all our righteous deeds are like a polluted garment (Is. 64:6). How wonderful that God created heaven and earth, foliage, grass, birds, fish, and all animals, for man's good! But a much greater kindness and mercy is that He sends the angels to minister to us. For this we should thank Him. But we must not worship the angels, for they are only the means and instruments by which God helps, they are like God's hands. If someone has helped you by his hand, you thank him and not the hand. When, then, God protects us by His angels, we are to thank Him alone, worship Him, and not the angels who do not desire this service (Rev. 19:10).

Furthermore, we should persevere in prayer to God that He would continue to permit His angels to be our angels. Like all gifts of God the protection of the angels is given in answer to prayer. When Cornelius prayed to God, he saw an angel in a vision who said to him: "Your prayers and your alms have ascended as a memorial before God" (Acts 10:4). Our prayer is the only effective messenger we can send to God if we wish to have the heavenly messengers with us. When the spiritual incense of prayer ascends from the altar of our heart, the angels of God join in it (Rev. 8:3, 4). The angels are sent to fight against the devil, yet we must not leave all to them but co-operate with our prayer that we enter not into temptation (Luke 22:46). The outward burning of incense does not drive the devil away. The spiritual incense of prayer must be employed if the angels are to defend us against the devil's power. In addition, we must crucify the old nature with its evil desires.

Thirdly, the Lord Jesus says in the holy Gospel for this day that we should not cause His little ones to sin, to stumble, not to place stumbling blocks in their way, for in heaven their angels always behold the face of His Father who is in heaven. If, then, we wish to have the angels with us, we must not be guilty of evil conduct that offends them. Often something is done secretly, particularly by the immoral and adulterous, in the hope that nobody will know because nobody sees or that if an important and otherwise honorable man were involved, it would be overlooked. But we learn here that the angels see all our deeds and doings; therefore we should fear to do evil in their presence and sight. At all times show your angel the respect due him. When they come before God's throne again, He will ask: "Have you considered my servant Job?" (Job 1:8.) Therefore let everyone reflect what answer the angels must give at times. If we would have them as protectors, we must be heirs of salvation through faith. It is written that the angels are indeed ministering spirits (Heb. 1:14), but the same sentence states that they are sent forth to serve for the sake of those who are to obtain salvation. They serve only such in this life as will be their companions in the life eternal. If we would have them as protectors, we must live in the fear of God. True, it is written that the angel of the Lord encamps (Ps. 34:7), but he "encamps around those who fear Him," that is, fear the Lord. If we would have the angels guard us, we must walk in the ways of our calling. For while it is written that "they will bear you up lest you dash your foot against a stone," it is also written that they are "to guard you in all your ways" (Ps. 91:12, 11). To have the angels' protection, we must truly repent, for our Lord said not only that there is joy before the angels of God over one sinner, but He added "who repents" (Luke 15:10). God's grace and the angels' protection may not be separated, for their protection is a work of divine grace. If, then, a man is not in the state of grace, he may not take comfort in the angels' protection. Where there is no repentance, there is no divine grace. When a man does not repent, there is no protection of the angels. Wherever Christ is not, the angels do not wish to be. Christ lives only in the faithful and repentant heart; therefore only such a heart may derive comfort from the angels' protection. Wherever the old nature, the sinful flesh, still rules, Christ does not dwell, and there is no guardian angel. If the angels are to come and minister to us, as they did in the wilderness after Christ's temptation (St. Matt. 4:11), we must fight valiantly against the devil with the sword of the Spirit, the divine Word, as Christ did. If we would have these heavenly spirits with us, we must have heavenly thoughts, seek the things that are above and not the things of earth. The angels are holy and pure spirits. If they are to be near us, we must "cleanse ourselves from every defilement of body and spirit and make holiness perfect in the fear of God" (2 Cor. 7:1). Our holiness and purity is not perfect, as that of the angels, since evil desires still cling to us, but the angels will not permit this to keep them from living with us and serving us if only we make Christ's perfect righteousness and holy obedience our own by faith and strive after a holy life, which is done when we pay attention to the Lord's admonition in this day's holy Gospel. If our eye, our hand, our foot, causes us to sin, we are to pluck out the eyes, cut off the hand or foot. That is, when evil desires tempt us to do evil through the eye, foot, or hand, we are to quench such evil desires and not entertain them. So we shall put to death what is earthly in us, as St. Paul admonishes us (Col. 3:5).

Finally, if we would have the holy angels with us, we must strive after true humility, of which our Lord also speaks in the holy Gospel. When the disciples asked who is the greatest in the Kingdom of Heaven, He put a child in the midst of them and said: "Unless you turn and become like children," that is, walk in God's ways in childlike humility, "you will never enter the Kingdom of Heaven." This humility is clearly illustrated in the angels. They are the noblest creatures, yet are not ashamed to serve little children too. They are perfectly pure, and among men none is wholly clean of sins, yet they are not ashamed to render service to us men. Why, then, does man elevate himself unduly? How can he comfort himself with the protection of the angels and desire their service if he will not serve others in love and humility? Pride is the devil's seed. Let all who wish the angels to live with them beware of pride, and let it not take root in their hearts. May God help us through Christ.

THE EIGHTEENTH SUNDAY AFTER TRINITY

The Church has now brought before us the chief internal graces of the Christian character, purity, singleness of heart, patience, and humility. But we are not to be satisfied with passive graces and must rise from these to the practical, active, and useful. The believer's life must be a life not only of holy emotions but of holy activities. On this and the following Sundays we are instructed in Christian duty and how it is to be done in the right spirit and to the best advantage. The present Sunday gives a summary of all Christian duty.

The Introit. "Reward them that wait for Thee, O Lord, and let Thy prophets be found faithful. Hear the prayer of Thy servants and of Thy people Israel. I was glad when they said unto me, Let us go into the house of the Lord."

The Antiphon is from the apocryphal Ecclesiasticus, whose thirty-sixth chapter contains a prayer for the Church against her enemies. The Psalm Verse is the first verse of Psalm 122. God's house today represents the heavenly Jerusalem; therefore the verse from the Song of Zion. We leave the world of strife, unrest, and persecution, and enter into the peace of the holy place. God's "servants" and "people," the new "Israel," looking forward with fervent hope to something yet to come, sing of the home of the soul, the place of communion and loving worship: "I was glad when they said to me, Let us go to the house of the Lord!" Here is the song of the Father's family on this earth, longing to be found faithful for the glories to be revealed. Give us eternal salvation, so that the prophets who pictured Thy return in such glowing colors may be found faithful.

The Collect. "O God, forasmuch as without Thee we are not able to please Thee, mercifully grant that Thy Holy Spirit may in all things direct and rule our hearts."

This very ancient little Collect must be prayed in the light of the Epistle. Conscious of our natural condition of impotence, we pray for divine mercy. We anticipate the tender assurance of the Epistle that the grace of God was given us in Christ Jesus; that in every way we were enriched by Him; that God is faithful, by whom we were called into the fellowship of His Son, Jesus Christ, our Lord. We pray that the Holy Spirit may in all things direct and rule, guide and give, tell us how and inspire us to do.

The Epistle, 1 Corinthians 1:4-9. As the Church Year nears its end, we look back and thank God for the manifold graces given us. The Epistle briefly covers the story of the family's founding, its nurturing, its maintenance, its purpose, its hope, and its goal. Here is a great commentary on the niches of Holy Baptism, through which God has opened this wondrous relationship to us. We thank for the grace of God given us in Christ Jesus, that we were enriched with all speech and all knowledge, that the testimony to Christ was confirmed among us, that we lack not in any spiritual gift. The purpose of all this is that God's family be sustained to the end, waiting for the coming of our Lord Jesus Christ, and to be found guiltless in that Day. How rich are God's children! Not a single grace is lacking. Also today God will sustain us to the end in the Holy Communion. Presupposed is that we wait for the coming of our Lord and that our chief concern is to be guiltless in the day of His return. We look backward and forward, back with thanks and peace of conscience, forward to the Great Day.

The Gradual. "I was glad when they said unto me, Let us go into the house of the Lord. Peace be within Thy walls, and prosperity within Thy palaces. Alleluia! Alleluia! Oh, praise the Lord, all ye nations! Praise Him, all ye people. Alleluia!"

Both the *Common Service Book* and *The Lutheran Hymnal* capitalize the pronoun before "walls" and "palaces." The words seem to be addressed to Jerusalem. The thought of Christ's coming prompts us to go again to the house of God, where peace and security reign. The waiting, faithful servants of the Lord, the spiritual Israel, call upon all nations and peoples to praise and extol Him.

The Proper Sentence. "Alleluia! O Lord, deal with Thy servant according unto Thy mercy, and teach me Thy statutes. I am Thy servant, give me understanding, that I may know Thy testimonies. Alleluia!"

Or: "Alleluia! Blessed be the Lord God of our fathers; praise Him and highly exalt Him forever. Alleluia!"

The Gospel, St. Matthew 22:34-46. The Great Commandment appears again, not as inspiration for practical application in the form of teaching a specific mark of the believer. We have prayed in the Collect that the Holy Spirit direct our hearts in all things. This is done when in the holy Gospel our Lord answers the question: "Which is the great commandment in the Law?" It is the great commandment of love to God and love to our fellow man. In answer to our prayer that the Holy Spirit in all things rule, the Church directs our attention to our Lord's question: "What do you think of the Christ? Whose son is He?" No one was able to answer Him a word. He is David's Son and God's Son, and the Holy Spirit rules us in all things if we truly believe this. It is the rule of faith. There can be no life of duty, no life of faith without the life of love; there can be no life of love without the life of faith. There must be the simple answer of the surrendered heart: "My Lord and my God!" This is to wait in faith, to be guiltless. To recall what love is and what fellowship really is, we must read 1 Corinthians 13 and 1 John 4:7-12.

The Proper Preface. "Who with Thine only-begotten Son and the Holy Ghost art one God, one Lord. And in the confession of the only true God we worship the Trinity in Person and the Unity in Substance, of Majesty coequal."

OUTLINE FOR SERMON ON THE EPISTLE

It is impossible for the intelligent and attentive worshiper not to be struck with the wisdom that so carefully arranged the orderly sequence of the Church Year's lessons. In the eucharistic Propers we have a guide to be closely followed, both in private meditation and in public teaching and preaching, as to the whole inward and outward Christian life. This Sunday gives us a summary of all Christian duty. The short Epistle deals exhaustively with the doctrine of grace. All of us have work to do for God and man, and all have received grace to do it. The same grace that filled the infant church of Corinth is at the disposal of every Christian and congregation.

The Equipment of Grace

A. The Channel of Grace. Grace is given us not merely by Jesus Christ, but "in Christ Jesus." All our enrichment as Christians comes not only from the Lord Jesus as its one and only source but from continual union with Him as members of His Church. We are not to seek the grace of God in isolation but as members of a body and by means of the Word and Sacraments. These Sacraments are social ordinances, as though to teach us that we are to be made perfect through fellowship with others in Christ. In the Church no man is to live for himself, but has a work provided for him to do and a power provided for him with which to do it. So will the Church prosper, the world be influenced, and every Christian be enriched in character and ability.

B. The Variety of Grace. The church of Corinth had not one gift but many. They were enriched with everything needed for the Christian life, in knowledge of the truth of God, in faith to realize it, and in speech to proclaim it. The perfection of the Church is to be the aim of the individual Christian. Christ is to be manifested in the visible body of His Church, but this can be only in sundry parts and divers manners. The riches of Christ cannot be fully seen in any one Christian but only in all Christians.

C. Growth in Grace. Perfection could not be all at once, and so the Corinthians were ever to be looking forward and waiting for the coming of the Lord Jesus Christ. It is not said that perfection will be reached before death, for death is not even mentioned, but only "the day of our Lord Jesus Christ." We have to begin by grace and to be confirmed by grace and by union with Christ cultivated and sanctified in every appointed way, and then Christ will complete our completeness that we may be "guiltless in the day of our Lord Jesus Christ." God grant in His mercy that we know what it is to be guiltless at the end and, in order to know this, that we may be guiltless all the way.

OUTLINE FOR SERMON ON THE HOLY GOSPEL

A. The Two Essentials. (1) Love to God. This is the first essential of perfection, namely, the desire of perfect service. This is to be the main and chief article of our lives. When we cease to live with this aim, we live below our nature; and instead of being able to plead our infirmities, we stand chargeable with negligence. He who does not desire perfection cannot plead imperfection, for if he had any object at all, his object was to be imperfect and not to love God with all his heart, soul, and mind. (2) Love to man. This is the second essential, but it is not second in importance, for it "is like it," like the first essential. It stands on the same level and is enforced by the same reasons. I am to love my neighbor as I love myself, because God loves him as He loves me. I am to love him for God's sake, if not for his own.

B. The Third Essential. It might have been expected that the holy Gospel would have ended with "on these two commandments depend all the law and the prophets." The Church has thought otherwise and has added faith in Christ in His humanity as the son of David and in His divinity as David's Lord. This does not mean that this is a third essential and that man has three. Faith in Christ is the one power that makes man able to do his two natural duties. We may say: (1) Faith in Christ has made easy the love of God, for to see God in Christ is to love Him. By the sacrifice of Himself, Christ has also removed the barrier of guilt which caused God to be an object of dread. Fear casts out love, but Christ has cast out fear. (2) Faith in Christ makes easier the love of man. Christ has taught us to love men as He loved them, and for His sake. If, then, faith in Christ is a third essential of duty, it is that which makes easy the other two great duties. The love of God and man is made possible for all who believe in Christ, who is God and man in one.

THE NINETEENTH SUNDAY AFTER TRINITY

With this Sunday we enter upon the final cycle of the Sundays after Trinity. The end of the Church Year is approaching. Progressively the Kingdom of Righteousness has been presented, its declaration and its founding. It has been described to us, and we have learned the life demanded to be a citizen. We now approach its completion, its fulfillment, and enter the cycle of the Last Things. The end of the Church Year not only closes a complete round of instruction but is a dramatic parable of the close of life. The believer's life closes with the opening of the glories of the heavenly home, but he who has no wedding garment is cast into outer darkness. The tone of this cycle rings clear with promise but also with solemn, awful warning.

The central teaching of this Sunday is found in the words of the Epistle: "Put off your old nature . . . and be renewed in the spirit of your minds." The first note of this cycle of Sundays is struck when the Introit announces: "Say unto my soul, I am thy Salvation." In the holy Gospel our Lord reveals Himself as the Savior of body and soul. He proves by a miracle that He has the power to forgive sins. In the Nicene Creed, which is spoken or chanted after the reading of the holy Gospel, we say: "I believe one holy Christian and Apostolic Church. I acknowledge one Baptism for the remission of sins, and I look for the resurrection of the dead and the life of the world to come." Between the confession of our belief in the family, the Church, and the confession of our hope in the resurrection and in the world to come, we confess our faith in Baptism for the remission of sins. The Epistle shows the effect of this forgiveness in our soul and life: "Put off your old nature . . . put on the new nature." All this in preparation for the Lord's coming. The Collect prays: "Keep us" from all hurtful things, make us free in body and soul to do Thy works, the works of the renewed nature. Today's central teaching is "The Life of Renewal."

The Introit. "Say unto my soul, I am thy salvation. The righteous cry, and the Lord heareth. He delivereth them out of their troubles. He is their God forever and ever. Give ear, O My people, to My law; incline your ears to the words of My mouth."

As we enter the house of God, Christ comes to meet us and speaks a word of comfort but also of admonition. "I am with you, your Deliverance, your God. Let your only concern be to keep My law, My commandments."

The Collect. "O almighty and most merciful God, of Thy bountiful goodness keep us, we beseech Thee, from all things that may hurt us, that we, being ready, both in body and soul, may cheerfully accomplish those things that Thou wouldst have done."

This is a prayer of pilgrims. We walk toward the eternal home, but the devil and our own lower nature cling like lead to body and soul. We pray for removal of the hindrances, so that we may cheerfully accomplish God's will.

The Epistle, Ephesians 4:22-28. Our most important task and duty in life is to put on the new nature in righteousness and true holiness. The old nature, the old man of the flesh and the lusts thereof, corrupt through deceitful lusts, palsied in sin, is to be awakened to newness of life, to the new nature, by the voice of the Savior. The new man, created after the likeness of God, is to arise. The Lessons teach us of things preparatory to the end and of life in the light of them, which is living toward the end.

The Gradual. "Let my prayer be set forth before Thee as incense, and the lifting up of my hands as the evening sacrifice. Alleluia! Alleluia! Oh, sing unto the Lord a new song, for He hath done marvelous things. Alleluia!"

The incense of our prayer rising up to God and the lifting of our hands as an evening sacrifice may be regarded as symbols of our longing for heaven.

The Proper Sentence. "Alleluia! O Lord, deal with Thy servant according unto Thy mercy, and teach me Thy statutes. I am Thy servant, give me understanding, that I may know Thy testimonies. Alleluia!"

Or: "Alleluia! Blessed be the Lord God of our fathers; praise Him and highly exalt Him forever. Alleluia!"

The Gospel, St. Matthew 9:1-8. Loving, serving brethren carry the palsied man into the presence of the Savior, who heals the needy man by first comforting and healing the soul and then mending the body. This man is a picture of our own selves. We, too, experience such a cure. We, too, were once lamed in our soul, but the Lord healed us. This happened at our Baptism. Every Sunday, also this day, has baptismal grace as a starting point and purposes to unfold it and bring it to maturity. But there is still much lameness in the soul. The world, our natural self, our lower nature, are like weights that keep our soul from soaring to loftier heights and keep us from rising above the earth. For this reason Christ has instituted the Sacrament of Holy Communion, to give us ever new momentum and to heal us of our spiritual disability and lameness of soul. The Eucharist is to make us ready for our heavenly home. So the holy Gospel joins the past, Holy Baptism; and the present, the Holy Communion; and the future, the Second Coming. On the Last Day it will be true also of us: "He rose and went home."

The Proper Preface. "Who with Thine only-begotten Son and the Holy Ghost art one God, one Lord. And in the confession of the true God we worship the Trinity in Person and the Unity in Substance, of Majesty coequal."

OUTLINE FOR SERMON ON THE EPISTLE

The subject of this Sunday is the life of renewal, a twofold renewal, not merely of the heart but of the whole life and conduct. In the Epistle the Apostle reminds the Ephesians that as members of Christ's mystical body they must no longer live as the Gentiles do, and admonishes them to put off their old nature and put on the new.

Renewal of Heart and Life

A. Renewal of the Heart. "Put off your old nature, which belongs to your former manner of life and is corrupt through deceitful lusts." In the verses preceding the text St. Paul gives a picture of man apart from Christ, of the old nature that is corrupt through deceitful lusts. The natural man has no true conception of the object and meaning of life. His mind becomes a prey to delusions, the understanding is darkened. From the mind, sin passes to the heart, and men become not only strangers to God but estranged from Him. Sin is no longer felt as pain, for the conscience becomes callous. Man plunges into every unhallowed thing with the greediness of lust. These results are not always seen at once but are gradual. The tendency is always there. When renewal has begun, man presents a very different picture. He has come under a new influence, received a new nature which conquers the old nature and character. The baptismal regeneration is completed by entire renewal in the spirit of the mind.

B. Renewal of Life. The inward nature must be manifested in outward conduct. This is the essential lesson of this Sunday. Certain evils are to be cast off, and opposite features of good are to be put on. "Put on the new nature, created after the likeness of God in true righteousness and holiness." (1) Falsehood. This is to be replaced by truth. To deceive one's neighbor is to deceive oneself, for it is as if one member of the body deceived another. The word of a Christian is to be as good as his bond, and his bond is his baptism into the body of Christ. (2) Sinful anger. Only such anger is to be endured as is not sinful, that is, on the right occasions, against the right objects, exercised only in a right degree and for the right duration. Anger is a natural remedy against injustice, but undue anger may itself come to be unjust. Unrestrained, it gives room for the devil in the heart and in the Church. (3) Dishonesty. This must be replaced by laborious toil, so that instead of taking from others we may be able to give to others. Happy those whose toil and thrift are so blest as to free them from improper dependence upon others and from the temptation to do wrong by others! (4) Evil language. This must be replaced by words which will bring a blessing and help to others. How beautiful to impart grace by our converse! Sometimes we rather drive it away. (5) Unloving tempers. We have here not only a catalog but a genealogy of bad passions. All such feelings are inconsistent with the presence of the Spirit, with His sensitiveness of holiness and His sensitiveness of love. They are inconsistent in those who have received forgiveness in Christ, full, free, continually repeated, and wholly undeserved, and should show the like toward others. So should the renewed nature be manifested in renewal of outward life.

OUTLINE FOR SERMON ON THE HOLY GOSPEL

The holy Gospel closely illustrates the doctrine of renewal taught in the Epistle.

A Miracle of Renewal

A. The Need of Renewal. Our state by nature is like that of the palsied, for we are weak in will and principle. Our weakness is, as may be that of palsy, the direct result of sin indulged till we are past feeling, as described in the Epistle. As was the palsied, we are unable to do anything to effect our cure. We must learn our need and prove our sincerity by breaking through every hindrance of prejudice, pride, and inherent shrinking, till we reach the feet of Christ, who alone is the Lord of every disease and can cure the palsied conscience, affections, understanding, and will. When we come so, we shall not be repulsed.

B. Renewal of the Heart. The miracle teaches most clearly (1) the blessing of renewal. It is a blessing more necessary even than the cure of a palsy. Others would have thought that the sick man desired bodily health most of all, but Christ saw deeper into his inward burden and misery and gave the greatest blessing first. (2) The conditions of renewal. These may be learned from this miracle, from which it is plain that Christ will not withhold forgiveness from those who feel their need of it and are more anxious for this blessing than for any other; who seek it from Him and break through every hindrance in order to gain His presence; and who, lastly, desire to be forgiven in order that they may afterward serve more devotedly. These three conditions are, in fact, repentance, which feels our need; faith, which seeks Christ; and obedience, which desires to serve Him. (3) The assurance of renewal. Christ not only forgave the man sick of the palsy but assured him of His forgiveness and bade him to be of good cheer because of it. He desires, therefore, that we should both be forgiven and know this so as to be happy in the knowledge. He has commanded His

Church to convey this blessing to those who have observed its conditions. He has appointed a ministry of reconciliation, whose great object is to announce forgiveness. He has ordained Sacraments, each of which is a channel and seal of forgiveness, for both the water and the blood are for the remission of sins. He gives the assurance of His Word and Spirit to assure our hearts before Him.

C. Renewal of Life. This is symbolized by the command to rise and walk. To walk in newness of life is at once the object and test of renewal. The miracle of healing was the test of Christ's power to forgive sins, for it was impossible to doubt His power to heal the soul when He had so clearly healed the body. So the great test that we have received the invisible benefit must be supplied by the visible tokens of a sanctified and invigorated life.

THE TWENTIETH SUNDAY AFTER TRINITY

The message of the day is stated in the words of the Epistle: "Look carefully, then, how you walk, not as unwise men but as wise, making the most of the time, because the days are evil." It is an exhortation to wisdom, not the cleverness of the Unjust Steward but the keenness and wakefulness of the child of God who, though still in the world, is only passing through it; to buy up every opportunity of grace, of service, of life in communion with God and His children, knowing that every failure to do so turns to the advantage of his foe. To avoid repetition, we may emphasize the admonition to address one another in psalms and hymns and spiritual songs, to sing, to give thanks, and so make the subject of the day "Cheerful Service." The holy Gospel speaks of the feast of joy God has prepared. The Introit seems to have in mind the casting out of the man without a wedding garment into the outer darkness when it declares that the Lord is righteous in all the works that He has done, and has us pray to be dealt with according to His steadfast love. The Collect asks for the blessing of the merciful God's pardon and peace, though the attribute of mercy is not named in the holy Gospel.

The Introit. "The Lord, our God, is righteous in all His works which He doeth, for we obeyed not His voice. Give glory to Thy name, O Lord, and deal with us according to the multitude of Thy mercies. Great is the Lord and greatly to be praised in the city of our God, in the mountain of His holiness."

The first verse of the Antiphon is from Daniel's prayer for his people (Dan. 9:14), in which he confesses that Israel brought God's visitation upon itself by its sins, "therefore the Lord has kept ready the calamity and has brought it upon us." So we today enter God's house as exiles who bear the bitterness of life in the spirit of repentance. But our souls long for the heavenly home, which we see prefigured in the holy place. We pray that God may glorify His reputation by dealing with us according to His steadfast love. We glorify Him by singing His praises in the city of God, in the mountain of His holiness, in His house, before the altar that symbolizes His presence, in the congregation of His faithful people.

The Collect. "Grant, we beseech Thee, merciful Lord, to Thy faithful people pardon and peace that they may be cleansed from all their sins and serve Thee with a quiet mind."

We are not rebels as were the men in the holy Gospel who made light of the king's invitation and treated his servants shamefully and killed them. We are God's faithful people, and we ask that in mercy He would forgive us our sins, that we may serve Him with a quiet mind, which is the peace of God, and that He would grant us earthly peace that we may serve Him with a quiet mind.

The Epistle, Ephesians 5:15-21. As pilgrims walking through this world on their way to the heavenly home, the Christians are to make the most of their time by being cleansed of their sins, by walking in the law of the Lord, undefiled in the way. St. Paul speaks of a twofold intoxication. We are not to be drunk with wine and with earthly things in general, but we are to be filled with the Spirit. He describes the latter condition: "addressing one another in psalms and hymns and spiritual songs, singing and making melody" of praise in our assemblies.

The Gradual. "The eyes of all wait upon Thee, O Lord, and Thou givest them their meat in due season. Thou openest Thine hand and satisfiest the desire of every living thing. Alleluia! Alleluia! Out of the depths have I cried unto Thee, O Lord! Lord, hear my voice. Alleluia!"

In the place of Ps. 130:1 the *Common Service Book* has Ps. 105:1 as the Alleluia Verse. The Gradual expresses our longing for the heavenly home and the confidence that the Lord will supply His pilgrims with the *viaticum,* His Holy Supper, all the way.

The Proper Sentence. "Alleluia! O Lord, deal with Thy servant according unto Thy mercy, and teach me Thy statutes.

I am Thy servant, give me understanding, that I may know Thy testimonies. Alleluia!"

Or: "Alleluia! Blessed be the Lord God of our fathers; praise Him and highly exalt Him forever. Alleluia!"

The Gospel, St. Matthew 22:1-14. The parable of the Marriage Feast must not be confused with the parable of the Great Supper. On the Second Sunday after Trinity we had a picture of grace and an illustration of men's response to God's loving invitation. The holy Gospel for this day presents a parable of judgment, and we see the sin of rebellion and the penalty of the outer darkness. The marriage is the work of salvation, Christ is the bridegroom, the Church is the bride, we are the wedding guests. The coming of the king into the hall is Christ's Second Coming, the wedding garment is the sanctifying grace. It is not enough to partake of the feast and sit in the hall, outwardly to be a member of some church. We must also live a life according to the will of God, possess the wedding garment of grace. A secondary interpretation of the parable may be permissible — that the holy Gospel is a picture of the Communion Service, the wedding hall is the house of God where the congregation of wedding guests has assembled, Word and Sacrament is the marriage feast, the Holy Communion at the same time the earnest and the prophetic picture of the heavenly marriage feast. The King appears and communes with the guests as a foretaste of the future coming. Our concern is that we be not the guest without the wedding garment.

The Proper Preface. "Who with Thine only-begotten Son and the Holy Ghost art one God, one Lord. And in the confession of the only true God we worship the Trinity in Person and the Unity in Substance, of Majesty coequal."

OUTLINE FOR SERMON ON THE EPISTLE

Last Sunday was the Sunday of renewal, when we heard the Savior say: "Take heart, My son, your sins are forgiven." The Authorized Version has: "Son, be of good cheer; thy sins be forgiven thee." It is quite fitting that this is followed by the Sunday of cheerful service, a service possible only for "a quiet mind," for which we pray in this day's Collect. The Epistle contrasts two apparently opposite views of religion in presenting:

The Joy of Service

A. The Seriousness of Religion. The Christian life demands
(1) Intense caution. In a world of so many inward and outward
enemies the Christian must "look carefully how you walk" and
must employ caution and wisdom in all the relations of life. Many
eyes are upon him, especially the eyes of God. (2) Active dili-
gence. We have fallen on evil days, and it is our duty to make
them better. We are therefore to make the most of the time, or
more accurately, to buy up the opportunity, at any expense of effort
and self-denial. Everything is so against us that we must make the
most of every passing help, influence, and means of grace. Our
sails must be set so as to catch every transient breath of favorable
wind. We must be alive also to every opportunity for doing good.
We must endeavor to discover the will of God and act upon it,
avoiding the folly of ignorance and the greater folly of disobedience.
We shall then be able both to gain and to impart good.

B. The Happiness of Religion. This happiness is a thing
commanded, for it is as much our duty to "be filled with the Spirit"
as not to "get drunk with wine." Certain features of this happiness
are to be noted. (1) Its source. It is the Spirit of God. We are
to seek for satisfaction not in the wine of earth but in the wine
of heaven. We are not to be content with any mere taste of it
but to be filled. (2) Its expression. This joy will find a vent in
holy intimacies and friendships, for we are to address one another.
It will show itself in the melody of the heart no less than of the
voice. Its inspiration will be gratitude to the Lord, who has redeemed us, and so will be like that of the songs of heaven. The
revelers in the wine of earth sing, and shall we not sing? We are
to sing in the Church on high, shall we not begin here? (3) Its
thankfulness. This is an essential element in Christian joy. We are
to be thankful always and for all things, for everything the Father
sends is good and for our good. (4) Its self-restraint. This joy
must not lead us to forget plain duty, as do the joys of revelry,
for we are to "be subject to one another." It is not inconsistent
with the utmost reverence, for amid all the joys of service we are
to remember that our Lord is One to be feared as well as to
rejoice in. These two views of religion here described are not

inconsistent. To take religion seriously is the only way to find a happy service, without misgiving and without remorse. A little religion will make us sad, but much will bring the joy of heaven. Heaven is only this Epistle carried out to the letter.

OUTLINE FOR SERMON ON THE HOLY GOSPEL

The parable of the holy Gospel reminds us of the parable of the Great Supper. The two have much in common, but there is a difference. The holy Gospel for the Second Sunday after Trinity illustrates our response to God's loving invitation. This day's holy Gospel is a call to rejoice. The man who gave a great banquet is here the King, seeking the happy service of His people. The parable of the Great Supper points to the sin of ingratitude. Today we see the deeper sin of rebellion and the penalty of the outer darkness. The invitation is a call to happiness and to enter into the joys of the Lord, but it is the invitation of the King. We may single out for special notice two points in connection with

The Feast of Joy

A. The Reason of Refusal. We cannot understand the refusal of happiness, still less the angry treatment of the servants. What was the cause of this bitter refusal? The answer is plain. These men would have none of the feast because they would have none of the King. Each man would go to his own farm or to his merchandise to show his independence of the King. But more than this, they were roused to active opposition of insult and violence. This was true of the Jews, and it is true of many today. Men reject the offer of happiness because it means service, a will and heart given to God. They resist and try to kill the messenger, conscience, and to discredit all the messengers of God. Let such opposition teach us that religion must be a very real thing, or men would not be so indisposed to accept it.

B. The Rejection of the Guest. Why was this one guest rejected? Evidently his lack of education was no impediment, for this is not to be sought among highways and hedges. His character was no objection, for bad and good were alike invited. What was, then, the wedding garment which he had not on? Evidently he came without the desire to be glad in that which was the joy of the King. The same disobedience which made others refuse made him, though present, to be unfit. The garment of renewal offered in Christ, and explained in the holy Gospel for last Sunday, was rejected. If any are cast into outer darkness, it will be because they will not put on the new man. If we miss the joy of service, it is because we will not serve.

SAINT LUKE THE EVANGELIST

October 18

The New Testament tells only a few facts regarding the Evangelist, but our inferential knowledge of him is considerable. His name is mentioned only three times. St. Paul refers to him Col. 4:14 as "Luke, the beloved physician"; again Philemon 24, where he is included in "my fellow workers"; and 2 Tim. 4:11: "Luke alone is with me." Eusebius tells us that he was born at Antioch in Syria. It has been thought that he was an emancipated slave. The fact that he was taught the science of medicine does not imply that he was of higher birth than the rest of the disciples, for slaves were often instructed in medicine to serve as family physicians. He was not born a Jew, for he is not included by St. Paul in "the only men of the circumcision among my fellow workers" (Col. 4:11). The first ray of historical light falls on the Evangelist in Acts 16:10, where the personal pronoun suddenly changes from "they" to "we" and "us." The resumption of "they" in 17:1 would indicate that the writer of the Acts was left behind in Philippi after having joined the missionary party in Troas. On the third missionary journey St. Luke apparently again joined the company at Philippi (Acts 20:5), after spending the intervening seven years in Philippi preaching the Gospel. Although the Revised Versions omit the postscript to the Second Letter to the Corinthians, it is commonly agreed that this epistle was written from Philippi by Titus and Lucas. If so, it is probably the Evangelist of whom the Apostle writes (2 Cor. 8:18, 19): "With him [Titus] we are sending the brother who is famous among all the churches for his preaching of the Gospel; and not only that, but he has been appointed by the churches to travel with us in this gracious work which we are carrying on." He again appears in St. Paul's company on the journey to Rome. He remained at his side during the first imprisonment. If the Second

Letter to Timothy was indeed written during the second imprisonment, then the testimony of the epistle shows that he continued faithful at the Apostle's side to the end. There is no reliable evidence that St. Luke shed his blood in martyrdom. His body was brought to Constantinople about A. D. 357, and he was commemorated first in the East. He was the last of the Evangelists to be honored with a festival in Rome, and this was not until the tenth century.

The Introit. "The Lord God said unto me: Write all the words that I have spoken unto thee into a book for a memorial. His name shall endure forever; His name shall be continued as long as the sun."

The Collect. "Almighty God, who calledst Saint Luke the physician to be an Evangelist and physician of the soul, heal, we beseech Thee, all the diseases of our souls by the wholesome medicine of Thy Word."

The Epistle, 2 Timothy 4:5-15.

The Gradual. "Their sound is gone out into all the earth, and their words to the end of heaven. The heavens declare the glory of God, and the firmament showeth forth His handiwork. Alleluia! Alleluia! I have chosen you out of the world that ye should bring forth fruit, and your fruit should remain. Alleluia!"

The Gospel, St. Luke 10:1-9. Perhaps this holy Gospel was chosen because St. Luke was supposed to have been one of the Seventy, but there is not a shred of evidence for this. The introductory words of his Gospel say only that he compiled his narrative of the things just as they were delivered to him by eyewitnesses. This would imply that he was not an eyewitness.

The Proper Preface. "Because Thou didst mightily govern and protect Thy holy Church, which the blessed Apostles and Evangelists instructed in Thy divine and saving truth."

THOUGHTS FOR SERMON ON THE EPISTLE

The Epistle appointed for this day is a part of St. Paul's last letter, written during his second imprisonment in Rome to his young assistant Timothy, pastor of the church at Ephesus. The Apostle had been released from his first imprisonment in 64.

But in the following year a great fire consumed more than half of the city, and Emperor Nero accused the Christians of having instigated it. Then began the most awful persecution, and St. Paul was imprisoned the second time. Awaiting his execution, he wrote to Timothy: "I am already on the point of being sacrificed; the time of my departure has come." The note of Christian triumph rings through the entire letter, but in the Epistle for this day we sense also loneliness. He pleaded with Timothy to come soon and to bring Mark with him. His co-workers and companion Crescens had gone to Galatia, Titus to Dalmatia, both to advance the King's business. "Demas, in love with this present world, has deserted me and gone to Thessalonica," the Apostle states sadly. There is one sentence that strikes us and assumes special significance as we commemorate St. Luke the Evangelist. It is: "Luke alone is with me."

Who was Luke? Was he bound to the Apostle by close ties of blood or nationality, that he faithfully remained at St. Paul's side even in prison? No, the two were not related. St. Paul was a Jew and St. Luke a Gentile. Not many years before, they were separated by the widest of chasms. Yet here we find them bound together by the closest bonds of friendship and brotherhood. They now were brothers because they were servants of the same Lord and had experienced the redeeming love of a common Savior. At one time they had been far from each other and from God, but they had been brought together by the blood of Christ.

We do not know when or how Luke became a Christian. Scripture does not tell us even where he was born or where he grew up. But we do know that he was a believer in the Lord Jesus Christ. Even more, he was a believer who had dedicated his life to preaching the Gospel. He was an assistant to the great Apostle Paul and helped him in his ministry, and he was appreciated for being a comfort and loyal aid, as the text indicates.

Another fact we know is that Luke was a physician, for St. Paul speaks of him as "the beloved physician." When the Lord Jesus became his Lord, He did not call upon him to discontinue the practice of medicine, to abandon his old profession and to take up one altogether new. He performed other services not part of his medical profession, but he performed them as a physician. A physician he was at the time of his conversion, and a physician he remained. The Collect for this day refers to this fact. God called St. Luke the physician to be a physician of the soul, and we pray that all the diseases of our souls be healed by the wholesome medicine of the Word which the Evangelist preached.

This is not unusual. God's call to most of us is not into new fields of service. True, for some to yield to God is to be called into the ministry as pastors and preachers or to be called into the foreign field. But for most of us to put ourselves into Christ's hands is to toil at the same task, to work in the way we have been working, but to do this in the inspiration of a new power and in the joy of a new fellowship. Dorcas did not throw away her needle when she became a Christian, but she was full of good works and acts of charity, and the widows showed Peter coats and garments made by her when she was with them. She simply consecrated her needle and ability to Christ. St. Luke did not throw away his bandages and healing medicines when he surrendered to Christ, but used them to the glory of God and the welfare of Christ's body. The man of business is not required to quit his business, if it is honorable, but to conduct it as a good steward of Jesus Christ. God does not ask that all do the same thing. We cannot all render the same service. But we can all render some service. St. Luke could not preach like St. Paul, and St. Paul could not heal like St. Luke. A physician like St. Luke has a task all his own, and it would be hard to find a person capable of being used more to the glory of God. The physician who goes to his work as God's man carries something to his patients that is better than his skill, however skillful he may be. Blessed the patient in the hands of a physician whose powers have been dedicated to his Lord and who may heal the soul as well as the body.

However, Luke, the beloved physician, did more than preach and practice medicine. He was also a writer of great brilliancy and power, and as such he has brought the whole world into his debt. There are sixty-six books in the Bible, and sixty-four of these were written by Jews. Only two of them were written by a Gentile, and the Gentile who wrote these was St. Luke, the Christian physician. The two, the Third Gospel and the Book of Acts, are about as choice bits of literature as the Scriptures contain. St. Luke's Gospel is considered by most as the finest of the four. It tells the same story as the other three, yet there are touches that make it quite different. It was written not to the Jews but to the Gentiles, especially for us. Naturally he does not always place his emphasis where the other Evangelists place theirs. For example, St. Luke goes to great pains in emphasizing the universality of Christ's forgiving love. St. Matthew, having the Jews in mind, has the Wise Men from the East ask: "Where is He who has been born King of the Jews?" But St. Luke gives no prominence to the Jewish claim. "An angel of the Lord appeared to them [the shepherds], and the glory of the Lord shone around them, and they were filled with fear. And the angel said to them: Be not afraid; for, behold, I bring you good news of a great joy which will come to all the people; for to you is born this day in the city of David a Savior, who is Christ the Lord." Then St. Luke proceeds to tell incident after incident in which he emphasizes the fact that the good news of a great joy is really meant for "all the people."

In the city of Jericho there was a man named Zacchaeus, a chief tax collector. He had sold himself to a foreign power and wore the livery of hated Rome. Therefore he was despised more than if he had worn the garb of a slave. This man was rich, but he was hated and shunned, and every door to decency was shut in his face. But one day the Lord Jesus said to him, "I must stay at your house today." Later He told him, "Today salvation has come to this house." St. Luke alone tells us this incident.

Again, one night there was a feast in the house of a certain Pharisee, and our Lord was a guest. During the meal there was a disturbance when a fallen woman of the streets stole in from out of the dark, fell down at His feet, wet them with her tears, and wiped them with the hair of her head. Simon, the host, shuddered with horror because the Master allowed Himself to be touched by this soiled rag of womanhood. But our Lord declared that she loved so much because her sins, which were many, had been forgiven. We owe this precious bit to St. Luke.

But the finest story ever written has not yet been mentioned. Our Lord told it, and St. Luke recorded it. It begins like this:

"There was a man who had two sons; and the younger of them said to his father, Father, give me the share of property that falls to me. And he divided his living between them. Not many days later the younger son gathered all he had and took his journey into a far country, and there he squandered his property in loose living." It is needless to tell the whole story, for it is about the most familiar in the literature of the world. The reason it is so familiar is that above all stories it reveals the compassionate and tender heart of our heavenly Father. It tells us how eternally eager He is to give heaven's best even to those who have rejected Him. Hereby St. Luke again makes most plain the universality of God's forgiving love.

What kind of man was St. Luke? We would like much to know him better, but he reveals little about himself. Nevertheless, some facts are quite noticeable. (1) He was a scholar. He was one of the best-trained men of his time, a man of wide reading and accurate information. He was capable of mental fellowship with St. Paul, one of the intellectual giants of all times. (2) Another fact St. Luke cannot conceal about himself is his modesty. He took a notable part in the events recorded in the Book of Acts, yet he never once mentions his own name. Neither does he give his name as the author of his Gospel. He presented us with two of the most excellent and helpful books ever written, but his name is not written on the title page. A modest man was St. Luke. (3) He was also lovable. St. Paul calls him the beloved physician. The love of Christ dwelt in his heart and reflected itself in his life and made him attractive and winsome, even as the Lord, whom he served. (4) He was steadfast. He was scholarly, modest, and loving, but this did not keep him from having the heart of a lion. As a physician, his healing touch was soft, yet he was a man of the hardiest courage. In the text St. Paul is writing from prison. The sword hangs over his head. The Christians were unpopular with the government and with the people. Many weak Christians were deserting the ranks of Christ's army, among them Demas. Then, with an appreciation that set his burdened heart to singing, the Apostle wrote: "Luke alone is with me." St. Luke was loyal and steadfast.

What a fine virtue is steadfastness! How God needs men and women in the Church today who can be relied on! Every church has some, and it does not take a pastor long to know who they are. When the family of God meets for worship, they are there. When things need to be done, they set to work. When the going gets rough or stormy, they stand by and are on hand. They are dependable, steadfast. To them God will say: "Well done, good and faithful servant."

"Luke alone is with me." The man who writes this pathetic little sentence is in disgrace and in prison. But Luke did not choose his friends because of their popularity or because of their success in the eyes of the world. He could be counted on when things were running smoothly, but no less in the days of adversity. A great, brave, noble, loyal soul! Modest, lovable, steadfast.

May you and I take St. Luke as an example for ourselves. This is the Church's purpose in placing him before us and bidding us to remember him this day. We may not have the special talents he had. We may not be scholars, write a Gospel, be physicians. But we can put ourselves into the service of Christ, our King. We can imitate St. Luke in his modesty, in his lovableness, and in his loyalty and steadfastness. We can let Christ come into our hearts to rule and live there.

THOUGHTS FOR SERMON ON THE HOLY GOSPEL

While our Lord lived here on earth, He trained and sent out three groups to spread the glad news of the Kingdom. The first group consisted of the twelve Apostles, and they were to have no successors. The second group was composed of the Seventy, who were chosen from the ranks of those who had become followers and were sent out to perform a definite task during our Lord's ministry. The third group was the Church He established. At the time of Pentecost this group numbered 120 besides the hundreds, and perhaps thousands, who believed and, in a way, followed Christ during His earthly ministry. They were the faithful group who remained in Jerusalem and prayerfully waited for the promised coming of the Holy Spirit. This nucleus was the center for the larger Church which grew and multiplied after Pentecost. The holy Gospel for this day invites us to discuss the ministry of the Seventy, that splendid group of men whom Christ sent out two by two for a specific service.

The Apostles may or may not have been included. We do not know. The Seventy certainly were faithful followers of the Lord Jesus, who heard His call to salvation and service and enlisted under the banners of this wonderful Teacher and Savior. Doubtless they had been instructed for some time and trained along with the Apostles while observing the Master's miraculous power and hearing the wonderful teachings embodied in His parables. They had received plain, definite instructions in the finest of the fine arts, soul winning. Evidently they caught their Teacher's spirit, acknowledged His Lordship, and yielded their lives as instruments of the divine will. Let us examine the instructions our Lord gave to these Seventy as He started them out on a soul-winning campaign.

1. "The Lord appointed seventy others and sent them on ahead of Him two by two." They were to go two by two. This was for mutual protection, companionship, strength, and power. This example has since then been followed by thousands with glorious results. One disciple re-enforces and complements the other. The two can pray together. They will be company for each other. One can render one sort of service and the other a different sort. Both can do personal work and be of mutual help and strength to each other.

2. The Lord "sent them on ahead of Him, into every town and place where He Himself was about to come." They were forerunners of Christ announcing His coming, introducing the Kingdom of God and telling of the loving Savior and miracle-working Teacher who was to come into their city or neighborhood with the words of life and salvation. Probably their ministry was to be among Jews, though there is no specific instruction as to this, but it seems to have been in keeping with our Lord's ministry at this time. He revealed Himself to His own, and His own received Him not. This does not mean that He did not come to save the whole world but that He was to be introduced to the whole world through the Jewish race.

3. The Lord started out the Seventy with the command "Pray the Lord of the harvest to send out laborers into His harvest."

The binding force of this command has pressed upon the hearts of God's people during all the centuries since, does today, and will in the future until the end. These Seventy, with the Apostles, were the first to be sent out in answer to this prayer of our Savior and of the early disciples for harvesters in the Kingdom. It is to the praise of God that Christ's disciples through the centuries have obeyed this command and have sought to pray out and call out the laborers who have been leaders in carrying the Gospel into all the world and in building the Kingdom. It is our duty today to obey this command and pray this prayer constantly. The pastors and preachers, the teachers and parents and children, the workers in the Kingdom everywhere, should constantly pray the Lord of the harvest to send out laborers into the harvest. It has been in answer to some worker's prayer that the meager supply of workers has been furnished. All the thousands of missionaries in foreign fields are the answers to somebody's prayers. All the hundreds of thousands of ministers throughout Christendom are the answers to somebody's prayers. It is urged upon Christian people everywhere to pray this prayer. We should do our best to call out and train more workers for Christ's Kingdom.

4. The Lord warned the Seventy as to the dangers they were to meet and the foes they were to antagonize. "I send you out as lambs in the midst of wolves." He wanted them to know that there would be enemies seeking their destruction. The enemies of Christ through the ages have been characterized by the wolf spirit. Of His messengers, however, the King expects the character of lambs, meek and yet bold, humble and yet courageous, pure and yet aggressive. The character of the ministry must never change, because through the spirit of meekness, humility joined with courage, and purity the spirit of the world is to be changed.

5. Their equipment was to be very simple. "Carry no purse, no bag, no sandals, and salute no one on the road." The meaning is that they were not to burden themselves with earthly supplies and baggage, not to become involved in worldly transactions. They were to proceed straight to their destination without time-robbing wayside conversation and social visits, and all their needs would be supplied by the people to whom they delivered the message of

the Kingdom. Evidently their ministry was not to be long, nevertheless He wanted them to have the spirit of dependence upon Him and the people to whom they brought the glad news of peace. Christ believed that their work would produce a spirit of gratitude and liberality in the hearts of those who believed and that this spirit would have the force and power to supply amply the needs of His ministers. This has been true in the main. This liberality has never enriched the ministry, but it has been sufficient to take care of the workers in Christ's Kingdom, often meagerly but usually in a substantial way. The two extremes of commercializing and of pauperizing the ministry should be avoided. "The laborer deserves his wages." The laborer in the Kingdom should be given sufficient support to reasonably care for his family, educate his children, provide clothes, shelter, books, and the other necessities of the ministry, an amount sufficient not only for the necessities of life but to enable him to give for the support of the cause of Christ.

6. The Lord instructed the Seventy: "Whatever house you enter, first say, Peace be to this house! And if a son of peace is there, your peace shall rest upon him; but if not, it shall return to you." They were to go in peace and carry peace to the homes and cities where they were to go. They were to pronounce their peace upon the people. If the people refused it, their peace would return to them. If Christ's messenger and his greeting of peace is rejected, the messenger's peace shall return to him and in multiplied measure rest upon him. If men cast him out, the Lord will receive him and confirm to him that he is at peace with his Lord. If people refused the peace offered, the messenger was to shake off the dust from his feet as he left that house or town (Matt. 10:14). Our Lord wanted His workers to have self-respect and to protect themselves from the cruel persecutions and rejections of indifferent people.

7. Our Lord told the Seventy: "Remain in the same house, eating and drinking what they provide, for the laborer deserves his wages; do not go from house to house. Whenever you enter a town and they receive you, eat what is set before you." He expected the spirit of hospitality from those who were beneficiaries

of the Gospel. The right way to do the work of the Kingdom is not to touch lightly here and there but to gain a firm foothold and to instruct willing hearers thoroughly in the mysteries of the Kingdom. Constant or frequent moving from house to house or town to town makes this difficult, if not impossible.

8. The Seventy were to do two things: "Heal the sick in it, and say to them, The Kingdom of God has come near to you." The Lord gave His messengers power over serpents and devils and diseases and death. Upon their return the Seventy joyfully reported: "Lord, even the demons are subject to us in Your name." He gave them also the power to preach the Gospel of God's coming Kingdom. They were to tell what they knew of the Messiah, the King of the Kingdom, and the principles and doctrines He had already taught them. He had tried to tell them that He was the Lamb of God and was to be slain as a sacrificial offering in the place and stead of men under the wrath of God. They did not fully understand the doctrine of the Atonement at this time, but they certainly had had some intimation of it. Their Gospel, as they understood it, was not a complete Gospel. It was only initiatory and in its beginnings, but it was sufficient in its simplicity and power to save.

In conclusion, some everliving points of instruction to all soul winners. First, we get our orders from Christ to go and to go together, to preach that the Kingdom is near, to teach through schools and churches, to win the lost world to Him through the Gospel and all Gospel agencies, to heal the sick through our prayers and all health agencies. Blessed is the man who gets his orders from Christ to go. When He told the Seventy to go by two and two and to work in harmony, He gave a tremendous message in co-operation to His people everywhere. Secondly, He gives us power over sin. This power is all His. By faith and obedience and surrendered wills He transfers a sufficient portion of it for the performance of our tasks. He promises to provide all necessities for the journey, and we may confidently go out trusting Him for support and power. Thirdly, our message is the message of the Kingdom, of the whole Gospel to the whole world. There is nothing selfish, provincial, or narrow in it. It represents all

God is and has and gives to lost men, and to all lost men. The heart of the message is to repent and believe, to turn away from sin and believe the Lord Jesus Christ and follow Him in blessed service. Finally, we are to carry peace and not a sword, a peace that God alone gives. It is a peace that comes from hidden spiritual sources. We are not to stir up strife, but to quiet the heart and the fear of men everywhere. We are to be lovers and makers of peace. When our task is completed in every heart, there will be no more war, international, national, local, or domestic. The Gospel of Christ is God's peace for all the world.

THE TWENTY-FIRST SUNDAY AFTER TRINITY

Most of us probably find it difficult to determine one thought that is common to the Propers for this day and gathers them under one harmonious subject. Any suggestions of Roman or Anglican scholars avail little, for they are not dealing with the same Propers. As always in the Trinity Season, the *Roman Missal* has the holy Gospel that is appointed for the following Sunday in the Lutheran Lectionary. The *Book of Common Prayer* has neither Introits nor Graduals, the Collect for this Sunday is that for last Sunday in the Lutheran arrangement, and the Epistle includes verses 18—20. The Epistle speaks of the spiritual enemies that threaten the Christian constantly and exhorts to "stand," "be strong in the Lord," and to "put on the whole armor of God." The holy Gospel shows how faith grows and becomes stronger in and through trial and affliction. The Collect prays that God's household and family may be free from all adversities and devoutly given to serve God. It will be noted that the armor and weapons mentioned in the Epistle are all protective, except one, the aggressive and all-conquering "sword of the Spirit." What are we to defend? On the Fifth Sunday after Trinity we learned that God manifests His love by giving the blessing of peace to His people in their trials and dangers. Today we learn that this gift of peace must be defended, must be employed in service and not in idleness. "Sure I must fight if I would reign" (*The Lutheran Hymnal,* No. 445).

The Introit. "The whole world is in Thy power, O Lord, King Almighty; there is no man that can gainsay Thee. For Thou hast made heaven and earth and all the wondrous things under the heaven. Thou art Lord of all. Blessed are the undefiled in the way, who walk in the Law of the Lord."

The source of the Antiphon is frequently given as Esther 13: 9, 10, 11. This does not refer to Luther's or any Protestant version, for the Hebrew Book of Esther has only ten chapters. The source is the Greek "Additions" to the Book of Esther incorporated into the Book of Esther by Rome. In Luther's translation of the Apocrypha the Antiphon is found under Additions to Esther 2:1-3. In the Introit the soul sees itself surrounded by many enemies as it enters the holy place. But it sings of brave confidence as it faces the battle with courageous heart. "With might of ours can naught be done," but we trust in the "King Almighty." "The whole world is in Thy power, O Lord." In His power we shall endeavor to walk in the Law of the Lord undefiled and blameless.

The Collect. "Lord, we beseech Thee to keep Thy household, the Church, in continual godliness, that through Thy protection it may be free from all adversities and devoutly given to serve Thee in good works, to the glory of Thy name."

The Church prays for protection. The King Almighty is implored to be the Protector of His family, to free it from all adversity, that it may be devoted to His name in good works.

The Epistle, Ephesians 6:10-17. St. Paul pictures the enemy against whom we must contend. The King Almighty will supply protection and furnish a whole armor which will enable us to stand against the wiles of the devil.

The Gradual. "Lord, Thou hast been our Dwelling Place in all generations. Before the mountains were brought forth or ever Thou hadst formed the earth and the world, even from everlasting to everlasting, Thou art God. Alleluia! Alleluia! They that trust in the Lord shall be as Mount Zion, which cannot be removed but abideth forever. Alleluia!"

This is an echo of the Epistle. The everlasting God is our Helper in the battle against our enemies. We trust in Him; therefore we shall not be moved.

The Proper Sentence. "Alleluia! O Lord, deal with Thy servant according unto Thy mercy, and teach me Thy statutes. I am Thy servant, give me understanding, that I may know Thy testimonies. Alleluia!"

Or: "Alleluia! Blessed be the Lord God of our fathers; praise Him and highly exalt Him forever. Alleluia!"

The Gospel, St. John 4:46-54. We have here the story of a faith that grows, becomes stronger and greater, reaches for, and lays hold on, the power of Christ, and stands firm.

The Proper Preface. "Who with Thine only-begotten Son and the Holy Ghost art one God, one Lord. And in the confession of the only true God we worship the Trinity in Person and the Unity in Substance, of Majesty coequal."

OUTLINE FOR SERMON ON THE EPISTLE

This is an epistle of war and teaches us that we are to gain and keep the peace of God through inward and outward struggle. We learn two secrets of assured peace.

A. Power. Peace is for the strong, who are strong not in their own strength but "in the Lord and in the strength of His might." We must fight, not against men like ourselves, weak as we are weak, but against the prince of evil, with his terrible resources of invisibility and cunning, and against a mighty host of evil ones, the spiritual forces of wickedness around us, "the world rulers of this present darkness." The world is this darkness, and this darkness is under the rule, in a degree, of evil spirits. Our danger is so great that, apart from Christ, we cannot but fall. Let us realize our peril, and let us secure the only strength that can save us. He who was so strong for Himself can be strong for us.

B. Protection. We must stand. This is to be our position, ever on the watch. We must withstand. This is our work, to drive back attack. Then we may be able to stand. This is to be our reward, to have gained everlasting acceptance and security. In order to do this we must be armed, not from any arsenal of our own but with the armor of God. We must take not only armor but the whole armor, the panoply of God. This complete and divine armor is supplied to us, and we must put it on, and we must put on every part of it. (1) The Christian belt or girdle. This is truth or sincerity. Conscious reality gives a sense of power and firmness to the whole character. (2) The Christian breastplate. This is righteousness or true principle, which will defend the body from mortal wounds. Is. 59:17: "He put on righteousness as a breastplate, and a helmet of salvation upon his head." No backplate is provided for the Christian, for he may not seek safety in flight but in fight. (3) The Christian sandals. That readiness for all obedience and service which comes from peace with God. A well-shod man feels ready for anything. His shoes seem to send up life and energy into his nature. Such sense of peace sent the Apostles marching through the world, and many others since. (4) The Christian shield. Faith in the Father shields from all distrust as to outward things; faith in the Son from all inward alarms as to acceptance with God; faith in the Spirit from all temptations to gross evil. (5) The Christian helmet. This is the hope of salvation or final victory, sure to be ours through Christ, which nerves us to persevere. (6) The Christian sword. The Word of God is a sword both to cut and to parry. It was forged by the Spirit, is the gift of the Spirit, and only the Spirit can enable us to use it. With this the Christian may both conquer the world and defend himself. Christ came not to bring peace but a sword, and this sword of Christ brings peace.

OUTLINE FOR SERMON ON THE HOLY GOSPEL

The peace of God, which is to be our stay in the conflict against sin, is to be our very present help in trouble. The miracle of the healing of the nobleman's son teaches that this peace depends upon faith and comes only to the believing. There are three distinct stages in the journey of the nobleman, of which each has its own lesson.

A. The Journey of Sorrow. His rank and position purchased no exception from sorrow for the nobleman, for those separated by birth from the common herd of men are by birth exposed to the common herd of trials. The more we have, the more we have to lose; and the more we love, the more possible sources of sorrow we have. When Christ sends an arrow of chastening, He can readily find a tender place in which to plant it. Sad, tremulous, and excited was this journey, and yet it was a journey of faith, though mixed with fear. Without faith he would not have come; with less faith he would have sent. Faith was present, but feeble, for, unlike the centurion, he thinks that Christ could not heal without coming and that if the son died before He came, all would be over. Little faith has little peace.

B. The Journey of Hope. He who had faith to come needed a greater faith to go away. So Christ nurses feebleness into strength by discipline. Who can describe this return journey, with its struggle between faith and unbelief and the arrangement that the servants should meet their master by the way! The journey of faith may be shorter than we fear, and the message of peace may be already on its way.

C. The Return in Peace. The last part of the return journey, so different from the first! The very servants have echoed the word of Christ "Thy son liveth" and have told of the cure so absolute and so immediate that there is no further room for doubt, and the journey of sorrow ends in peace. May it be so with our life journey, as Christians, and may we learn the lesson that our peace will ever be in proportion to our faith. Then the sadness of the journey will be forgotten in the joy of coming home.

THE TWENTY-SECOND SUNDAY AFTER TRINITY

As we approach the end of the Church Year, the Propers turn our thoughts more and more to the end of all things, the end of human life, of the world. Constantly we are exhorted to watch and be ready. Constant is the comfort of divine grace and love, so that we need not fear or doubt but can rejoice and trust. Also the description of the Christian character now draws to a close. Most fitly we are led therefore to consider the graces needed for the close of the Christian life. Renewal and glad cheerfulness are the grace of the morning, peace sustains us during the burden and heat of the day. Now as the evening of life draws on and hearts grow weary, we are encouraged to endure to the end and not to lose what we have been given but to gain our full reward. This is the Sunday of perseverance, and the great lesson of the day is that perseverance is not of ourselves but the work of God, a fruit of the righteousness which comes through Jesus Christ. Twice the Epistle refers to "the Day of Jesus Christ." The holy Gospel brings a note of warning, which is constantly sounded throughout these final weeks, regarding our heart's relation with others. The servant is the direct opposite of what the Epistle demands.

The Introit. "If Thou, Lord, shouldest mark iniquities, O Lord, who shall stand? But there is forgiveness with Thee, that Thou mayest be feared, O God of Israel. Out of the depths have I cried unto Thee, O Lord! Lord, hear my voice."

With repentant earnestness and troubled soul we come today into the holy place. Burdened by sins we cry out of the depths to the Lord for forgiveness. Stirred to the depth of serious contemplation of life with all its weakness and sin, we declare that we have risen to the high plane of peace. We humbly confess that if the Lord should mark iniquities, we could not stand, but trustingly we assert that there is forgiveness with God.

The Collect. "O God, our Refuge and Strength, who art the Author of all godliness, be ready, we beseech Thee, to hear the devout prayers of Thy Church, and grant that those things which we ask faithfully we may obtain effectually."

We address God as our Refuge and Strength. This sincere, confident, trusting prayer contains no particular petition but summarizes our daily and weekly petition for faithful, persevering fulfillment of our calling and for increase in perfection as we approach the day of completion.

The Epistle, Philippians 1:3-11. The great pastor of souls, St. Paul, speaks to his favorite congregation, breathing innermost love, yes, tenderness. His deepest concern is that the good work begun in them will be brought to completion at the day of Christ's return. They are to be like trees laden with fruit, that their love may abound more and more.

The Gradual. "Behold how good and how pleasant it is for brethren to dwell together in unity! The Lord commanded blessing, even life forevermore. Alleluia! Alleluia! The Lord healeth the broken in heart and bindeth up their wounds. Alleluia!"

In the battle against the world and hell the Christian finds comfort in the holy community, a united congregation, a happy and blessed family. "Behold, how good and pleasant it is when brothers dwell in unity! . . . For there the Lord has commanded the blessing, life forevermore" (Ps. 133:1, 3). The Epistle calls this family of God "partnership in the Gospel," where love abounds more and more, with knowledge and all discernment, filled with the fruits of righteousness which come through Jesus Christ. We are being prepared to hear the holy Gospel for the day.

The Proper Sentence. "Alleluia! O Lord, deal with Thy servant according unto Thy mercy, and teach me Thy statutes. I am Thy servant, give me understanding, that I may know Thy testimonies. Alleluia!"

Or: "Alleluia! Blessed be the Lord God of our fathers; praise Him and highly exalt Him forever. Alleluia!"

The Gospel, St. Matthew 18:23-35. We meet the servant who owed his lord so much that he could not even hope to pay the debt, for he had nothing with which to pay. "If Thou, O Lord, shouldest mark iniquities, O Lord, who shall stand?" Yet upon the servant's plea to have patience came the instant, free, and full pardon and forgiveness. "There is forgiveness with Thee." The servant leaves the presence of his lord only to face immediately a like experience. A fellow servant who owed a negligible sum, infinitesimal in comparison with what he had owed, pleads: "Have patience with me." But there is no compassion, no patience, no forgiveness, but the unyielding, unforgiving condemnation of the untouched heart. The coming of Christ is the great day of the accounting. God is kindly in His forgiveness. He is ready to forgive sin here on earth, but only under the condition that we practice forgiving love. If we are to find a merciful judgment, we must belong to the fellowship of the forgiven and the forgiving. Lovelessness and mercilessness will be strictly punished. In the Holy Communion we are reminded of the magnanimous act of the King, the Lord's dying on the cross. He pardons my enormous debt. In return my reciprocating gift must be love of my neighbor.

The Proper Preface. "Who with Thine only-begotten Son and the Holy Ghost art one God, one Lord. And in the confession of the only true God we worship the Trinity in Person and the Unity in Substance, of Majesty coequal."

OUTLINE FOR SERMON ON THE EPISTLE

The keynote of this Sunday is struck in the words: "He who began a good work in you will bring it to completion at the day of Jesus Christ." St. Paul marks three stages in the Christian life and shows that each is gained only by grace.

A Prayer for Perseverance

A. The Good Work Begun. Religion is a good work in us, not merely a round of external services, however valuable and right, nor some outward and formal obedience, however strict and accurate, but something inward, something good within, something solid, real, substantial, a good work within, which has been begun in us by God alone. St. Paul gives his grounds for confidence that this work has been really begun in the Philippians, whereby we may test our own reality. (1) Their Christian partnership or fellowship. This is not merely "in the Gospel," that is, in the blessings, comforts, hopes, and joys of the Gospel. The American Standard Version translates "in furtherance of the Gospel," that is, their fellowship shown in their united interest, zeal, labor, and liberality. The first proof is our earnest churchmanship. (2) Their Christian experience. St. Paul could feel that they were partakers with himself, not only in works but in grace. The same grace by which he suffered, contended, and toiled was plainly and strongly working in them. Hence his hope of them was steadfast. He longed after them "with the affection of Christ Jesus (ASV: "in the tender mercies of Christ Jesus"), but his love was all joy and no pain. The second proof of reality is Christian feeling and our likeness in heart to the saints. When we work like the saints and have the experience in us which is recorded in their writings, we have evidence that God has begun a good work in us.

B. The Good Work Carried On. This work, if it is real, must grow. We are apt to be satisfied with continual beginnings. St. Paul is not so certain of the Philippians that he can leave them out of his prayers. On the contrary, he prays for them. (1) That their love might ever grow and grow, springing ever from a deeper root in the love of Christ for them. (2) That through love they might attain to ever-advancing knowledge. Love without knowledge is wild and undisciplined, but knowledge without love is nothing at all. Love is the key of knowledge, and slow learning comes from cold loving. (3) That through love they might attain to all-Christian instinct and perception. The loving Christian attains a delicate perception and sensitiveness of spirit as to what is right and wrong, true and untrue, fitting and unfitting, kind or unkind. Just as the musical ear detects want of harmony in sounds, so true love to God detects at once the discords of sin and instinctively discovers the true best in everything and the truly excellent in action and conduct.

C. The Work Completed. St. Paul pictures the complete Christian character (1) In its freedom from sin. It will be sincere, that is, pure, unsullied, and without blemish in the sight of God. It will be "pure and blameless," without fault of conduct before men. (2) In its active usefulness. It will be filled with the fruits of Christian influence and power. These fruits will spring not of a mere good nature or of mere human culture but from connection with Christ and from the motive of the Cross. They are necessary to our own safety at the last and to the glory of God. This is the description of the complete Christian character. Let us beware of a Christianity that does not tend this way. Let us be sure that we have the aim to be like this, for no man was ever more fruitful than he intended to be; but for our comfort let us remember that St. Paul speaks not of death as the goal but of the day of Jesus Christ.

OUTLINE FOR SERMON ON THE HOLY GOSPEL

The Epistle leads us to think of our perseverance, but St. Paul has taught us that we should rather speak of God's perseverance with us, which is so great that He will not fail to complete the good work of His grace, unlike men who begin to build and are not able to finish. We who cry so often, "Lord, have patience!" must show a like patience toward others. We must not only forgive as we have been forgiven but persevere with others as God perseveres with us. This is the practical lesson of the holy Gospel, in which we learn:

Perseverance with Others

A. The Limit of Perseverance. There is no such limit, for seventy times seven stands obviously for infinity. To fix a limit to their own patience is not to be endured in those who themselves depend upon the continued patience of God. To ask: How often shall I forgive my brother? is, in fact to ask: How often shall I be forgiven? For Christ has promised that the one answer shall be the measure of the other. No man will willingly limit the divine mercy to be shown to himself.

B. A Parable of Patience. We learn from this parable the reasonableness of any demand on our patience, however great it may seem. (1) The hopelessness of our debt. Our debt is ten thousand talents, probably ten million dollars, a debt beyond all payment, hopeless, unreasonable, and guilty. It is enough to mention our sins of omission, of imagination, of temper and spirit, of heart and nature, and that we have sinned against light, knowledge, and conviction, against vows, promises, and good resolutions without number. (2) The completeness of our forgiveness. "The lord of that servant released him and forgave him the debt." It was general. "I forgave you." It was also particular. "All that debt." God forgives each the sins of his individual character and history. It was absolute. "He could not pay." We have nothing that is not sin or stained by sin; we have nothing to pay, for all that we have is His by right already. This parable does not hint at the later truth that forgiveness, though free to us, was not free to God, and that we can be forgiven only because the world's ransom was paid for us. (3) The fairness of the one condition. It is no more than fair that we should make some acknowledgment, and the acknowledgment required is only that we should forgive the twenty dollars to whom God has forgiven the ten million dollars. We exaggerate offenses against ourselves; we forget our offenses against God.

SAINT SIMON AND SAINT JUDE, APOSTLES

October 28

These two Apostles are placed together in the list of the chosen Twelve (Luke 6:14-16). St. Simon is listed as "Simon who was called the Zealot." The Zelotes, a very strict sect of the Pharisees, were conspicuous for their fierce advocacy of the Mosaic ritual and their endeavor to realize the Messianic hope by force. He is called "Simon the Cananaean" (Mark 3:18; Matt. 10:4). The King James Version translates "the Canaanite," Luther *"von Cana."* But Simon was neither a Canaanite nor from Cana. *Kananaios* is said to be the equivalent of *Zelotes,* which would exclude reference to Canaan or Cana.

St. Jude is listed in St. Luke's Gospel and the Acts as "Judas of James," and the translators have supplied the word "son." Others have supplied the word "brother," believing him to have been the brother of the Apostle James the Less and therefore a cousin of our Lord. They point to Matt. 13:55 (cf. Mark 6:3): "Is not this the carpenter's son? Is not His mother called Mary? And are not His brothers James and Joseph and Simon and Judas?" These "brothers" could have been the sons of Joseph by a previous marriage. More probable is that they were the sons of the Virgin Mary's sister, also named Mary, and that they were cousins of our Lord. The difficulty, implied by John 7:5, that "even His brothers did not believe in Him" is not insurmountable. St. Matthew and St. Mark list St. Jude as Thaddaeus. St. John speaks of him as "Judas (not Iscariot)" (14:22).

Traditions regarding the two Apostles are plentiful but contradictory. They are said to have labored together in Persia and to have been martyred there on the same day. There is no certainty as to where St. Simon preached, and it is doubtful whether he died a martyr's death or died peacefully. In the West it is generally thought that he died a cruel death, but in the East it is said that his end was peaceful. In the West it is generally supposed that St. Jude was a martyr, but the Greeks state that he fell asleep in peace but that the next month he was hanged on a cross and run through with javelins.

The Introit. "The Spirit of Truth will guide you into all truth, for He shall glorify Me. Ye shall be My witnesses, because ye have been with Me from the beginning. Blessed are ye when ye are persecuted for My sake, for the kingdom of heaven is yours The Lord is my Light and my Salvation. I will sing, yea, I will sing praises unto the Lord."

The Collect. "O almighty God, who hast built Thy Church upon the foundation of the Apostles and Prophets, Jesus Christ Himself being the Head Cornerstone, grant us to be joined together in unity of spirit by their doctrine, that we may be made a holy temple acceptable unto Thee."

The Epistle, 1 Peter 1:3-9.

The Gradual. "The mouth of the righteous speaketh of wisdom, and his tongue talketh of judgment. The Law of his God is in his heart; none of his steps shall slide. Alleluia! Alleluia! The righteous shall flourish like the palm tree; those that be planted in the house of the Lord shall flourish in the courts of our God. Alleluia!"

The Gospel, St. John 15:17-21.

The Proper Preface. "Because Thou didst mightily govern and protect Thy holy Church, which the blessed Apostles and Evangelists instructed in Thy divine and saving truth."

SERMON ON THE EPISTLE

According to Joseph A. Seiss

From time immemorial this 28th day of October has been set apart for the commemoration of the Apostles St. Simon and St. Jude. If there was any particular reason for selecting the passage before us as the Epistle for the festival, this reason does not appear. The Epistle has no direct connection with either of the Apostles, except that it sets forth the common Gospel of hope which they preached and in whose joys they shared. We consider:

The Gospel of Hope

A. What Christian Hope Involves. "Blessed be the God and Father of our Lord Jesus Christ! By His great mercy we have been born anew to a living hope through the resurrection of Jesus Christ from the dead." As creatures of God all men are God's children. "Have we not all one Father? Has not one God created us?" (Mal. 2:10.) "We are indeed His offspring" (Acts 17:28). But as Christians we are God's children in a special sense which applies to Christians only. "Israel is My first-born son" (Ex. 4:22). "Ye are the sons of the Lord, your God" (Deut. 14:1). God has taken this people into a relation far higher and closer than that of other nations. So those who have living hope in Christ are God's sons and daughters, because they have been raised to a still more blessed spiritual nearness of relation to Him. This mystic sonship is separably connected with a new putting forth of divine power. God sent His Son into the world, who by His obedience unto death has purchased eternal redemption for us. "There is therefore now no condemnation for those who are in Christ Jesus . . . who walk not according to the flesh but according to the Spirit" (Rom. 8:1, 4). Believing this and putting our whole confidence in it, we are forgiven, accepted, and pass from the state of condemned criminals to that of beloved children. With the exercise of faith there is wrought in us a new life and a new spirit, by which God is recognized as a loving Father and we are set to the obedience of true and dutiful children.

The true Christian hope involves fundamentally a new birth by the awakening of the soul to the embrace of the Gospel and to faith in the saving mercies it propounds. The Holy Spirit brings us to faith in Christ, and we are "born anew" by the power of grace to a Christian hope. We need not even wait till our faith is proved by our works, for the very moment we believe with a will to obey, we are already in condition to cherish Christian hope, and are cherishing it. Faith, regeneration, and sonship are involved and presupposed in true Christian hope.

B. To What This Hope Looks. "All who are led by the Spirit of God are sons of God. . . . And if children, then heirs, heirs of God and fellow heirs with Christ" (Rom. 8:14, 17). Having been brought into the relation and estate of children, we are in the way of inheriting as children. So the text rates our being born anew to a living hope as born "to an inheritance" to which that hope goes out. This is further described as "a salvation ready to be revealed in the last time."

Christian believers are saved now. The moment they exercise faith in Christ as their Lord and Savior they enter upon great and blessed possessions. They have forgiveness. They are in a state of freedom from all condemnation. They stand before God as citizens of the heavenly commonwealth. They are no longer aliens and strangers, but fellow citizens with the saints and children in the household of God. Yet their salvation is largely a matter of hope. It remains to be "revealed," made manifest, brought into full actuality, "in the last time," "at the revelation of Jesus Christ." Meanwhile they rest in Paradise, but the fullness of their inheritance awaits the coming of their Savior at the resurrection time.

What is that future inheritance? "It does not yet appear what we shall be" (1 John 3:2), yet there are glimpses given and assurance of much with which to feast and refresh our souls. Joint heirs with Christ must inherit with Christ. Whatever portion of glory and blessedness falls to Him we shall share. Suffering with Him we shall also "be glorified with Him" (Rom. 8:17).

What is this patrimony? When Christ had completed His work and satisfied all the demands of violated Law, God raised Him up again from the dead. Now death cannot hold the believers. Through Christ they no longer dread its power and soon shall be eternally delivered from its grasp. The Lord Jesus is now at the right hand of the Father, who has appointed Him a kingdom, dominion, and glory, and put all His enemies under His feet. As coheirs with Him it is our high privilege to become participants in that same glory. The assurance is that we shall be like Him. His own promise is: "He who conquers, I will grant him to sit with Me on My throne, as I Myself conquered and sat down with My Father on His throne" (Rev. 3:21).

It is also proclaimed as the Lamb's portion "to receive power and wealth and wisdom and might and honor and glory and blessing," to which "every creature in heaven and on earth and under the earth and in the sea and all therein," are to give their acquiescence and accord (Rev. 5:12, 13). In all that we are to share. "For Thou wast slain and by Thy blood didst ransom men for God from every tribe and tongue and people and nation, and hast made them a kingdom and priests to our God, and they shall reign on earth" (Rev. 5:9, 10). St. Paul's last farewell to this life was: "Henceforth there is laid up for me the crown of righteousness, which the Lord, the righteous Judge, will award to me on that Day, and not only to me but also to all who have loved His appearing" (2 Tim. 4:8). St. Peter could admonish his co-workers in the holy ministry with the promise "When the chief Shepherd is manifested, you will obtain the unfading crown of glory" (1 Peter 5:4). The great voice from heaven announced the completion of the consummation: "Behold, the dwelling of God is with men. He will dwell with them, and they shall be His people, and God Himself will be with them; He will wipe away every tear from their eyes, and death shall be no more, neither shall there be mourning nor crying nor pain any more, for the former things have passed away" (Rev. 21:3, 4).

This, then, is some indication of that "inheritance which is imperishable, undefiled, and unfading," to which the text refers, the "living hope" to which God has born anew all those "who by God's power are guarded through faith for a salvation ready to be revealed in the last time." It is eternal life, life that ever grows and never dies, life with Christ in God. It is salvation, deliverance from all sin, from all evil, from the disabilities and sorrows of earth, from all power of death. It is to rule with Christ a kingdom which cannot be moved. It is eternal kingdom and priesthood with the Son of God.

C. On What It Rests. The inheritance is reserved and kept for us, and we Christians are reserved and kept for the inheritance. The hope of God's children is assured and certain. What is the guarantee? We have God's promises, which are sufficient. But we should like something more tangible and convincing, something to give practical proof and pledge. God in His mercy has not left us without such demonstrative assurance. He has given it "through the resurrection of Jesus Christ from the dead." The great seal of the Gospel is Christ's resurrection. It was the underwriting of the eternal Father to the divine Sonship of Christ and His confirmation as the world's Redeemer. It was the demonstration that hell and death are conquered and that there is a life of glory beyond death's reach and power. It gave the proof that the whole penalty of the Law was exhausted when Christ died, and the whole debt paid. It was the bursting into effective being of a new potency by which justification came to the guilty, life to the spiritually dead, and the impulse and beginning of a new life to the whole suffering creation. It was already the potential opening of the new world of eternal life and blessedness. The judgment of believers passed in Christ's death, and we have even now by regeneration entered upon the possession of so much that all else included in the inheritance must necessarily follow. Justified in His justification, His resurrection is virtually our own. Risen with Him to the new life of faith, and brought into the new relation of sonship, we already have, in living fact, all the beginnings of the full realization. As Christ went down under the penalty of our sins, He never could have risen again except by the complete doing away of that penalty. Delivered for our offenses, His coming forth again in the powers of an endless life was the practical demonstration not only that the old condemnation is gone but that all else of our perfect redemption is in actual process of accomplishment and on the way to its consummation. "But now is Christ risen," and that settles everything. With that established, the Gospel stands, and all that it holds out to men is sure and certain. In it is our unfailing security and warrant as Christian believers. On this our hope rests.

D. How It Helps. St. Paul wrote: "If in this life only we have hoped in Christ, we are of all men most to be pitied" (1 Cor. 15:19). But his faith and anticipation enabled him for the sake of Christ to be content with weaknesses, insults, hardships, persecutions, and calamities (2 Cor. 12:10). So it was with the saints in general. Of his Christian brethren St. Peter says in the text: "In this you rejoice . . . with unutterable and exalted joy."

The source of their joy was their living hope, to which they were born through the resurrection of Jesus Christ. There is a gladdening power in Christianity. If there is any substantial joy in anything, this can furnish it. A somber and unhappy Christian is an anomaly. He does not rightly understand what he professes or half appreciate what has been done for him. He has yet to come into the true light of life. He may believe after a fashion, but he has not yet entered upon the privileges and comforts of faith. The Gospel is to bring us up out of the horrible pit and the miry clay and to set our feet in a large room. We live beneath ourselves if we cannot rise up and bless our God and Father for that abundant mercy by which we have been born again to a living hope.

Is there nothing in full and free cancellation of all our sins in the Savior's blood; nothing in being the very children of God, heirs of God, and joint heirs with Christ? Is there nothing in all this to be glad over? Shall the angels shout at the doings of Almighty Goodness in our behalf, and shall we find no ground of joy in the saving mercies exercised toward ourselves? Shall we behold the holiest treasure of eternity given that we might live forever, and all the blessedness and honors of an imperishable heaven open and sealed to us by the blood and triumph of our God-appointed Savior, and see nothing in it to start a lasting current of joyous gratitude and exultation in our hearts? We should be an abnormity in God's universe, for it is the purpose of Christianity to create in us a faith and hope to comfort, console, and rejoice us with joy unutterable and exalted.

Nor can afflictions or trials in this world extinguish the joy of Christian hope. The people to whom St. Peter wrote were scattered abroad among the Gentiles, driven from their homes, deprived of their country and possessions, and made to suffer all manner of hardship in their exile. But, with all, their Christian consolations did not fail them. "You rejoice, though now for a little while you may have to suffer various trials." They believed, and their souls were full of peace and exultation notwithstanding the sadness of their external condition. Anticipating the far more exceeding and eternal weight of glory to come to them at the revelation of their Lord, they still rejoiced with unutterable and exalted joy.

Many are the afflictions, trials, sorrows, and hardships of this present world, and Christians are as liable to them as any others. Faith will not keep off sickness, or exempt from pains, or deliver from the thousand ills to which flesh is heir. It will not drive off poverty or prevent accident, calamity, and want. It will not do away with bereavements, losses, crosses. It often brings special trials, exposes to persecution, and has its own peculiar tribulations. But it has in it something to uphold and comfort us in them all. "Who shall separate us from the love of Christ? Shall tribulation, or distress, or persecution, or famine, or nakedness, or peril, or sword? . . . No, in all these things we are more than conquerors through Him who loved us."

The gracious and merciful God has a reason for not exempting us from suffering in this present life. Affliction is part of His discipline to make His grace dearer to us, to make us feel our need, to keep us humble, to stimulate our prayers and piety, and to prepare us for our inheritance. It is for the testing and refining of our faith, so that "the genuineness of your faith, more precious than gold which though perishable is tested by fire, may redound to praise and glory and honor at the revelation of Jesus Christ." If there were no sorrow or suffering in the world, there would be fewer saints, less piety, and less fruit of righteousness. It is the very preciousness of gold that causes it to be put into the fire that its dross may be purged. The greater the trials of God's people, if submissively endured, the sublimer is their portion at the last. At worst, they are only temporary, "for a little while," and are meant to work for us the greater glory. Faith knows and sees all this, and it helps to turn grief to joy and lamentations into songs.

It is true that our confidence must rest in an unseen Savior; but that is no hindrance to our Christian joy. We can love and trust in the risen Christ without having Him visible to our sight. "Without having seen Him you love Him; though you do not see Him, you believe in Him." As matters stand in this world, we can have a truer and better conception of Him without seeing Him and can be the more blessed by loving Him without seeing Him. It is enough that our hearts take hold on Him and that our hope in Him is fixed and living. This is ample to give us joy in sorrow and triumph even in death.

Sermon on the Holy Gospel

By Johann Gerhard

When Joseph in Egypt parted from his brothers, he said to them: "Do not quarrel on the way." They were to conduct themselves in a brotherly way and to travel together in upright love. So we read in this day's holy Gospel that when our Lord, the heavenly Joseph, was about to part from His disciples, He commanded them to love one another. They would suffer much in a world of hate and therefore need to love among themselves. We consider:

    I. *Christ's Admonition to Brotherly Love*
   II. *Consolation Against the World's Hate*

I

Our Lord had said to His disciples: "You are My friends if you do what I command you." Then He continued in the text: "This I command you, to love one another." He would have them know what was the command they were to obey as proof that they were His friends. In His farewell address He admonished repeatedly that they love one another. "A new commandment I give to you, that you love one another, even as I have loved you, that you also love one another. By this all men will know that you are My disciples, if you have love for one another" (John 13:34, 35). "Abide in My love. If you keep My commandments, you will abide in My love. . . . This is My commandment, that you love one another as I have loved you" (John 15:9, 10, 12). Nevertheless He repeated the command to love once again in the text, because He realized that the depravity of our nature makes us prone to forget this command and permits love to grow cold in our hearts — as will be true especially toward the end of time (Matt. 24:12) — and because He wished to emphasize love particularly and to leave the command as a precious bequest. We are therefore to make the command to love our special concern:

1. Because our Lord Jesus Christ gave it. He is our Creator, who has given a heart and a soul that we may love. It is only right and reasonable that we submit to this command. He is our

Redeemer, who has brought us into His Kingdom of Grace. It is only fair and proper that we follow the rules and regulations of His Kingdom. He is our Lord. It is our duty to follow Him as obedient disciples. He is our soul's Bridegroom. It is only reasonable that we love Him and lovingly obey this command. He is our eternal King. It is only right that we subject ourselves to Him and dutifully obey His command. He is our Head. It is only natural that we as members of His spiritual body follow His directions, as He said: "By this all men will know that you are My disciples, if you have love for one another" (John 13:35). From this the opposite, that whoever will not follow this command of love is not as yet Christ's disciple, is to be concluded.

2. Because it is part of our Lord's farewell address, part of His last will and testament. Obedient children remember throughout life the instructions the parents gave before their death. How much more should we remember this command of Him who did endlessly much for us and whose love was far superior to that of parents!

3. Because this is our Lord's one and only new commandment. "A new commandment I give to you," He said, "that you love one another," as though He would tell them: This is My commandment, My one and own commandment. I will not burden you with many statutes as Moses did, but instead of all others I give you the command of love. When love governs all your words and deeds, yes, your heart, there is no need for many commandments. Should we, then, not fulfill this command of Christ willingly and gladly?

4. Because it is an easy commandment. "His commandments are not burdensome" (1 John 5:3). For what is easier and more pleasant than to love? Love is not only agreeable and delightful in itself but also makes its objects pleasing and delightful. There is nothing as bitter as death, yet when one willingly gives one's life out of love for another, even death is beautiful and agreeable. Should we, then, not follow this lovely command of Christ? Christ does not demand love in the highest degree by compulsion and pressure as did Moses, but in a friendly manner He entices us to love, gives the Holy Spirit into our hearts, powerfully reveals His own sweet love so that we may be moved to love also and to

follow this command with willing spirit. Though our love is not so holy and perfect as it should be, He patiently bears with our weakness, covers our shortcomings, and by His Spirit works constantly in us that our love may become more perfect.

5. Because the love Christ here commands is a lofty and precious thing. "God is Love" (1 John 4:8). He does everything out of love and is the essence of eternal love. Whoever loves abides in God, and God in him. St. John could not have raised love to a loftier plane than to say that God Himself is Love.

Love is certain evidence of true faith. Only "faith working through love" is of any avail (Gal. 5:6). Love is active through faith. "Show me your faith apart from works, and I by my works will show you my faith" (James 2:18). Therefore where there is no love, there can be no true, genuine faith but only a false semblance.

Love is a glorious fruit of the Spirit (Gal. 5:22). Where therefore this fruit of the Spirit is not in evidence, the heart is not as yet a temple and dwelling of the Holy Spirit.

Love is the bond that unites all members of Christ's body, and it is said: "Put on love, which binds everything together in perfect harmony" (Col. 3:14). In the Old Testament the curtains of the tabernacle were coupled with clasps (Ex. 26:4 ff.). So the hearts of the faithful, in whom Christ has His dwelling, are bound together by the clasps of love. Where there is no love, there is no true and living member of the spiritual body of Christ.

Without love all other gifts and graces, be they ever so lofty, are nothing. 1 Cor. 13:1: "If I speak in the tongues of men and angels but have not love, I am a noisy gong or a clanging cymbal." Without love there is no genuine Christianity, no good and God-pleasing life. As we value our Christianity, we should be concerned about loving one another.

Love will also endure in the life of eternity, yes, will then become all the more perfect. For this reason St. Paul gives it preference over faith and hope (1 Cor. 13:13). As the fire from heaven and the golden vessels were brought from the tabernacle into the temple of Solomon, so the gold and fire of love will be brought out of the Church Militant on earth into the victorious and triumphant Church in heaven. Therefore we must permit the

Holy Spirit to kindle the fire of love in this life, and we must tend and maintain it faithfully if we would have it perfected in the heavenly Jerusalem, the City of God.

All this is to commend most forcibly Christ's command to love one another. If anyone wishes to examine himself whether he has such love, let him study 1 Corinthians 13, in which the noble tree of love and its excellent fruits are described gloriously. Where these fruits are found, there is the true love. However, the fruits of the tree at times appear fair on the outside but are worm-eaten and rotten on the inside, as is said particularly of the apples of Sodom that they appear healthy and good but that when they are touched and handled, they turn to dust and ashes. So the works of hypocrites sometimes appear good yet have a hidden worm and rottenness, such as self-love, self-glorification, a desire for personal advantage, and the like. Whoever, then, outwardly assumes a friendly pose but in his heart hates his neighbor, or does good works in the neighbor's behalf for the sake of his own honor, is not doing good works prompted by upright love of the neighbor. There is a hidden worm in such works that ruins them. O God, Thou Essence of love, warm our hearts with the fire of love. Write this command of Christ in our heart that we may willingly obey it. Remove all hellish seed of the Serpent and all evil tares of hatred, envy, anger, discord, and the like, that the blessed fruit of love may grow in us. May the heavenly dew of Thy grace refresh the precious plant of love in us that it may prosper to eternal life.

II

After the Lord Jesus had so admonished His disciples to love one another, He spoke to them of the world's hate and persecution, in order to arm them with patience and consolation. The admonition to love is followed immediately by comfort against the world's hate, because the disciples were to overcome all adversities and particularly the world's hate by brotherly love.

In comforting His disciples our Lord directs their attention first to His own example and then to the reason for the world's hate. The first source of comfort He gives in the words: "If the world hates you, know that it has hated Me before it hated you." Do not allow the world's hate to keep you from loving one another, but remember that I experienced the same at the hands of the world and was hated and persecuted no less. "He who does not take up his cross and follow Me is not worthy of Me" (Matt. 10:38). "If any man would come after Me, let him deny himself and take up his cross [daily] and follow Me" (Matt. 16:24; Luke 9:23). "Consider Him who endured from sinners such hostility against Himself, so that you may not grow weary or fainthearted" (Heb. 12:3).

Then Christ points to the reason why the world hates His disciples. "If you were of the world, the world would love its own; but because you are not of the world [that is, of those who are earthly, worldly-minded, and who put their trust in this world] but I chose you out of the world, therefore the world hates you." The world's hate and persecution should frighten you as little as it grieves you that you are not of the world. You should rejoice when you are hated and persecuted in the world, even as you rejoice that you are chosen out of the world. "Not frightened in anything by your opponents. This is a clear omen to them of their destruction but of your salvation" (Phil. 1:28).

Then Christ goes back to the first source of comfort and again directs them to His example. "Remember the word that I said to you, A servant is not greater than his master. If they persecuted Me, they will persecute you; if they kept My word, they will keep yours also." He refers them to His word recorded Matt. 10:24, Luke 6:40, John 13:16. Remembering His own experience, they will not be frightened or offended that their teaching is despised and they are not only hated but persecuted because of it, since their Lord and Master fared no better.

Next our Lord returns once more to the second source of consolation and points out the reason why they will be hated and persecuted. "But all this they will do to you on My account, because they do not know Him who sent Me." Some opponents will wish to be regarded as men who know the true God and preserve His honor, but because they do not know the Son, they do not know the Father who sent Him (John 5:23). In the verses following the text our Lord declares that this ignorance cannot serve to excuse the world's opposition. "If I had not come and spoken to them, they would have no sin," that is, the opponents

would still have something to excuse their sin of refusing to accept
My teaching, "but now they have no excuse for their sin," because I proclaim the very teaching attributed to the Messiah by the
prophets. "He who hates Me hates My Father," who is of the
same indivisible essence with Me, whose teaching I teach, and by
whom I was sent into the world. "If I had not done among them
the works which no one else did, they would not have sin; but
now they have seen and hated both Me and My Father." They
have seen that I did the works which the prophecies ascribe to the
Messiah. They hate the Father who has done these works through
Me. "It is to fulfill the word that is written in their Law, They
hated Me without a cause" (Ps. 35:7; 69:4). All this is said to
assure His disciples that the world's hate is without cause and to
encourage them to bear it patiently.

What our Lord said to His disciples in the night before His
death is to be our consolation also when we are hated and persecuted for Christ's sake. What is there that can seem hard and
heavy to our flesh and blood and will not be bearable when we
consider Christ's example? He is the Son of the Most High, come
to earth that He might suffer and die for the world's sin, yet the
reward He reaped from the world was hatred, envy, affliction,
defamation, and persecution. Therefore we must not find it strange
that we receive the same treatment. Why should the members be
more fortunate than the Head? Whoever will not suffer with the
Head cannot be a true member of this spiritual life. Though we
may not expect to be rewarded for our suffering, it should be
gratifying that we have become like our Lord. For then we may
boast with St. Paul that we bear on our body the marks of Jesus
(Gal. 6:17), and with St. John that we share the tribulation, the
Kingdom, and the patience of Jesus Christ (Rev. 1:9).

Again, by its hate and persecution the world proves that it is
alien to the true knowledge of God and therefore also to eternal
salvation, and we have a deeper concern about the poor world
than about our suffering. Its suffering is eternal and endless, ours
temporary and passing. The world hates the true God and will
be hated by Him, but we are at peace with God. The worldling
is a slave of sin and has no excuse for his sin, but we are servants
of God, to whose glory we patiently suffer in dutiful obedience.

Thirdly, our persecution and adversities in this world are a sign that we are chosen out of the world. "For those whom He foreknew He also predestined to be conformed to the image of His Son" (Rom. 8:29). Not only that, but He has carefully weighed by what and by how much affliction He would make the elect to conform to the image of His Son. If, then, we are parties to the process of conformation, we have within ourselves the witness that we are chosen out of the world. "Through many tribulations we must enter the Kingdom of God," said St. Paul (Acts 14:22). If, then, we walk the way of sorrow, we may be confident our path leads to life eternal.

Finally, God has not only ordained from eternity but has also declared in His holy Word that His own may expect only hate and persecution in the world. "All who desire to live a godly life in Christ Jesus will be persecuted" (1 Tim. 3:12). If this were not true, all the prophecies would not be fulfilled. This, too, gives comfort in all affliction and persecution, that the Lord God has such accurate knowledge of our sorrows and considers them so worthy and important as to have them foretold in His holy Word. Then let the world hate and persecute. It will not change God's decree of our salvation or His promise of future glory, which is to follow upon our sorrow. May God grant us this through Jesus Christ, His Son.

THE FESTIVAL OF THE REFORMATION
October 31

The Lutheran Liturgy is unique in appointing a Festival of the Reformation. The *Common Service Book* and the new *Service Book,* prepared by the Joint Commission on the Liturgy, list it among the Greater Festivals. It may be traced back to the annual commemoration of the translation of the Bible into the German language or to the annual Thanksgiving Service commemorating the introduction of the Reformation. Bugenhagen's orders for Brunswick provided for such a celebration as early as 1528. The Pomeranian set the date as St. Martin's Day, in memory of Luther's birth on St. Martin's Eve. Some orders appointed the Sunday after the Nativity of St. John the Baptist, since the Augsburg Confession was presented on June 25. After the Thirty Years' War the Elector of Saxony appointed it for October 31. The effect has been that an ancient and important festival has been overshadowed, All Saints' Day, on November 1. If the Festival of the Reformation must be observed on a Sunday, this should be the Sunday before October 31, in order that All Saints' Day be allowed an equal observance on the Sunday after November 1. The trend has been to move weekday festivals to the nearest Sunday. Perhaps the time has come for serious and persistent effort to train our people in observing the weekday festivals on the appointed days. Such efforts were successful in regard to the midweek Lenten services. The Festival of the Reformation is distinctly Lutheran and offers a splendid opportunity to make a beginning, without exposing our people to Roman concepts which at times color the "keeping" of Lent.

It is not amiss to remind Lutherans that, like all other festivals of the Church Year, the Festival of the Reformation is observed to the glory of God and not to glorify Luther or the Lutheran

Church or any branch of the Lutheran Church. Nor is the object of the observance to present the evils of the Papacy. The purpose is to thank and praise God for the blessings of the Reformation. Luther's person will inject itself of necessity, but he was merely the instrument God employed to do great things for His Church. For this reason it is gratifying that the festival is not observed on Luther's birthday, for only the Lord Jesus Christ and St. John the Baptist are accorded the honor of having their birth commemorated by the Church. If Luther's birthday is to be commemorated, this may be done without subtracting an additional Sunday from the Trinity Season, especially if the Festival of the Reformation has been observed only one or two Sundays before.

The Introit. "The Lord of hosts is with us; the God of Jacob is our Refuge. Therefore will not we fear though the earth be removed and though the mountains be carried into the midst of the sea. God is our Refuge and Strength, a very present Help in trouble."

The text is from Psalm 46, which is usually associated with the Reformation. When the hymn *Ein' feste Burg* first appeared, it bore the title "Der XXXXVI Psalm." It is more than a metrical paraphrase. It is really an original production on the theme of David's psalm, with some phrases reminiscent of the Biblical text.

The Collect. "O Lord God, heavenly Father, pour out, we beseech Thee, Thy Holy Spirit upon Thy faithful people, keep them steadfast in Thy grace and truth, protect and comfort them in all temptations, defend them against all enemies of Thy Word, and bestow upon Christ's Church Militant Thy saving peace; through the same Jesus Christ," etc.

This prayer is from the Saxon Order, 1539—40. The *Common Service Book* brings a second Collect, which first appeared in 1918.

The Epistle, Revelation 14:6,7. This text appears to lend itself poorly as basis for a sermon. It seems difficult to separate the angel and his message from the context, for a second and a third angel follow and deliver their message of doom. The King James Version translates "the everlasting Gospel," the Revised Standard "an eternal Gospel." What the angel proclaims is "a Gospel everlasting," not another Gospel but the Gospel as its contents shape themselves in its address to the nations when "the hour of His judgment has come." Luther once said that he did not like this book, because its spirit did not agree with his feelings as to the Gospel. His great soul, permeated through and through with the very life and spirit of reconciliation in Christ Jesus, felt that here is something different, just as the Christian is disturbed by the imprecatory Psalms. The message of the angel is Gospel, but it is the Gospel in the form it takes when the hour of judgment has set in. Perhaps the Epistle appointed in the *Common Service Book* is to be preferred (Gal. 2:16-21), in which the central doctrine of the Reformation, the justification through faith, is gloriously expounded by St. Paul.

The Gradual. "Great is the Lord and greatly to be praised in the city of our God, in the mountain of His holiness. Walk about Zion; tell the towers thereof, mark well her bulwarks, consider her palaces, that ye may tell it to the generation following. Alleluia! Alleluia! For this God is our God forever and ever. He will be our Guide even unto death. Alleluia!"

The text is from Psalm 48, also usually associated with the Reformation. Jehovah revealed Himself as the great Lord, the God of salvation, and is to be praised exceedingly in Jerusalem and on Mount Zion, where He resided in the midst of His peculiar people. The city of God and Mount Zion were prophetic pictures of the holy Christian Church, the Communion of Saints, which the Holy Spirit calls, gathers, enlightens, sanctifies, and keeps with Jesus Christ in the one true faith. In this Church the Lord is great and praised exceedingly. Walk about Zion, surround and encircle her, as Israel walked about Jericho. Survey the perfect state of her defenses. Count her towers to see if any of them have been demolished. Set your heart to her ramparts, apply your mind, give attention, observe closely, examine her palaces on the inside, that you may recount the result of your inspection on the outside, the sound state of the defenses, as an emblem of the safety which the Church enjoys, that you may tell it to later or future generations. For this God, our God, forever and ever, for eternity and perpetuity, will be our Guide even to the end of life.

The Gospel, St. Matthew 11:12-15. The *Common Service Book* suggests St. John 8:31-36. *Country Sermons,* Volume IV, by the Rev. F. Kuegele, contains an excellent sermon on the holy Gospel from St. Matthew.

The Common Preface.

NOTES ON THE HOLY GOSPEL

Adapted and translated from *Das Evangelium Matthaei* by Dr. Oskar Pank. C. Ed. Mueller's Verlagsbuchhandlung, 1920, Halle.

"He who has ears to hear, let him hear." We know the serious tone of these words. Whenever our Lord employs them, it is to impress deeply some especially significant truth. In this instance, as always, His Word strikes the consciences of Lutheran Christendom like a hammer blow, on this anniversary of the day when four and one-half centuries ago Luther's hammer struck mightily on the doors of the Christian Church. The text takes us back to the greatest days this world has ever seen, when the Kingdom of Heaven came into this world in the person of the Lord Jesus Christ, when in St. John the Baptist the Old Testament reached its most radiant climax and the New Testament dawned. In the morning hour the Baptist appeared, of whom our Lord said that no one greater has risen among those born of women. Yet he who is least in the Kingdom of Heaven is greater than he. The least in God's Kingdom of the New Testament is greater and richer, because St. John had only the promise, stood merely on the threshold, whereas the humblest sinner who by faith has laid hold on Jesus Christ as his Savior stands within the holy of holies and has more abundant grace than he who still asks, "Are you He who is to come, or shall we look for another?"

Of the days when the New Testament dawned our Lord said: "From the days of John the Baptist [from the time he disappeared from the stage] until now the Kingdom of Heaven has suffered violence [or has been coming violently] and men of violence take it by force." He was not referring to the violence of enemies who persecute and kill to destroy the Kingdom of Heaven. It is a holy violence that takes it and really gets possession of it, a violence which makes men heirs of God. The force employed is spiritual, not physical, the violence is done with the heart and soul, not with the fist. It is violence in which God takes great delight. In those early days souls desiring salvation and hungering for it took the Kingdom by storm. A spirit laid hold upon the people that would not be denied. By their faith, contrition, and prayers they strove and fought, and the Kingdom was their spoil and prize.

The world will not and cannot see such days of holy violence again. Yet the history of the Christian Church records similar times when men took the Kingdom by force. Upon periods of decline followed periods of spiritual force. When the Kingdom of God seemed almost to have disappeared and been forgotten, hearts again took possession by violent assault. This was true in the great days of the Reformation.

After Luther had vainly wrestled for peace in the monk's cowl of renunciation and mortification and when at last heaven opened to his soul "by faith alone," he stormed the very gates of heaven by the power of his faith until he took it. Later he stormed heaven again and again by prayer. Truly the greatest and noblest quality of this hero in God's Kingdom was the faith by which he stormed and took heaven violently and forcefully. In the night before he appeared at the Diet of Worms he was heard to pray as if he were determined to draw heaven down to earth by violence and force of faith: "O God, O God, Thou art mine, Thou art my God! Stand by me against all men's reason and wisdom. Thou must do it, for when I turn my eyes that way, I am done for, the bell is already cast, and the sentence is pronounced. Be with me, I rely on no man!" At the sickbed of Melanchthon he demanded in prayer that the devil be not permitted to destroy this instrument of God. In a letter to the timorous Melanchthon in Augsburg he wrote: "God has assigned this matter a place which is beyond and outside your rhetoric and philosophy. This means: Believe! . . . If Christ were to lose the title 'King of kings and Lord of lords' in Augsburg, He will have lost it also in heaven and on earth."

As Luther, so were the heroic believers of that day who followed his banner and thousand and thousands who were seized by the power of evangelical preaching. A violent emotion ran through men in all walks of life. Hungrily men took hold on the Kingdom of Heaven, stormed it, and did it violence. Commenting on the text, Luther once wrote: "The Gospel is not preached in vain; there are people who hear it and love it violently, so that they hazard body and life for the sake of God's Word. When they hear the Gospel, their conscience drives them on, so that none can keep them away." They virtually laid siege to the churches of evangelical preachers. Luther's writings and hymns could not be printed fast enough to keep up with the demand. Again and again entire congregations interrupted a Catholic sermon by singing one of Luther's hymns and so compelled the priest to leave the pulpit. All this was doing violence to the Kingdom of Heaven, of which our Lord speaks in the text.

How do we compare with these heroes of the faith? This day is not an occasion for lamentations and accusations while the good of our days is ignored. It may be said without hesitation that we are living in a time of growth in the Church's history. Many who once cared little for the Kingdom of God are learning to seek it. But it is not a matter of merely seeking it, but of fighting and doing holy violence. He who would attain heaven must be fully in earnest. Yet where are the people who today actually strive and strain with Luther's holy determination? Where are the heroes who by their faith overcome God, who by their prayers take heaven by storm? If persecution were to come upon us, and all who go to church and profess to believe the Gospel were to lose their position, possessions, and means of livelihood, how many of us would be seen in church? How many would remain faithful and true to our profession unto death? Let us be honest though we might be ashamed. We look like dwarfs by the side of the heroes of the Reformation.

> Rise again, ye lionhearted
> Saints of early Christendom.
> Whither is your strength departed,
> Whither gone your martyrdom?
> Lo, love's light is on them,
> Glory's flame upon them,
> And their will to die doth quell
> E'en the lord and prince of hell.

ALL SAINTS' DAY

November 1

The Feast of All Saints had its beginning in Syria circa 360. It was there observed on the Friday after Easter in honor of all holy martyrs. The Greeks commemorated all saints on the Octave of Pentecost, the West on May 13. In Rome, Agrippa built the Pantheon in honor of Augustus for all gods of the seven planets in the year 27 B. C. This building was given to the Pope, and Boniface IV rededicated it as a Christian basilica in A. D. 610, and according to report twenty-eight wagonloads of the remains of early martyrs were "translated" from the catacombs to this church, dedicated to the memory of Mary and all holy martyrs on May 13. Gregory IV appointed November 1 as the date of the feast and confirmed its title as All Saints' instead of All Martyrs'. The feast recalls the memories of all the faithful departed and the triumph of Christ over all false gods. At the very end of the tenth century an additional feast, All Souls', was initiated and officially accepted by the Roman Church in the fourteenth century. It commemorates the souls in Purgatory who are not technically regarded as saints. After the Reformation the Lutherans in many parts of Germany and generally in Scandinavia, and the Anglicans, continued to observe All Saints' but rejected All Souls' Day because of its unscriptural implications. The *New Service Book,* prepared by the Joint Commission on the Liturgy, makes All Saints' Day a major festival of equal rank with the Festival of the Reformation. It is a more fitting occasion for the commemoration of the faithful departed than a *Totenfest,* than the Last Sunday after Trinity or St. Sylvester's Day, on December 31.

The Introit. "A great multitude which no man could number stood before the throne and before the Lamb, clothed with white robes and with palms in their hands, and cried with a loud voice, saying: Salvation to our God, which sitteth upon the throne, and unto the Lamb. Rejoice in the Lord, O ye righteous, for praise is comely for the upright."

In the *Common Service Book* the Introit is Rev. 7:14, 15 a, Ps. 33:1.

The Collect. "O almighty God, who hast knit together Thine elect in one communion and fellowship in the mystical body of Thy Son, Christ, our Lord, grant us grace so to follow Thy blessed saints in all virtuous and godly living that we may come to those unspeakable joys which Thou hast prepared for those who unfeignedly love Thee."

This prayer is by English Reformers, composed in 1549.

The Epistle, Revelation 7:2-17. This Lesson leads us into heaven. St. John permits us a glimpse of the Church in glory, and we see the great multitude of saints gathered around the throne of God, singing holy hymns. A number, a great but countable number, came from the Jews, but innumerable multitudes from the Gentiles. All have been cleansed from sin by the blood of the Lamb and now bear palms of victory in their hands.

The Gradual. "Oh, fear the Lord, ye His saints, for there is no want to them that fear Him. They that seek the Lord shall not want any good thing. Alleluia! Alleluia! Come unto Me, all ye that labor and are heavy laden, and I will give you rest. Alleluia!"

Here we are led back to earth and shown the way to heaven in preparation for the hearing of the holy Gospel, which is about to be read.

The Gospel, St. Matthew 5:1-12. The Epistle shows us the saints in heaven and the holy Gospel the saints on earth. The Lessons picture the blessedness of the saints in heaven and the blessedness of the saints on earth.

The Common Preface.

OUTLINE FOR SERMON ON THE EPISTLE

We are observing the Feast of All Saints, consecrated for many centuries to the memory of those whom the Lord removed by death and transferred into the Church Triumphant in heaven. The Epistle is a portion of St. John's vision of heaven. He saw God on the throne. Before the throne were twenty-four elders, representing the Church, who fell down in worship and adoration before Him who sat upon the throne. In the midst stood the Lamb, who took the book of seven seals containing the counsels of God in regard to men and opened six seals. But before the seventh was opened, before God's final acts, St. John saw four angels standing on the four corners of the earth, holding the four winds of the earth, which if released would destroy the earth in final Judgment. Another angel cried with a loud voice not to release the final destruction until the servants of God were sealed upon their foreheads and the elect of God gathered in. The number of the elect was 144,000. The number twelve symbolizes perfection and completeness. Twelve times twelve is completeness multiplied by completeness. Thousand signifies greatness. So twelve times twelve thousand is a large and perfect number. St. John saw a great multitude which no man could number, from every nation, from all tribes and peoples and tongues, standing before the throne and the Lamb, clothed in white robes of purity and righteousness, with palm branches in their hands. This vast multitude cried out with a loud voice: All praise and honor for our salvation belongs to our God, who sits upon the throne, and to the Lamb! And all the angels standing round the throne and round the elders and the four living creatures fell on their faces before the throne and worshiped God with a sevenfold magnificat.

One of the elders now said to St. John: "Who are these, clothed in white robes, and whence have they come?" He knows, but he questions in order to teach. When then St. John answers him, "Sir, you know, he answered him": "These are they who have come out of great tribulation; they have washed their robes and made them white in the blood of the Lamb." There is a continuous pouring in of the elect from the world of care to the realm of peace. Because they have washed their robes white in the blood of the Lamb, "therefore are they before the throne of God and serve Him day and night within His temple, and He who sits upon the throne will shelter them with His presence." He will dwell among them, spread His tabernacle over them, as He did in the wilderness. "They shall hunger no more, neither thirst any more; the sun shall not strike them, nor any scorching

heat. For the Lamb in the midst of the throne will be their
shepherd, and He will guide them to springs of living water;
and God will wipe away every tear from their eyes."

We have here a glimpse of the departed believers. They are
not yet in their glorified state, as they will be after the Last
Judgment, when their bodies shall live again. This glorified state
will be ushered in at Christ's Second Coming. In the text we see
them between the Second Coming and their earthly life. The
Church of God is still divided, part on earth and part in heaven.
Having placed this vision, we now look at:

Our Friends Who Are Already in Heaven

A. Where do we see them? Before the throne and before the
Lamb. These words give us no clue to the locality of heaven.
We do not need it. Any part of "the Father's house" is home to
His children. There is something of far greater interest and importance here: the state of the saints rather than the place. "Before
the throne." While in the flesh they had a consciousness of God's
presence, but here they are far more conscious of the immediate,
all-surrounding, and all-pervading presence. "Before the Lamb."
On earth they saw the Savior with the eyes of faith, whom having
not seen they loved. Now they see Him. The veil of sense and
the limitations of earth no longer obstruct their sight. They are
forever with their God, in His immediate presence, where they
wished and longed to be.

B. What is their appearance? They are "standing." They
stand, but God sits upon the throne. This standing is a sign or
token of subjection and service. They have white robes. White
stands for purity and righteousness. On earth they were sinners
as all men and had their garments spotted by sin. But they washed
their garments in the blood of the Lamb. The blood of Jesus
Christ, His Son, cleanses us from all sin. So they appear before
God pure and spotless, arrayed in the garment of Christ's righteousness. Pure and holy, they are fit to mingle with the angels and
to stand before God. They have palm branches in their hands.
This reminds us of the Jewish Feast of the Tabernacles, the most
joyous observance of Israel. It came at the close of the year's

outdoor labors, when the season of rest began. It commemorated God's care during the wilderness period and His continued care by the gifts of His providence in the Promised Land. One of the chief features of this festival was the carrying of palm branches. So St. John sees the saints who are coming out of great tribulation bearing palm branches. The troubles of the wilderness are ended, the harvest home of the Church has come. The days of labor are over, now comes rest.

C. Whence come they? "From every nation, from all tribes and peoples and tongues." Sin brought about this separation and confusion on earth. That is done away with in Christ. Its effects disappear in heaven. All barriers caused by diversity of language will cease. The final union in the heavenly state will present the true solution of the question that concerns the unity of the human race and vexes us here on earth. There it will be apparent at last that God made of one blood all nations of men.

D. How come they here? The answer is twofold. First, they come by the pathway of a common experience. They have come out of the great tribulation. Wars, famine, pestilences, persecutions, revolutions desolate the earth and make life one great tribulation. But they have left it all behind. They are free from it now. The words have been fulfilled: "We must through much tribulation enter into the Kingdom of God." (Acts 14:22)

Again, they reach heaven on the ground of a common redemption. The atoning sacrifice of the Lord Jesus availed for them all. The cleansing power of a Savior's grace purified them all. "They have washed their robes," that is, in their earthly life they experienced this sanctifying grace.

E. What do they miss? "They will hunger no more, neither thirst any more; the sun shall not strike them, nor any scorching heat." On this earth their bodily frame demanded incessant attention. The activity of the spiritual life was often interrupted by the demands of the fleshly life. The flesh lusted against the spirit. The spirit was willing, but the flesh was weak. On high such clogs burden them no more.

All sorrow has passed away. "God will wipe away every tear from their eyes." This is perhaps the tenderest little sentence in the whole Bible. We who are still in the great tribulation can hardly conceive of a state when there shall be nothing to cause a single tear to flow, no dying, no sorrow, no pain, no longing. Picture the vision! From all nations the saints stream into heaven out of the great tribulation, their cheeks wet with tears, and God tenderly wiping away all tears and saying comfortingly: "So, that is all over."

F. What do they enjoy? For one thing, the real presence of God. "He who sits upon the throne will shelter them with His presence." It is impossible to clothe the presence of God in human words; so the elder paraphrases the thought that they enjoy intimate communion with the Sovereign of all. The presence of God shelters them as a tent, covers them, they are secure eternally. He will spread His tabernacle over them. In the wilderness the tabernacle was the visible symbol of God's presence among His people. Over it hovered the pillar of cloud by day and the pillar of fire by night. "The Lamb . . . will be their Shepherd." In His relation to God, Christ is the Lamb, in His relation to His people He is a tender Shepherd. He will feed them the bread of heaven and guide them to springs of the water of life. Here they had but crumbs, there they have in abundance. Here they had but drops, there they have the fullness of the fountain. Here the bread and water of life reached them through earthen channels, a printed book and human lips, there they are at the fountainhead. What do they enjoy? Entire satisfaction, perfect security and repose.

G. Finally, how are they occupied? Only one aspect of their occupation is given here. They "serve Him day and night within His temple." For details regarding this service we must wait until we die. We have presented to us merely the service of praise, the giving of honor and praise for salvation equally to God and the Lamb, to the Father and the Son. This service of praise is unwearied, day and night. Never do they tire of singing God's praises for His unmerited mercy and grace shown when He sent the Holy Spirit with His message of Christ Jesus and worked faith by the Gospel and kept them in faith until the end.

H. Application. This is the picture St. John paints of the saints in heaven, for us who are still in the great tribulation. Some of us may have come here today sorrowing over the loss of some sainted loved one, but as we open our eyes to the vision of the Epistle, it is as if God even now wiped away every tear from our eyes. Our grief appears selfish. We are thinking only of our loss and not of their gain. In spite of all our pain caused by separation, we would not wish them back. They have come out of the great tribulation. For us there remains only the wish to be with them.

This wish to be with the saints is gratified in a measure today at the Lord's Table, as we commune with our Lord and all the saints. If we would feel close to our loved ones who died in the Lord, the place is not on the cemetery, where only their physical covering found a temporary sleeping place. The place to have communion with them, to be close to their real selves, is at the Lord's Table. The Holy Communion is the Sacrament that links us to the saints in heaven.

The text tells us that the Lamb in the midst of the throne will be their Shepherd, feeding them with the bread of heaven. Today this same Lamb is truly present here, the Lamb of God, who gives us heavenly food, His very Body and Blood together with the Bread and Wine, heavenly manna, His very Self.

The saints stand before the throne and the Lamb, praising God for their salvation. The angels join in the praise. Today we also join in the song of heaven in the Holy Eucharist. We acknowledge: "It is truly meet, right, and salutary that we should at all times and in all places give thanks unto Thee, holy Father, almighty, everlasting God. Therefore with angels and archangels, and with all the company of heaven, we laud and magnify Thy glorious name." Then we break forth in the jubilant Sanctus, the song of the angels from Isaiah's vision: "Holy, holy, holy, Lord God of Hosts, all the earth is full of Thy glory." So sing not only we but angels and archangels, yes, all the company of heaven, the saints in glory, our blessed dead.

We read that the saints have palm branches in their hands and sing: "Salvation belongs to our God." So we today greet our Lord as He comes to us in the Holy Sacrament and sing as did the people when He came to Jerusalem. Then they waved palm branches and sang: Hosannah! Bring now salvation! Blessed is

He that cometh in the name of the Lord! Hosanna! Salvation belongs to our God!

The saints are arrayed in white garments. Because they washed their robes in the blood of the Lamb, they stand before God. We come rejoicing and wash our robe in the blood of the Lamb. By eating and drinking in faith we declare: He gave His Body for me, He shed His Blood for me. My sins are all forgiven, washed away. I, too, even now am arrayed in Christ's righteousness, and therefore I, too, shall stand before the throne of God. As the saints in the text ascribe all honor for their salvation to God and the Lamb, so we declare by our coming to the Holy Communion: I am one whom the Lord redeemed by His suffering and death. All my hope is built on this, that He gave His Body and shed His Blood for me.

So we could continue indefinitely to show that never are we closer to heaven and our sainted loved ones than in Holy Communion with Christ, with one another, and with the members of the Church who have come out of the great tribulation. Here we have a foretaste of the bliss which the saints enjoy in heaven. Here is the Lamb, here He feeds us with Himself, here we occupy ourselves as do the inhabitants of heaven. May we, as we gather before the throne and the Lamb today in praise and adoration, become conscious of the fact that we are experiencing a foretaste of heaven and are in communion also with the saints.

NOTES FOR SERMON ON THE HOLY GOSPEL

The Epistle and the holy Gospel describe the two-sided lesson of All Saints' Day. The Epistle shows the saints who have reached the rest remaining for the people of God and assures us of their safety and unclouded bliss. Their troubles all over, their temptations all past, their sins all forgiven, triumphant and rejoicing they stand before the throne and the Lamb. The holy Gospel describes the saints on earth. It places before us a well-known portion of the Bible, the Beatitudes from the Sermon on the Mount. The King issues a proclamation to the citizens of His Kingdom. He lays down the laws that are to govern the citizens. At the same time He describes the people who are His saints here on earth and will be His saints in heaven.

These declarations have been much misunderstood and often misapplied. Men have taken the Beatitudes and with them painted a picture of a most unfortunate, almost ridiculous creature, who has been compelled to renounce almost every characteristic of a self-respecting human being. The saint on earth, the citizen of Christ's Kingdom, is represented to be a penniless, sniveling, spineless, spiritless individual, an object of contempt and scorn to every red-blooded man or woman. This is, of course, a gross misconception of Christ's words. Our Lord did not come to make us poor and miserable and contemptible, but to make us rich, rich in every quality that makes for real manhood, rich in our outlook on life and its meaning, rich in the things that truly and lastingly satisfy the cravings of the human heart. He came not to detract from life but to make it more abundant.

Every Beatitude begins with the word *Blessed.* The word used here is different from the word translated with "blessed" in Matt. 23:39 and 25:34. Some, when they hear this word in the Beatitudes, think of pleasure, others of good fortune, still others of happiness. But blessedness is far more than that. The word is derived from a Greek word meaning "great." It was applied to a man who was wealthy, powerful, honored. The Greeks called their gods blessed, not because they were good and perfect and happy, but because they had power, dignity, because they were masterful. The Bible takes this word and gives it a higher and nobler meaning. When our Lord said, "Blessed is the man," He meant to say, "Powerful, dignified, masterful, is the man," he has attained to what God intended him to be. He is perfect, beyond the reach of every ill, his life is restored to its fullness, he lives in perfect harmony with God. He has acquired dignity, power, absolute mastery of life and its environment. He has gotten hold of that which restores his broken life and brings him into harmony with the Author of his being and all the higher laws of life.

A. "Blessed are the poor in spirit, for theirs is the Kingdom of Heaven." Poor in spirit stands in contrast to self-sufficiency. It describes the man who is so poor that he lives by begging. In his opinion he has nothing, no qualifications or qualities that enable him to meet life. He begs everything from God. In himself and by himself he has no power to fight life's battles, but he asks and receives that power from God.

This man is blessed, masterful, powerful, dignified. When the storms of life sweep over him, the self-sufficient man finds his resources inadequate, and he becomes frantic. The man who does not depend upon himself but upon God begs and receives counsel and strength from God, and he remains calm, collected, masterful. He has the solution for every problem. He is never defeated, able to handle every situation. For the Kingdom of Heaven is his. The Kingdom of Heaven is the realm in which the almighty God rules absolutely, in which there is no opposing will and purpose. It is the Kingdom that marches on victoriously through this time and shall be established in eternity. If this Kingdom is his, a man is bound to be on the winning side, to come out on top. He is marching with God to victory. God's eternal purposes will be accomplished in spite of all opposition. The poor in spirit yield themselves to the purposes of God, and so they belong to, and have a share in, the Kingdom of Heaven.

B. "Blessed are those who mourn, for they shall be comforted." This mourning is not the sorrow of which every man is capable, not the pain caused by losses and troubles. It is a deeper, an inward mourning of the spirit, closely related to the poverty of the spirit. It is a mourning over one's unworthiness, sinfulness, slowness of spiritual progress and improvement. To truly mourn over his unworthiness, a man must have stood on Golgotha and seen the great love of Christ. It is only there that he can feel true sorrow for his many sins against that great love, for his want of gratitude, for the coldness of his heart.

There under the Cross the citizens of the Kingdom also learn the blessedness of mourning. For they shall be comforted. He who calls, "Come to Me, all who labor and are heavy-laden, and I will give you rest," fulfills His promise. They lay their burden at the foot of the Cross and receive the assurance that their Savior took it all away. In the consciousness that all which stood between them and their God is cleared away, as men who are comforted with the lasting comfort of God, they are blessed.

C. "Blessed are the meek, for they shall inherit the earth." Meekness is an attitude of the spirit which we assume when another is acting in regard to us. To be and remain a citizen of the Kingdom of Heaven, a man must be meek, first of all, toward God. When God acts in his life, the meek man will accept His dealings as good. He will not dispute or resist. He will not fight against God, contend with Him. The natural reaction in a man when God deals with him contrary to his own wishes and desires is rebellion and resentment. This spirit of rebellion is the real source of all unhappiness. Blessed is the man who realizes his own folly and ignorance and yields himself and his life to God's superior wisdom, trusts God's unfailing love, and humbly submits. He is blessed, dignified, collected, in the midst of the greatest calamities.

Not only God, however, acts in regard to us. Men do also. There is a meekness toward men. It is willingness to take wrong patiently. It is a gentleness in dealing with others. This is a virtue not natural to men. The Holy Spirit must work it. First God makes a man poor in spirit, so that he has no false pride in him. Then He leads that man to Golgotha and lets him see the meekness and gentleness of Christ in the face of unspeakable insults and unjust abuse. Then He makes that man meek, so that he follows God's leadings and trusts in God's love to turn all things to his good. Now he is ready to be meek toward his fellowmen.

A meek man does not think overmuch of himself, his position, his dignity. He will not allow his temper to be ruffled by slights and provocations. He will not expect always to be treated with respect and reverence. He will do his duty in the station where God has set him, gently, lovingly, seeking not honor from men, ambitious only to be well pleasing to God.

Blessed is he, for he shall inherit the earth. The world does not believe that. Not the meek but the violent shall inherit the earth. The world will not learn that by the time the violent have done their work there is little of the earth left to inherit. The general conception of meekness is that it is weakness and cowardice, that manliness requires resentment of every slight and insult. But our Lord says that the meek shall inherit the earth. True meekness is found only in the follower of Christ. A follower of Christ is an heir together with the Son of God, an heir of the Kingdom that shall in the end come into its own and possess the earth. But the citizens of the Kingdom of Heaven need not wait for the consummation of the Kingdom to inherit the earth. The quiet strength of Christian meekness will win its way here and now, where violence fails. Meekness and lowliness of heart enabled our Lord to win. Had He applied force and violence, He would have failed utterly. Gentleness is a power in the world. It exerts a strange influence over rougher natures. Even when this is not true, it has a joy of its own, a deep inner contentment, a holy restfulness, which gives a sweetness to this present life on earth.

D. "Blessed are those who hunger and thirst for righteousness, for they shall be satisfied." Our Lord spoke first of the consciously poor in spirit; next of those who mourn over their poverty; then of those who are ready to receive whatever teaching or chastisement might be given. Now He speaks of those who have an earnest longing for that right relation to God in which they are so lacking. No seriously minded, thinking person can read and ponder our Lord's words without having aroused in him the desire to possess the qualities pictured here. Surely this hunger and thirst is ours in this hour. Blessed are we, for we shall be filled. This hunger will be satisfied. God never refuses these gifts to any who ask sincerely.

E. "Blessed are the merciful, for they shall obtain mercy." Powerful, masterful, are those who practice mercy. The mercy referred to here is not that almost negative quality usually understood, that we do not deal harshly, do not inflict punishment when due, spare an animal or a fellow man some unnecessary labor or pain. With mercy our Lord meant active kindness, the feeling of pity showing itself in action. By being kind, pitiful, merciful, in their dealings with their fellow men, men will be blessed, powerful, masterful. They will exert a mighty influence for the betterment of the world. The world has always reached out for its good in other ways and tried to improve its condition by other methods, but essentially it has failed utterly. It is essentially unmerciful, savage, brutal. Its final solution for every problem, its last argument is to blow the opposition into eternity with bombs. Natural man is morally incapable of making the proper use of scientific inventions.

In this world, helpless to advance itself toward its higher good, comes the call of the King to the citizens of His Kingdom: "Blessed are the merciful." Powerful, masterful, are the merciful. The power to improve the world lies with the merciful. What this poor world needs is not more inventions but to overcome selfishness, greed, injustice. It needs merciful men, men with the Christ-born spirit of brotherliness. It needs the exhibition of our King's gentle spirit, to have Christ's people demonstrate the power of mercy. Blessed, powerful, are the merciful, for they shall obtain mercy. Not that God's mercy is earned and merited. No, God first showed us mercy by making us His children in Christ Jesus. As children we are to be like our Father, have His nature, show the family trait of mercy. We are to be imitators of our Father, the God of mercy. So, reflecting the undeserved mercy of God toward us in our dealings with other men, we shall continue to enjoy the mercy of God.

F. "Blessed are the pure in heart, for they shall see God." In the language of Scripture, the heart stands for the whole moral nature of man, his understanding, emotion, conscience, will, the whole inner life. The man who is pure in his inner life is powerful, exerts a mighty influence, because his outward life and conduct conforms to the inward purity. Nothing that man can do will fit him to step into the presence of God. When he accepts Jesus Christ as his only Hope, his sins are forgiven. Upon this forgiveness follows the purity of a godly life, a new birth, a new nature. He no longer opposes the purposes of God but works together with Him in developing a pure, beautiful, radiant life.

Pure in heart. The very idea is scorned and ridiculed by the world as hopelessly Victorian. If there is one outstanding characteristic of our modern world, it is the utter unconsciousness of sin, the absolute indifference to the fact that impurity is the transgression of a God-given moral code, a code that cannot be ignored or violated without deadly consequences. Into this impure, immoral age comes the word of the Lord Jesus to the citizens of the Kingdom: "Blessed are the pure in heart." By not adopting the moral code of the impure world, but living righteously before men, the citizens of the Kingdom exert a mighty influence for the good of humanity.

"For they shall see God." The pure in heart, and only the pure in heart, shall see God. How can any man see the invisible God? With the natural eye this is impossible. But men can see God in that they experience Him. There is a relationship, a fellowship with God, a knowing of God that comes to those who are pure in heart. Whether we call it the vision of God, or communion with God, or the indwelling of God makes no difference. It is the comforting, soothing, vitalizing consciousness of His presence, the realization of His character, the assurance of a blessed relationship with Him who has come near to man in the person of Jesus Christ.

G. "Blessed are the peacemakers, for they shall be called sons of God." To be a maker of peace, a man must have peace himself, the highest and most needed of all forms of peace, the peace of which the angels sang on Christmas night, the peace with God which the Lord Jesus brought to earth. God is a God of peace, and His children must be lovers of peace. The Lord Jesus is the Prince of Peace, and His followers must be workers for peace. This poor world needs peacemakers. It has tried to make and maintain peace in its own way. Yet it seems that the world is bound to write also its future history in blood. We have international wars, racial wars, class wars, and movements, societies, organizations, international alliances show little progress in promoting and maintaining peace.

Into the war-weary world comes the cry of the King to the citizens of His Kingdom: "Blessed are the peacemakers, for they shall be called sons of God." They alone possess the power to make and keep peace on earth. The trouble with this world is that it is a stranger to God's peace. There is so much strife because men do not know the peace of reconciliation that God made with men while they were yet His enemies. This peace must be brought to the world first of all. Men must see the new value the Gospel puts on human life, the implications of the Gospel in their social life. Men of the Kingdom must demonstrate the power of the Gospel in making peace. Then they have done more to elevate life than by all other means together.

"They shall be called sons of God." To be called is to be. When the citizens of the Kingdom live in peace, make peace, encourage others to live in peace, men will see that they are children of the God of peace and will call them sons of God.

But better still. God Himself will own them and call them His sons, approve of them, tell them that they are like Him, and have His nature and qualities.

H. "Blessed are those who are persecuted for righteousness' sake, for theirs is the Kingdom of Heaven. Blessed are you when men revile you and persecute you and utter all kinds of evil against you falsely on My account. Rejoice and be glad, for your reward is great in heaven, for so men persecuted the prophets who were before you." When the citizens of the Kingdom live according to the laws of the Kingdom, they will be persecuted and reviled and mocked and defamed by the unbelieving world. But they must willingly take up their cross and follow their King. So long as they know that the utterances of all kinds of evil are false, they may rejoice and be glad, for all persecution on the King's account is proof of their citizenship. They suffer in good company, with the prophets who were before them and with the noblest and purest who have ever lived. The glorious company of the Apostles, the noble army of the martyrs, and the King Himself have trodden the same path. The Kingdom of Heaven is theirs. They are on the way to the sublimest honors. They will be compensated a hundredfold when the Kingdom is consummated. "Rejoice and be glad, for your reward is great in heaven!" Think of the myriads who now chant their alleluias by the crystal sea. Think of the destiny offered through simple faith, by which they were raised to stand before the throne and the Lamb. May it be our ambition to follow their steps, comforted and assured by their successes that we shall share their bliss.

THE TWENTY-THIRD SUNDAY AFTER TRINITY

A rubric in *The Lutheran Hymnal* directs that the Introit and the Collect for this Sunday be used on the last Sunday after Trinity in each year. When these Propers are used on the last Sunday, due consideration should be given to the fact that the Last Sunday after Trinity occupies a place of its own as the climax of the season.

The Introit and the Gradual for this Sunday are more joyful and comforting than those of the previous Sundays. We come to the holy place and are welcomed by the enthroned Lord with the joyful message that our exile is nearing its end. He is coming, not as our Judge but as our Savior, bringing peace and eternal salvation. For His own the Last Day will not be a day of wrath but a coming into the eternal home. The days of exile are at an end, the return home into the heavenly Jerusalem is near. Today the Church speaks to the lukewarm in tearful tones that they must not live as enemies of the cross of Christ, not make the belly their god, and not live for this earth. To the faithful, whose names are written in the Book of Life, she speaks words of encouragement. They feel themselves to be foreigners on earth and long for home; their commonwealth is in heaven, and from it they await a Savior, the Lord Jesus Christ, who will change their lowly bodies to be like His glorious body. In the holy Gospel the Lord Jesus reminds us that though we are even now citizens of heaven, we have a two-fold duty here on earth while waiting in exile to be taken home. We are to fulfill our twofold duty, toward man and toward God, to Caesar and to Christ. There is no contradiction here. The command to love includes God and the neighbor. God stands behind our superiors and sanctions their commands. The lesson of this Sunday may be summarized in the word *citizenship*. It is of only one kind, heavenly. Therefore the thought of the day could also be *heavenly-mindedness*. We considered last Sunday that by perseverance we advance toward the end of our Christian course. But when we gain heavenly-mindedness, it is as if the Holy City came down from heaven to meet us on our way. This grace is the last attainment of the Christian character. Surely, it is granted in order that we may escape the bitterness of death by anticipation of what is beyond death. It is the Land of Beulah, referred to in Is. 62:4 (RSV, "married") and in Bunyan's *Pilgrim's Progress* as the land of rest where pilgrims abide till death. To it come sounds and visions of the heavenly Jerusalem, that the Christian pilgrims may there await in peace their final passing of the river.

The Introit. I know the thoughts that I think toward you, saith the Lord, thoughts of peace and not of evil. Then shall ye call upon Me and pray unto Me, and I will hearken unto you; and I will turn your captivity and gather you from all nations and from all places. Lord, Thou hast been favorable unto Thy land; Thou hast brought back the captivity of Jacob."

The Antiphon is part of a letter written by Jeremiah to the exiles in Babylon, telling them that their captivity will last seventy years and then they will return to the homeland. As we enter the house of God, we hear the declaration that our exile soon will be over. God will not be a judge over us but a Savior and Bringer of peace. To us the word *peace* today means eternal blessedness. The Last Day is not to be for us a day of wrath but a coming to the eternal home. The Revised Standard Version translates: "I know the plans I have for you, says the Lord, plans for welfare and not for evil, to give you a future and a hope. . . . I will restore your fortunes and gather you from all the nations and all the places where I have driven you" (Jer. 29:11, 14). Also Ps. 85:1: "Lord, Thou wast favorable to Thy land; Thou didst restore the fortunes of Jacob."

The Collect. "Absolve, we beseech Thee, O Lord, Thy people from their offenses that from the bonds of our sins which by reason of our frailty we have brought upon us we may be delivered by Thy bountiful goodness."

In the Introit we heard: "Then shall ye call upon Me and pray unto Me." The Collect pours out our inmost desire: Absolve, loose us, Thy people, from our offenses, that by Thy bountiful goodness we may be delivered from the bonds of our sins, the slavery of serving the world. The bonds must be loosed. They are not fashioned by men as were those borne by St. Paul. But they are the bonds of sin.

The Epistle, Philippians 3:17-21. The statement "Our commonwealth is in heaven" probably was more meaningful to the Philippians than it is to us. They were citizens of Rome though they lived far away, surrounded by barbarians. So we are citizens of heaven though far from home, fighting enemies in defense of our commonwealth, waiting for our Savior to appear. The Philippians were proud of their Roman citizenship. There were things a barbarian might do but which were unbecoming a Roman. So citizens of heaven are to be ever conscious of their alienship and live a life worthy of their citizenship. "Join in imitating me, and mark those who so live as you have an example in us." The chief thought of the Epistle is: "We await a Savior, the Lord Jesus Christ, who will change our lowly body to be like His glorious body."

The Gradual. "Thou hast saved us from our enemies and hast put them to shame that hated us. In God we boast all the day long and praise Thy name forever. Alleluia! Alleluia! Ye that fear the Lord, trust in the Lord! He is their Help and their Shield. Alleluia!"

Perseverance is the chief thought on this Sunday. The Gradual encourages us to continue our battle against the enemies until the end. Psalm 44 is a song of confidence. "Through Thee we push down our foes; through Thy name we tread down our assailants. For not in my bow do I trust, nor can my sword save me. But Thou hast saved us from our foes and hast put to confusion those who hate us. In God we have boasted continually, and we will give thanks to Thy name forever."

The Proper Sentence. "Alleluia! O Lord, deal with Thy servant according unto Thy mercy, and teach me Thy statutes. I am Thy servant, give me understanding, that I may know Thy testimonies. Alleluia!"

Or: "Alleluia! Blessed be the Lord God of our fathers; praise Him and highly exalt Him forever. Alleluia!"

The Gospel, St. Matthew 22:15-22. Our commonwealth is in heaven, and our eyes are raised hopefully and longingly toward heaven, awaiting the appearance of our Deliverer. But we have a life to live here, the life that is the preparation for that to come, a life worthy of heavenly citizenship. The holy Gospel gives us instruction for our earthly walk as citizens of heaven. We are to render loyally every duty the earthly citizenship rightly imposes. To Caesar we are to give what is his, but to God what is His. The Christian will always be the ideal world citizen if he obeys his Lord; yet he is an alien here.

The Proper Preface. "Who with Thine only-begotten Son and the Holy Ghost art one God, one Lord. And in the confession of the only true God we worship the Trinity in Person and the Unity in Substance, of Majesty coequal."

OUTLINE FOR SERMON ON THE EPISTLE

The Christian lives in two spheres, the earthly and the heavenly, and has connection with each, an earthly and a heavenly citizenship. St. Paul draws two pictures in solemn contrast as he presents:

The Heavenly Citizenship

A. The Citizens of Earth. These are they who forget their heavenly sphere. They are the enemies of the Cross and of the principle of self-sacrifice, of which the Cross is the highest example. They live entirely to gratify their appetites, lusts, and passions. They glory in their shame, having no sense of anything higher or better. Their minds are set on earthly things, speaking and thinking only of the earth and of the cares, loves, and enjoyments of the transient present. It would seem that to such the Paradise of God is no more than a name, a dream, a fiction. Their treasures and their hearts are upon earth.

B. The Citizens of Heaven. The word *conversation* in the King James Version should be rendered commonwealth or citizenship. This citizenship is not future but present. It is now. Though absent from the heavenly city, we are nonetheless its citizens, for the Church on earth and the Church in heaven are in truth one, and the Kingdom of Grace is but a suburb of the Kingdom of Glory. As citizens of heaven we are to be more anxious about our interests there than about any of our earthly concerns. We are so to regard heaven as our native country that our thoughts turn to it as to our home. We are to be guided by its laws and possessed by its spirit of obedience, love, and praise. We must be evidently preparing in character and disposition for the future enjoyment of the rights we already possess, and we must be desirous of becoming more worthy of fellow citizenship with the saints. We are also to find our position and prospects a consolation in trial and an encouragement in toil.

C. The Completion of Citizenship. This will be the consequence of the manifestation of our King and will include (1) the salvation of the body. The body is now the body of our humiliation, vile, lowly. It has become this by being made the instrument of sin, the seat of temptation, and the object of sin's penalty of decay and of sin's triumph in death. The body is to be changed, restored to the likeness of Christ's glorified body. That by which we have been connected with a world of sin shall be our means of correspondence with a new earth in which dwells righteousness. (2) The restitution of all things. The power that will renew the body will renew also the world, now defiled by sin, stained with blood, its light polluted by scenes of wickedness, its night blackened with deeds of darkness, its very air the vehicle of curses and hideous words of blasphemy. The renewed body is the pledge of a renewed world, purified by disinfecting fire, to be the home of purified souls.

SERMON ON THE EPISTLE

The Epistle for this day is part of a letter written by the Apostle Paul while he was a prisoner in Rome. The letter is addressed to the Christians in Philippi, a city of Macedonia.

We shall better understand St. Paul's allusions if we bear in mind the circumstances of the Philippians. Near the city of Philippi a battle of decisive importance in the history of the Roman Empire had been fought. It was the battle between Brutus and Cassius on the one side and Anthony and Octavius on the other. As a result, Octavius became emperor under the name of

Augustus. Many veterans of the victorious army settled in Philippi, and Caesar Augustus made the city a Roman colony.

There was a vast difference between a Roman colony and a Roman province. At Christ's time Judea was a Roman province, ruled by a governor who was appointed by the emperor. The inhabitants had no rights whatsoever except that of paying exorbitant taxes and were ruled in a most cruel and bloody fashion. A colony, however, was a bit of Rome itself on foreign soil. The inhabitants and their children were Roman citizens and elected their own magistrates and own senate. The colony of Philippi was also free from taxation. One thing was expected of a colony. When barbarians threatened to invade the empire, it was bound to fight.

As Roman citizens the Philippians had the pride of Romans. A Roman knew only two kinds of people: Roman citizens and barbarians. Romans were so far superior to all other men that there was no comparison. The haughty look, the proud bearing, the contempt for barbarians, were characteristic of the Roman as he mingled with the rest of humanity. There were things which others might do and say but to which a Roman would not stoop. He was different.

So Philippi, far out on the borders of the empire, was a part of Rome, although in the territory of barbarians. Its citizens were surrounded by barbarians on every side and mingled with them in the streets. But one could identify the Roman at once by his conduct and attitude. His very bearing distinguished him from all others.

These Philippians understood when St. Paul wrote: "Our commonwealth [our citizenship] is in heaven." They lived here on this earth, but as Christians their home city was heaven. Though far from home, they were citizens of the Eternal City even now. They were an outpost of this city, far out along the boundaries, surrounded by barbarians.

They were in this world but different from the rest of the world. As citizens of heaven they had a certain dignity to preserve over against the world. There were things which others might do, but citizens of heaven could not stoop to that level. In the first chapter of his letter the Apostle had already reminded them that they were citizens of heaven living far from home, when he wrote:

"Behave as citizens worthily as becomes the Gospel of Christ," play the citizen in a manner worthy of the Gospel.

Here in the third chapter St. Paul returns to the subject. "Our commonwealth is in heaven." We are a colony of heaven, citizens of a city we have never seen, in which we never lived, the heavenly Jerusalem, the home of all believers. We live here on earth, but we belong to heaven. Our heavenly citizenship is a great privilege and honor, and we must show ourselves worthy and behave as it becomes such exalted persons.

"Brethren, join in imitating me, and mark those who so live as you have an example in us." Follow my example and that of all who are like-minded. Through this entire letter breathes the spirit of a man who sees clearly that he does not belong to this world but is the citizen of another commonwealth. Longingly he looks forward to the time when he will go home. All that is counted gain by the barbarians of this world he counts loss for Christ's sake. All that he loses in this world he counts gain. He lives according to the laws of the heavenly city. He fights for that city and is willing to give his life in the advancement of its interests. He writes to the Philippians: Live as I do, live as citizens of heaven in the midst of a perverse and crooked generation. Stand fast in one spirit, with one mind striving together for the faith of the Gospel, and in nothing terrified by your adversaries.

"For many, of whom I have often told you and now tell you even with tears, live as enemies of the cross of Christ. Their end is destruction, their god is the belly, and they glory in their shame, with minds set on earthly things." The Apostle is not speaking of the godless heathen in Philippi. Of them nothing else could be expected but to be enemies of the Cross of Christ, and he would not have spoken of their attitude and wept over it. No, he is speaking of people who outwardly were members of the Christian congregation, who professed to be believers.

So this outpost of Christ's Kingdom was not only surrounded by enemies on the outside, but there were also enemies within the gates. There were people who bored from within. They minded earthly things, concerned themselves with the things of this world. They did not live here as citizens of a far-off fatherland but lived as though they belonged here. They were perfectly at home in this world. Nothing was farther from their thoughts than that this is a foreign country in which they stopped for only a brief time on their way to the homeland. This world offered so much that was attractive and pleasant and comfortable. They wished to miss nothing and drank deeply of the pleasures offered. The cross of Christ, the self-denial which is a condition of following Christ, giving up things for Christ's sake, was not for them. They were full-fledged citizens of this world. Yet they professed Christianity and were regarded as Christians by the outsiders. Thereby they brought only shame and contempt on the cause of Christ and on the commonwealth of which they claimed to be citizens. They were indeed enemies.

That the Philippians might recognize these enemies more readily, the Apostle describes them more closely. "With minds set on earthly things." They have understanding only for the material. Their purpose in life is to enjoy things. They never think beyond what they can feel, taste, see, handle. Truth, honor, righteousness, justice, love, faith, have no meaning for them. Their eyes never fix on the stars; they have eyes only for the lower regions, the perishable things of earth.

"Their god is the belly." The highest and noblest they know is their stomach, fleshly appetites. They have lost sight of their relationship with God. They are not free children but slaves to their bodies, which will be eaten by worms. If you speak to them of a higher, nobler purpose in life, this is beyond their conception and understanding. Speak to them of the satisfaction derived from communion with God, from meditation on His Word, from self-denial, from the service of fellow men, and that is a language they cannot understand.

"They glory in their shame." They are not in the least ashamed of being reduced from citizens of heaven to slaves grubbing in the filth of this earth. They regard their slavery as an honor and are proud of it, even boast of their freedom from all moral and religious restraints. They believe themselves too intellectual and smart to be serious with the Word of God. They are not so stupid as to give time and effort to the advancement of the Kingdom. They live only for the slime and dung of this earth and are proud of their taste.

"Their end is destruction." God has so ordained, and so it shall be. No matter how long they live, how contented and successful they seem, their end is perdition. Therefore the Philippians were not to follow their example. St. Paul argues: If you are citizens of heaven, live as it becomes such highly privileged people. Show yourselves worthy of that high honor, follow my example and that of all who are of the same mind with me. Mind heavenly things, make Christ your Lord and God, and serve Him. Glory in your other-worldliness.

What the Apostle wrote to the Philippians he could write to us if he were alive. What was true of them is true of us. God has called us out of darkness into His marvelous light. He has separated us from the rest of humanity and has transplanted us into the Kingdom of His Son. Through Christ we are His children. As children of God we have our home not on this earth, which shall be burned with fire; we have our home with our Father in heaven. Our home is where our Father and our Big Brother are. Even now, while still on earth, we are citizens of heaven. We are no longer pilgrims and strangers, but citizens with the saints and of the household of God.

Our commonwealth is in heaven. We are an outpost of heaven here on earth. We live here but are at home in another city. We live for a time in this world but belong to another country. Our sentiments are with the mother city. We are strangers here and natives of heaven. What Philippi was to Rome, that earth is to heaven in our eyes, a colony on the outskirts of the heavenly empire, ringed about by barbarians, but we keep open all communications with home.

Walk worthy of your high calling! As citizens of heaven we must not be like the people who are at home here on earth. We must not stoop to the pastimes and occupations of the barbarians about us. There are things which are considered quite conventional in this foreign land, but citizens of heaven cannot forget their origin and destiny, and they cannot do these things. We are different from the people about us.

We belong to an unseen order of things that is in existence now. For us it lies in the future, but it is even now a present life to an innumerable company. St. Peter speaks of it as being ready to be unveiled. It is only behind a thin veil, close to us. Before long God will draw back the curtain, and there will blaze out what has always been, though we did not see it. It is so close, so real, that it is worth our while to try and feel its nearness. We simply must not be so wrapped up in the unreal things of this life and city on earth, such foolish slaves to our senses, that we treat the things which are as yet unseen as nonexistent.

As a colony of Rome the Philippians had delegated to them the task of defending the dominions of the empire against attack and of advancing the borders by conquest. So we, being citizens of a colony of heaven, must engage in defensive and offensive warfare. We are set down in this world, like a frontier guard, to push the conquests of the Kingdom and to win more ground for the King. In the performance of this duty we are hindered by people in our ranks who are enemies of the Cross of Christ. They profess to be Christians but do not live as it becomes citizens of heaven. They live according to the laws of this world. Their minds are set on earthly things. They have no taste for the things of God. Yet since they profess Christianity, the world judges Christianity by them. The world does not read and study the Bible; it reads only the character and actions of supposed Christians. When it sees these professing Christians whose mind is set on earthly things, it concludes that there is no sense in being a Christian only to continue grubbing around on the lowest level of existence. So we, too, have the enemy within our gates.

This, then, is the picture the Epistle paints. This life is living in a little outlying colony on the far-off edge of Christ's great empire, ringed about by wide-stretching hosts of aliens and barbarians, a constant battle against mighty forces who seek to invade the Kingdom and have, in fact, alienated many within the gates. This life becomes most trying over the years. A pronounced nostalgia creeps into the hearts of the colonists, they become homesick. They long to have the constant warfare come to an end. Eagerly they look forward to the time when their King shall come to take them home.

As far as the eye can reach, the barbarians and traitors cover the land. But we know that the King will come to His sorely beset outpost. Our eyes are fixed on the pass in the hills through which we expect His waving banners and gleaming spears to appear. "Our commonwealth is in heaven, and from it we await a Savior, the Lord Jesus Christ." Soon we shall hear the music and the shouts which tell of His coming. When He comes, He will raise the siege and scatter all enemies as chaff before the wind. Then the colonists, who held the post against seemingly overwhelming odds, will go with Him to the land they have never seen but which is their home.

Of course, we are not fit to enter the home city as we are, with our earthly bodies, flesh and blood stained by inherited and actual sin, bodies weakened and corrupted by the disease from which all suffer in this barbarous land. But our King will make us fit for the homeland. "Who will change our lowly body to be like His glorious body, by the power which enables Him even to subject all things to Himself."

As we wait with eyes straining for our King to come and take us home, He comes to the far-off colony, unknown to the surrounding enemies, to strengthen our hopes, lest we grow discouraged and despair of relief. He comes to us in Word and Sacrament to strengthen His weary colonists. He assures us that our sins are forgiven, that we are children of God, that our Father is keeping our inheritance in safety, that we are not cut off from the homeland, that communications are open. He bids us hold out just a little longer, assures us that He will come at the earliest possible moment and lead us in triumph through the gates of the heavenly Jerusalem. "I am coming soon; hold fast what you have, so that no one may seize your crown."

OUTLINE FOR SERMON ON THE HOLY GOSPEL

As members of the Church, we have a citizenship in heaven, but we have a citizenship also on earth. We must learn how these are related. The Church has shown admirable and practical wisdom in the selection of the holy Gospel. We are less concerned with the attempt of the Pharisees and Herodians to entangle our Lord in order to accuse Him either of impiety or disloyalty, than with His answer. It helps us to find the truth, to know what we ought to do, as citizens both of earth and of heaven.

Our Twofold Citizenship

A. The Claims of Caesar. The Christian has a duty to the world in which he lives, and to powers by which that world is governed. He must not make religion an excuse for being careless in respect of any earthly duty, in regard to his business, his family, his city, country, or government. If Caesar, a heathen Roman conqueror, had a just claim, how much more the rulers we have elected! The Roman tribute was a rendering back to Caesar an acknowledgment for benefits of law, security, and order enjoyed under his rule. Our tribute money is our bounden acknowledgment of far higher benefits of liberty, peace, confidence, religious freedom, social comfort, and prosperity.

B. The Claims of God. These also depend on what we have received from Him. Our Lord puts the two duties side by side, but this only shows how much the last is greater than the first. We are bidden to make a return to God for our creation, preservation, and all the blessings of this life, for the redemption of the world, for the means of grace, and for the hope of glory. Caesar is satisfied with the return of the things that are his; God demands the return of ourselves, for we ourselves are His.

C. The Consistency of These Claims. Christ answered the dilemma by the command to do both. The private duty to God is rarely inconsistent with public duty, and so long as Caesar demands no more than is his, he must be obeyed. Should he demand to rule conscience, he intrudes into the things that are God's, and must be resisted, even unto death. But in the main, duties to God and man are consistent, because they are not two duties at all but one. The division into sacred and secular is convenient, but it means no more than that some duties are directly paid to God, others indirectly through man to God. Our Lord drew no hard and fast line between the things of Caesar and things of God. If we are to eat and drink to God's glory, we are surely to do our public duties to God. Caesar is best served by those who serve him for God's sake. If Christ bids us render to Caesar, and we do it because Christ bids us, we serve not Caesar but Christ.

THE TWENTY-FOURTH SUNDAY AFTER TRINITY

If this is the last Sunday of the Church Year, the Introit and the Collect for the Twenty-third Sunday after Trinity shall be used. The *Roman Missal* appoints Propers for only twenty-three Sundays and the Last Sunday after Pentecost. If there are additional Sundays, the Propers are taken from Sundays after the Epiphany. The Introit for the Last Sunday is that of the Twenty-third, the Collect, the Gradual, and the Epistle are for the Twenty-fourth in *The Lutheran Hymnal*. The holy Gospel is Matt. 24:15-35. In the *Book of Common Prayer* the holy Gospel is the same as in *The Lutheran Hymnal,* the Epistle is lengthier, beginning with the third verse. In the *Common Service Book* the Gradual is Ps. 1:1, 2; 91:15, 16.

The ancient Church seems to have had no conception of a definite Church Year. There are indications that this Sunday was not the last Sunday of the Trinity Season but rather a transition to Advent, a fifth Sunday in Advent. The Collect begins: "Stir up," as do the Collects for the First, the Second, and the Fourth Sundays in Advent. The Advent Season was probably longer than it is now, which could account for the choice of the holy Gospel in the *Missal* for the Last Sunday after Pentecost and the First Sunday in Advent. The first is our Lord's own account of His Second Coming, and the second is Luke 21:25-33. The latter is the holy Gospel for the Second Sunday in Advent according to Lutheran use, with three verses added.

The Trinity Season is divisible into two halves, the first twelve Sundays dealing with Christian motives, the second twelve with the Christian character. We have seen that character in its internal graces and their manifestation in active service. Last Sunday it culminated in perseverance and heavenly-mindedness. Today we gaze on the final scene, to which all that has gone before is the long preparation. We see the final deliverance from guilt and sinfulness in the inheritance of the saints in light. The Church reaches the high level of complete confidence, not in herself but in her Head. She knows and is firmly convinced that nothing will be able to separate her from the love of God in Christ Jesus, her Lord. The Introit declares: "He is our God, and we are the people of His pasture and the sheep of His hand." This confidence is poured out in adoring praise: "Oh, come, let us sing unto the Lord; let us make a joyful noise to the Rock of our salvation!" The Church does not ignore the serious lessons of these last days before the end. She has risen above fear. She has heard and learned. With the growth of knowledge has come confident trust. On the Nineteenth Sunday she heard: "Put off your old nature"; on the Twentieth: "Make the most of the time"; on the Twenty-first: "Be strong in the Lord, recognize your enemies, take the whole armor of God, stand"; on the Twenty-second: "He who began a good work in you will bring it to completion at the Day of Jesus Christ; let your love abound more and more"; on the Twenty-third: "Our commonwealth is in heaven"; and today all is climaxed: "The Father has qualified you to share in the inheritance of the saints in light." Today's Epistle is the Church's prayer for her own who are passing through these last days in a world filled with the things that lure away. In the Collect she prays that any waning of enthusiasm, determination, and inspiration to persevere be prevented. Stir up, excite, stimulate, make enthusiastic, the will of Thy faithful people that they may attain to the reward of inheritance. The Gradual breathes out the note of confidence: "He hath delivered us, qualified us to share in the inheritance, transferred us to the Kingdom of His beloved Son."

The Introit. "Oh, come, let us worship and bow down, let us kneel before the Lord, our Maker. For He is our God, and we are the people of His pasture and the sheep of His hand. Oh, come, let us sing unto the Lord, let us make a joyful noise to the Rock of our salvation."

The Collect. "Stir up, we beseech Thee, O Lord, the wills of Thy faithful people that they, plenteously bringing forth the fruit of good works, may of Thee be plenteously rewarded."

This prayer has an Advent tone, at the end of the old year, that in the coming year of grace we may make the most of the time. The Reformers changed the original "the fruit of Thy divine service" to "the fruit of good works," and "the remedies of Thy tender mercy" to "plenteous reward." Perhaps the intention was to have us regard the Advent as the consummation of Christian life. Our growth in good works is to be tested at the final Advent, and for those who have been God's faithful people, there shall be plenteous reward in the commendation "Well done, good and faithful servant." Our prayer is for quickened wills, for greater fruitfulness, and for the final reward (Heb. 10:24, 25). The reward is not salvation, but it will be according to our works. Plenteous fruitfulness will be plenteously rewarded, but the will, the fruit, and the reward are all "through Jesus Christ, Thy Son, our Lord."

The Epistle, Colossians 1:9-14. This may be regarded not only as the prayer of St. Paul for the faithful Colossians but also as the Church's prayer for her children. She knows the glory to be revealed and prays that we may not lose our inheritance through any lack in faithful endeavor, through any weakness, temptation, or trial. St. Paul's and the Church's prayer is for the final perfection of the saints.

The Gradual. "Thou hast delivered my soul from death, mine eyes from tears, and my feet from falling. I love the Lord because He hath heard my voice and my supplication. Alleluia! Alleluia! With Thee is the fountain of life; in Thy light shall we see light. Alleluia!"

The Proper Sentence. "Alleluia! O Lord, deal with Thy servant according unto Thy mercy, and teach me Thy statutes. I am Thy servant, give me understanding, that I may know Thy testimonies. Alleluia!"

Or: "Alleluia! Blessed be the Lord God of our fathers; praise Him and highly exalt Him forever. Alleluia!"

The Gospel, St. Matthew 9:18-26. The original holy Gospel ended with the words "Instantly the woman was made whole." This would indicate that the lesson of the day is intended to concentrate not so much in the raising of the ruler's daughter as in the healing of the woman suffering from a hemorrhage. However, we have in the present Gospel a double manifestation of power, a double ministry to seeking, hungering faith that seals the promise of the Epistle's blessed message. "He is our God!" He is "the Rock of our salvation." "He shall call upon Me, and I will answer him . . . and show him My salvation."

The Proper Preface. "Who with Thine only-begotten Son and the Holy Ghost art one God, one Lord. And in the confession of the only true God we worship the Trinity in Person and the Unity in Substance, of Majesty coequal."

OUTLINE FOR SERMON ON THE EPISTLE

In the Epistle St. Paul prays for

The Perfection of the Saints

The text opens: "From the day we heard of it, we have not ceased to pray for you." The Apostle has heard good tidings of the Colossians. They were showing the three great marks of the Christian character that correspond to the three necessary relations of life, the relation with God, with man, and with themselves. In relation to God they possessed "faith in Christ Jesus," in relation to men they showed "the love which you have for all the saints," while in relation to themselves they were conscious of "the hope laid up for you in heaven." This progress was due, as everywhere, to the Gospel in its two aspects of truth and grace, giving them both a new standard of life and power to attain it.

This their past progress was to be the foundation for yet greater attainments in the future. What St. Paul has heard only stirs him up to more earnest prayers on their behalf. He prays for such progress as may know no limit whatever. Four times over he repeats the comprehensive "all." Absolute perfection, though never attained, is always to be before us as the goal and aim of our effort, and that in three directions:

(1) In knowledge. We must seek knowledge with a view to obedience, "the knowledge of His will," a knowledge so digested as to become wisdom in the mind and understanding in its practical applications to conduct.

(2) In holiness. We are to desire such a holiness as shall be worthy of our Lord, of the motives of His love, and the perfection

of His example; such holiness as shall be pleasing to God and shall produce every sort of good fruit toward men.

(3) In strength. We are to long to receive strength proportioned to the glorious power of its Giver, and especially such strength as is needed for cheerful endurance in the duties and trials of the Christian life.

There is to be no limit to the attainments in knowledge, holiness, and strength, which are open to us, and which it is our duty to secure.

OUTLINE FOR SERMON ON THE HOLY GOSPEL

The holy Gospel presents

Two Miracles of Deliverance

A. From the Disease of Sin. The poor woman, after twelve years of suffering and conscious uncleanness, came to Christ polluted, exhausted, disappointed, impoverished, and altogether hopeless (Luke 8:43). Such are the ravishes of sin. We learn from her example how to approach Christ in faith and humility and that no touch of faith, however hesitating, will escape His observation. No case, however desperate and long continued, is past His power to heal. But there must be, on our side, the touch of faith, a personal contact with the personal Lord of health, a contact hindered by no sense of inward guilt and impurity, and by no crowd of worldly impediments. We must touch the Savior if His salvation is to be ours, in our daily prayers and in His holy Word and Sacraments, when our hearts are dead, when sin tempts and evil thoughts arise, in the midst of daily duties and employments, and we shall never touch Him in vain.

B. From the Death of Sin. Sin is disease and, like disease, tends to death, but from this also Christ can deliver us. He delivers (1) by encouraging faith. Jairus had faith, as shown by his humble access and earnest prayer. Christ performed a miracle while He was on the way, to increase and confirm his faith. All Christ's dealings with us in our life's history have this as their object. (2) By the touch of power. Men may scoff, but their scorn only helps the truth by showing that if death be real, yet more real must be the power that conquers death. Christ's power, manifested in the silent chamber, is now manifested in the secret chamber of the heart, and one day it will be manifest in the silence of the tomb. This miracle is the converse of the last, which taught that deliverance must come through our touch of Christ, for here it was Christ's touch that aroused one who could not touch Him. To touch and be touched by Christ is the secret of deliverance.

THE TWENTY-FIFTH SUNDAY AFTER TRINITY

The last few Sundays have brought exhortation and promises. Today we enter on the final group of Sundays, dealing with the Last Things as the completion of the believer's life and the end which the unbeliever, too, must face. The first of these Last Things is the Second Coming of our Lord. Next Sunday's Lessons will tell of the final Judgment. The last Sunday will picture all this parabolically, but to the very end we have warning and exhortation to watch and be ready.

The ancient Church looked forward to the Second Coming with inmost longing. Adorned as the bride, bearing the palm of martyrdom, she went forth joyfully to meet her Lord and Bridegroom. The Maranatha, "Come, Lord Jesus," was the heart and culmination of all her prayers. The attitude of the Middle Ages was quite different. Wholesome terror and dread was awakened by the very thought of the Judgment. The *Dies irae* of the Mass for the Dead expresses this apprehension. This hymn of the thirteenth century, in translation, is Hymn 607 in *The Lutheran Hymnal* and Hymn 515 in the *Common Service Book*. It was first issued in England as a hymn for Advent. "Day of wrath, O Day of mourning! . . . What shall I, frail man, be pleading? Who for me be interceding When the just are mercy needing? . . . Nothing unavenged remaineth."

We feel neither longing nor terror. We no longer have the enthusiasm of the ancient Church nor the unaffected simplicity of the Middle Ages. What is to be our reaction? Our Lord spoke often of His Second Coming. In His eschatological discourse, of which the last three Gospels are a part, He gives many details. The Christian who lives his life with and in the Church should be familiar at least with the line of thought. The purpose is not to satisfy curiosity but to give the Christian life a mighty tension and tenseness. For it reaches its climax in the thought that the end is uncertain. This holds true also of death. For the individual, death is the return of Christ. Time ends with death, and eternity begins. There is no passing of time, no intervening time between death and Christ's coming. But from this side, the great conclusion is: We must be ready always. To emphasize this conclusion our Lord presented four parables, all of which teach the same: of the Thief, of the Faithful and Wise Servant, of the Wise and Foolish Maidens, and of the Talents. The sum of our Lord's address may be said to be: Life in the light of the Second Coming. To emphasize this seems to be the object of the Church in the Liturgy. She admonishes that in the light of Christ's return we are to become rich in the fruits of good works and increase in perseverance and patience.

The Introit. "Have mercy upon me, O Lord, for I am in trouble. Deliver me from the hand of mine enemies and from them that persecute me. Let me not be ashamed, Lord, for I have called upon Thee. In Thee, O Lord, do I put my trust; let me never be ashamed."

The faithful enter the house and presence of the Lord somewhat soberly, yet not timidly, but hopefully and confidently. "I am in trouble," in distress. The warfare against the world and the flesh and the Evil One grows bitter as the goal of my expectation and of my living draws nearer. Deliver me. I put my trust in Thee. Let me not be put to shame. Have mercy upon me. The Introit sings of the Church's confidence and trust in God's mercy and protection.

The Collect. "Almighty God, we beseech Thee, show Thy mercy unto Thy humble servants, that we, who put no trust in our own merits, may not be dealt with after the severity of Thy judgment but according to Thy mercy."

God's humble servants put no trust in their own merits. They humbly pray that through our Lord's merits they may pass through the Judgment to the glories of the life to come. "In Thee, O Lord, do I put my trust!"

The Epistle, 1 Thessalonians 4:13-18. Underlying the Apostle's words seem to be anxious care and loving anxiety that the believer continue steadfast even unto the end, unswerving in his allegiance, clinging to the great hope in his Lord and Savior. It appears that some in the church of Thessalonica had doubts and fears, some were hesitating in purposefully continuing in the Way. St. Paul addresses himself to a difficulty that resulted from the seeming delay in the Lord's return. They expected an immediate coming. But the Lord delayed, and believers were dying. The surviving grieved that those who had fallen asleep were at a disadvantage. "Comfort one another with these words." "We who are alive, who are left until the coming of the Lord, shall not precede those who have fallen asleep." "The dead in Christ shall rise first; then we who are alive, who are left, shall be caught up together with them in the clouds to meet the Lord in the air; and so we shall always be with the Lord." A precious, comforting, peace-filling song of the blessedness with which the glorified Lord crowns His own at His coming. The Epistle is filled with comfort and peace and glory for His own.

The Gradual. "Thine enemies roar in the midst of Thy congregations; they set up their ensigns for signs. Remember Thy congregation, which Thou hast purchased of old, the rod of Thine inheritance, which Thou hast redeemed, Alleluia! Alleluia! There is a river the streams whereof shall make glad the city of God. God is in the midst of her, she shall not be moved. Alleluia!"

"I am in distress." "Thy foes have roared in the midst of Thy holy place; they have set up their own ensigns for signs." Psalm 74 speaks prophetically of the distressing trouble of the Church both in the Old Testament and the New Covenant. The foes set their idols in the holy places and destroyed everything in the sanctuary. We pray: "Remember Thy congregation, which Thou hast gotten of old, which Thou hast redeemed to be the tribe of Thy inheritance." Then comes the confident note of trust from Psalm 46: "There is a river whose streams make glad the city of God, God is in the midst of her, she shall not be moved."

The Proper Sentence. "Alleluia! O Lord, deal with Thy servant according unto Thy mercy, and teach me Thy statutes. I am Thy servant, give me understanding, that I may know Thy testimonies. Alleluia!"

Or: "Alleluia! Blessed be the Lord God of our fathers; praise Him and highly exalt Him forever. Alleluia!"

The Gospel, St. Matthew 24:15-28. It is essential that particularly on this Sunday the preacher bear in mind that he is speaking to people who have declared in the Introit that they put their trust in God, who put no trust in their own merits, who have prayed that the Lord would not let them be put to shame but deal with them according to His mercy. The Church had these humble servants of God in mind when she appointed the holy Gospel for this day. Therefore we must not lose sight of the fact that our Lord did not intend to frighten but to comfort when He spoke of His Day. His intention is to gather His elect that they may share in the inheritance of the saints in light. The holy Gospel brings loving admonition but also the assurance of the Lord's concern for His faithful. The people who have on their lips the confession "I am in trouble" are not to be further troubled by a discussion of wherein later theologians differed with Luther in the explanation and application of this part of our Lord's eschatological sermon or by a lengthy explanation of the fact that many mistakenly identify the destruction of Jerusalem and the Second Coming. It is enough that the disciples asked: When will every stone of the temple be thrown down? and What will be the sign of our Lord's coming and the close of the age? Our Lord answered both questions by regarding the judgment over Jerusalem as the beginning of an era of final judgment, as a picture of the last Judgment. When will this be? When the desolating sacrilege has made of Jerusalem and of the world a putrifying carcass that pollutes the air with its stench. Then the eagles, or vultures, of God's judgment will remove the city and the world from the scene. What will be the signs? Certain signs will announce the coming of Jerusalem's destruction. But no such special and particular signs will announce the judgment of the world. "For as the lightning comes from the east and shines as far as the west, so will be the coming of the Son of man. Wherever the body is, there the eagles [vultures] will be gathered together." When the world has become a hopeless, polluting carcass, the end will come, without special preceding signs, suddenly, unexpectedly. Therefore be ready always. Where does Daniel speak of the desolating sacrilege standing in the holy place? Undoubtedly Dan. 11:31 is to be preferred to 9:27.

The Proper Preface. "Who with Thine only-begotten Son and the Holy Ghost art one God, one Lord. And in the confession of the only true God we worship the Trinity in Person and the Unity in Substance, of Majesty coequal."

SERMON ON THE EPISTLE

At the end of the Church Year the Propers speak much of the end of all things, the end of human life, and the end of the world. This is not to awaken fear in the faithful but joyous expectation. The Church does well by her children in appointing lessons for the close of the Church Year which not merely warn and admonish but also encourage and comfort. For also the faithful are prone to become depressed and apprehensive at times, as we sing in one of our hymns: "Though the night of death be fraught Still with many an anxious thought." When we stand at the open grave of our loved ones or when we contemplate that we ourselves are also subject to death and corruption, these anxious thoughts will come. The normal attitude of the Christians is joyous expectation, for we know that the moment of our death will be to us individually the moment of our resurrection, of Christ's return in glory, and of our entrance into the eternal home, for we shall have left behind us the concept of time and entered upon timeless eternity. Normal for the Christian is a joyous looking forward to our Lord's coming in power and glory and the resurrection of our bodies to a new life. To maintain this joyous anticipation it is necessary that we recall constantly the hope we have and what the Scriptures say of the resurrection. We consider, then:

The Comforting Hope of the Resurrection

A number of remarks in the First Letter to the Thessalonians lead us to believe that the Epistle was occasioned by a report made by Timothy on the state of the church at Thessalonica. St. Paul heard much to gladden his heart, of the faith of the Christians, of their zeal in serving the Lord Jesus Christ, and of their patience in tribulation and affliction. But Timothy reported one disquieting fact which would have prompted the Apostle to go to Thessalonica immediately. Since circumstances made such a visit impossible, he had to content himself with a letter. His beloved Thessalonians were still hazy and unclear regarding the resurrection of the dead. They expected an immediate return of the Lord. As time went on, some of the congregation died, and there was deep concern whether their beloved who had fallen asleep would have part in the Kingdom of Jesus Christ when He returned in glory or whether they were at a disadvantage, to say the least. Therefore the Apostle wrote what we read in this day's Epistle regarding the resurrection of the dead and concluded with the words "Comfort one another with these words."

A. "We would not have you ignorant, brethren, concerning those who are asleep, that you may not grieve as others who have no hope." The Apostle writes that the Thessalonians had no cause to grieve at the death of their loved ones, as did others who have no hope. The comforting hope of the resurrection was not to be concealed and hidden from them. There were people for whom death was hopeless and comfortless. The unbelievers had various ideas as to what became of them after death. They imagined that their body returned to its original material and assumed some other form. The soul or spirit roamed about in search of some other living being in which to exist. A resurrection to a new life was to them ridiculous. Unbelievers today have similar ideas. At best, words about a great beyond and even of a reunion after death are mouthed, but there is no faith, no looking forward with confidence. When death occurs, these hopeless unbelievers numbly resign themselves to the inevitable.

To have hope, it is necessary to be like the Thessalonians, with their mind set not on earthly but on heavenly things, looking forward confidently for the inheritance kept for them in heaven. To them this world meant so little that they kept the Lord's coming constantly before their eyes and thought and spoke much of His bringing this world to an end and revealing His heavenly Kingdom. Apparently only one question caused them concern, and that was whether their loved ones who had fallen asleep in Christ would enter with them into the glory of this Kingdom. To such people the message of the resurrection brings hope, and to them alone.

Death and all its woes are a result and consequence of sin.

Christians know this and happily thank God that through Christ they have been freed from sin and its curse and therefore will not remain in death but pass from death into the life eternal. Life on this sinful earth is distasteful to them, and they long to be with the Lord, where they will sin no more but serve God in perfect righteousness. Such people have a receptive, open heart for the hope of the resurrection. When they stand at the grave of a loved one or grow momentarily apprehensive about their own death, they hear the Apostle calling to them: "Be of good cheer! The dead in Christ will rise again! The Lord will awaken them and take them to Himself." So the heart is comforted, gloomy thoughts are banished, and the soul is filled with a sweet hope. It is here that many of us fall short. Our minds are still set on earthly things. We have greater knowledge regarding the resurrection than the Thessalonians had, yet there are times when our faith and our love for the Savior fail us and we feel no desire to depart and be with Christ. We lose sight of the fact that it is a great privilege and unspeakable grace to be taken out of this wicked world and in peaceful sleep wait for the day of resurrection. We must accustom ourselves to give more thought to the resurrection and its meaning. The text offers the opportunity to make a beginning, by telling us, secondly, wherein the comforting resurrection consists.

B. "Since we believe that Jesus died and rose again, even so, through Jesus, God will bring with Him those who have fallen asleep." Because we believe that the Lord Jesus died and rose to save us from death and to bring us life, we cannot fear that our fellow believers who have fallen asleep in Him will be excluded from the glory He will bring at His coming. These believers did not really die but only fell asleep and are united with Christ, through Him have attained the promise of life. When He comes in glory to lead His own into life eternal, He cannot disregard these sleeping believers. He will not leave them in sleep but awaken them and have them with Him always.

For the comfort of Christians, the Apostle states that the dead of whom he speaks have fallen asleep. Their death in Christ is only a sleep. Even in death they are still His, and since they merely sleep, there must be an awakening. Their Lord will awaken them. He Himself spoke of the death of His beloved as a sleep. Of His friend Lazarus He said: "Our friend Lazarus has fallen asleep." Of the daughter of Jairus He said: "She is not dead but sleeping." All men, also the unbelievers, must rise from their graves at His coming. But the resurrection of the unbelievers is not the resurrection of which the text speaks as a comfort. The certainty that he will rise is in itself no comfort for the sinner. When a criminal is found guilty and led to his cell, he finds no comfort in the knowledge that when he is sentenced by the judge on another day he will be taken from his cell. The unbeliever can find no comfort in the knowledge that he will be called from the grave only to revive an eternal sentence from the Judge. "The hour is coming," said our Lord, "when all who are in the tombs will hear His voice and come forth: those who have done good, to the resurrection of life, and those who have done evil, to the resurrection of judgment" (John 5:28, 29).

For the Christian, however, the resurrection is comforting. "God will bring with Him those who have fallen asleep." When God raised Christ from the dead and exalted Him to glory, He did not separate the Head from the members. The believers remain united with Christ also in death. Therefore God will raise them also from the dead and bring them to glory with Christ. The believers are sinners when they die, but they do not die the death of sinners. They fall asleep through Christ, are His own also in death, and therefore they have forgiveness and His righteousness. They have the assurance that they will not come into judgment. All the terrible threats against sinners do not apply to them. When Christians think of the day of the resurrection, they look forward to the day when through Christ they stand before God as justified and the Lord will say to them: "Come, O blessed of My Father, inherit the kingdom prepared for you from the foundation of the world."

How comforting this confident hope is when we stand at the grave of our loved ones! We look beyond the grave and see them living again, full of a new life, standing among the great multitude of the saints, and arm in arm with them following the Lamb to the eternal home. How comforting to have this hope in the hour of our own death! "O Death, where is thy sting?" we say. "Take what is yours, what is perishable about me. This perishable nature must put on the imperishable, and this mortal nature must put on immortality. I know that my Redeemer lives, and because He lives, I shall live also!"

C. Human reason finds the article of the resurrection of the body hard to believe. Nothing seems to contradict reason more flatly. The wise of this world tell us that it is a beautiful thought but that it cannot be true. Man's body turns to dust, dissolves into atoms that are scattered and even mixed with other atoms. How can these atoms be reunited after a long time and become the original body once more? Every attempt at a natural explanation is useless. Do we Christians consider this when we say: "I believe in the resurrection of the body"? Certainly we do! But our faith is based on a foundation that overcomes every doubt. The Apostle states in the text: "This we declare to you by the word of the Lord, that we who are alive, who are left until the coming of the Lord, shall not precede those who have fallen asleep." This word concerning the resurrection is a word of the Lord. This word is firm and immovable, for it is the word of Him who performs what He promises and is able to create what He wills. He has given all things their nature and being, why should it be impossible for Him, yes, even difficult, to renew the nature and being of His creation? Attempts have been made to explain the resurrection scientifically. It has been argued that as in spring new life comes to nature, so the life of the dead shall again break forth at the restoration of all things. This may be a beautiful comparison, but it proves nothing. Who would base his faith and hope for time and eternity on such an argument? But when we are told: "This we declare to you by the word of the Lord," that is an utterly different manner of speaking. "For the word of the Lord is upright, and all His work is done in faithfulness" (Ps. 33:4).

This word of God gives us another basis for our faith in the resurrection of the body. "Since we believe that Jesus died and rose again." In this way God Himself supplies a foundation for our faith. Consider that Jesus died and rose again. Why and for what purpose? For you, for your salvation. Is it possible that He should have sacrificed His life to save you from death and you should nevertheless remain in death? Should it be possible that your Head came forth from death to eternal life and leave you,

His members, in death? No, we Christians are too closely united with Christ in this life. We live in Him, and He lives in us. Our body is His temple, the temple of His Spirit. Is this a life of this world, perishable, a life death can destroy? Indeed not. The life we live in Christ is a divine life. Death cannot touch it. Therefore in the faith that Jesus died and rose again we have a sure foundation for our hope of a blessed resurrection. Those who do not believe are not united with Him, are outside of Christ, and have no part in His resurrection. But we who believe and put our trust in Him will be united with Him in all eternity.

D. Finally, the Apostle describes how the comforting hope of the resurrection will become the reality. "For the Lord Himself will descend from heaven with a cry of command, with the archangel's call, and with the sound of the trumpet of God. And the dead in Christ will rise first; then we who are alive, who are left, shall be caught up together with them in the clouds to meet the Lord in the air; and so we shall always be with the Lord." The Lord will descend from heaven, not in humility as at His first coming, but as a mighty Conqueror, surrounded by His heavenly army. His mighty command will be heard, like a thousand thunders the trumpet of the archangel will resound, and as the walls of Jericho fell at the sound of the trumpets, so the entire structure of this world will collapse. But before the dissolution of all things begins, the Lord's own will be removed from the scene of judgment. Those who are alive at His coming shall not precede those who haven fallen asleep. The dead in Christ are not at any disadvantage. They shall rise immediately, their bodies shining like the sun. At the same moment those who are alive at His coming will be changed in the twinkling of an eye, and be caught up together with the awakened sleepers to meet the Lord in the air. Then the Lord will have His whole congregation of elect before Him, clothed in indescribable glory. Then will be fulfilled what the Son asked of the Father for His own: "Father, I desire that they also whom Thou hast given Me may be with Me where I am, to behold My glory which Thou hast given Me in Thy love for Me before the foundation of the world" (John 17:24). Then our mouth will be filled with laughter, and our tongue with shouts of joy" (Ps. 126:2).

May God help us that this comforting hope of the resurrection ever continue a living conviction in our hearts and draw us away from this sinful, perishing world, to a constant waiting for the blessed hope and revelation of our Savior's glory.

SERMON ON THE HOLY GOSPEL

When the wicked city of Sodom was to be destroyed with all its inhabitants, God sent two angels to warn righteous Lot of the impending doom. They urged him to lead his family out of the city, and when he lingered, they seized him and his wife and two daughters by the hand and brought them forth and set him outside the city and said: "Flee for your life; do not look back or stop anywhere in the valley; flee to the hills, lest you be consumed!" Something similar is told us in the holy Gospel for this day. Here, however, Christ Himself is the messenger of doom. He warns His disciples of the approaching destruction of Jerusalem and advises them: "Let those who are in Judea flee to the mountains."

Our Lord and His disciples were leaving the temple, where He had pronounced His sevenfold woe over the scribes and Pharisees and uttered His lament over Jerusalem. In plain words He had announced the fearful doom awaiting them, their city, and their nation. As they walked, the disciples, still thinking of His prediction that the temple would be forsaken and desolate, drew His attention to the massive strength and solidity of that structure, as if half questioning whether such a magnificent building could ever be destroyed till all the earth would be shaken to its very foundations. Our Lord's answer was: "There will not be left here one stone upon another that will not be thrown down." He then passed over Kidron and sat on the Mount of Olives, looking upon Jerusalem and the temple on the opposite hill as if musing on the fearful ruin that was to fall on both. The disciples came to Him privately and asked Him to explain when these things would be and what would be the sign of His coming and of the close of the age. In response, our Lord gave a prophetic discourse whose immediate application was to the destruction of Jerusalem and of the temple. The forty years between this prediction and the event brought a striking fulfillment of His prophecy. But the disciples had also asked what would be the sign of His coming and of the end of the age, and our Lord treated the two questions as one, applying His answer also to the end of the world. We consider, then:

The Judgment upon Jerusalem as a Call to Prepare for the Last Judgment

A. The Sign of Its Coming. "When you see the desolating sacrilege spoken of by the prophet Daniel, standing in the Holy Place (let the reader understand), then let those who are in Judea flee to the mountains."

1. The reference undoubtedly is to Dan. 11:31: "Forces from him shall appear and profane the temple and fortress, and shall take away the continual burnt offering. And they shall set up the abomination that makes desolate." The first meaning is of Antiochus Epiphanes, tyrant and king of Syria. What he and his helpers, the apostate Jews, did to the temple as Daniel prophesied, was a picture of what was to happen again at the time of Jerusalem's destruction. The desolating sacrilege was Israel's falling away from Jehovah, their covenant God. They refused to accept their Messiah, disregarding the witness of the Apostles to the risen and exalted Christ. As a people they rejected Him and so turned from the true God and in His place put a false god, a product of their phantasy and imagination. They replaced the true worship of God with a pagan worship of ungodly self-righteousness. This sacrilege made its way into the very holy place, the temple. Sacrifices were no longer offered to the true God through faith in the Messiah but to an idol by self-righteous, self-seeking service. When this falling away from the Messiah became general, the end had come. Outward evidence of this inner falling away was that the Zealots and other parties did not hesitate to desecrate the holy place by scenes of abomination, murder, and bloodshed. Israel was ripe for judgment.

Whether our Lord had in mind a special act of profanation we have no means of knowing. Nor is it needful that we should know. The people to whom these words were first addressed and to whom the sign should serve as a warning could understand it, and were exhorted to understand it, that they might profit by it. The abomination and the desolation which it brought were before their eyes and pointed to the coming of the Roman legions whose din should resound in their ears. To us the special sign and what it portended lie in the past, and the whole presents itself to us as an example of divine judgment and of divine mercy forewarning of its coming.

2. But just for that reason the desolating abomination before our eyes now in the holy place is a call to us to prepare for the judgment, whose coming it forebodes. Such an abomination St. Paul describes 2 Thess. 2:3, 4: "That Day will not come unless the rebellion comes first and the man of lawlessnes is revealed, the son of perdition, who opposes and exalts himself against every so-called god or object of worship, so that he takes his seat in the temple of God, proclaiming himself to be God." The abominations which have been admitted into Christian churches and Christian homes by the indifference and coldness and callousness of Christians, not to say by utter unbelief, are manifold. So great is the liberalism and rationalism and sentimentalism that now passes for progressive Christianity that a man who adheres strictly to the words of the Lord is regarded as a relic of the Dark Ages who has not learned the gospel of enlightenment and the advanced charity of disenthralled humanity. Recklessness in morals keeps pace with indifference in doctrine. A conscientious service of God in the vocation He has given is represented as a superstition which increased intelligence has banished, and the fear of God is barely tolerated as a childish sentiment of an uncultured mind that must not be permitted to hamper business with its crudeness. The desolating abomination is among us and indicates that the end of all things is at hand.

B. The Warning to Escape. "Then let those who are in Judea flee to the mountains." The immediate application is to the catastrophe that threatened Jerusalem. But it applies to us also, urging us to prepare for the coming end of all things. It bids us flee, to stop at no importance, to make haste, to pray for help and deliverance to Him who alone can rescue us from the threatening ruin.

1. Many of the Jews heeded the warning and fled to Pella when the Roman legions approached. There they were safe from

the horror that raged in the Holy City. But where shall we flee? There is no hiding place in all the world. Yet there is a refuge for us where all are secure. "God is our Refuge and Strength, a very present Help in trouble. Therefore we will not fear though the earth should change, though the mountains shake in the heart of the sea" (Ps. 46:1, 2). Not only are we permitted to run to that refuge, but the Lord calls us to come and find safety.

2. "Let him who is on the housetop not go down to take what is in his house; and let him who is in the field not turn back to take his mantle." When they should see the desolating abomination in the holy place, the people of God were to make their escape by the speediest way possible and were not to permit any thought of rescuing property to interfere with rescuing their lives. Those on the housetops were to descend by means of the staircase on the outside wall and, without stopping to enter the house, leave the city by the quickest route. Those who were in the field were not to think of going back to their homes to save at least their clothing. Without the slightest delay they were to hasten and save their lives.

This warning is also for us. The desolating abomination has appeared, and the end is coming. Flee for your lives! Do not think of first securing or enjoying this or that earthly prize or pleasure. What would it profit you if you gained the whole world and lost your soul? Let nothing deter you from getting ready for the Lord's coming. Seek first the Kingdom of God and His righteousness. All else, even though the Lord's coming be long delayed, will then be amply provided for. Attend to these eternal things now, for now is the day of salvation.

3. "And alas for those who are with child and for those who give suck in those days! Pray that your flight may not be in winter or on a Sabbath." Our Lord here injects a note of infinite compassion and tenderness. He deeply sympathizes with His people under the peculiar trials of this sudden and hurried flight. He thinks of winter and stormy weather, and how these fugitives would suffer if compelled to undertake this flight at such a time! He bids them pray that the necessity might not fall in so unfavorable a period. He thinks of the restrictions of the Jewish Sabbath, when the gates of the cities were closed, all journeys intercepted, and all sympathy for those not conforming to the custom entirely withdrawn, and

how they would be disadvantaged and hindered if compelled to flee on that day. He thinks of the burdened and expectant mothers and of the little children and laments the sorrows and trials this necessary flight would bring to them. Every kind of exposure, peril, and disadvantage He takes into consideration and provides against them with the utmost tenderness. It is impossible for us half to understand the depth of our Lord's compassion for them who trust in Him. It might seem foolish to think of influencing the march of the Roman armies or the orders of Roman generals by the prayers of a few Christians in the obscurity of their homes and little assemblies. Yet so our Lord directed. Whatever philosophers and skeptics may say of it, the disciples did as they were commanded, and the result was as they prayed.

To carry a child was a hindrance to speedy flight. The weather and the roads of winter were impediments to a hasty flight, and the law of the Sabbath forbade a journey of more than a mile on the holy day. These things were not to be a hindrance in fleeing from the impending judgment. But their mention shows us that everything on earth, though it be father or mother or son or daughter, the best and dearest this life has, must be regarded as a calamity when it stands in the way of or hinders us in, fleeing from the wrath to come. The one absorbing thought must be to escape the destruction and find a refuge that is safe. Therefore pray for deliverance from every power and every entanglement that endangers your life by hindering your flight. You have not the power in yourselves to break the bonds that constitute the danger; you have not the power in yourselves to flee; you have not the power in yourselves to make your flight a success. Ask God for light and life and strength. We have a God who hears prayer and is ever ready to help. Call upon Him. He will hear you and give you what you need to comply with His warning, that you may escape.

C. The Coming Tribulation. "For then there will be great tribulation, such as has not been from the beginning of the world until now, no, and never will be." The destruction of Jerusalem brought, and the end of the world will bring, terrible things which all should wish to escape.

1. The text refers to the tribulation that befell Jerusalem in its siege and destruction by the Romans. It was a scene of horror unparalleled in the annals of time. War and famine and pestilence combined to make it a calamity beyond the power of human language to depict. Josephus estimates that there were three million people in the city when the Romans surrounded it at the time of the Passover. Within such a limited space such a number cannot remain healthy, and a terrible pestilence raged. Food became so scarce that some mothers killed their children, boiled and ate them. One million are said to have died, ninety-seven thousand were sold into slavery for a cheap price.

2. Great will be the tribulation also when the final judgment comes which is prefigured by Jerusalem's destruction. When all the vast fabric of God's creation will have accomplished its end and will fall to pieces in a final crash, even the strongest hearts will quake with fear if they have not sought security in Him who has provided a refuge for His people. "The Day of the Lord will come like a thief, and then the heavens will pass away with a loud noise, and the elements will be dissolved with fire, and the earth and the works that are upon it will be burned up" (2 Peter 3:10). The distress and terror of the ungodly will not cease when the destruction of the world is past and the end of all things has come. Their tribulation only begins in the eternal doom of those who have rejected God and are now rejected forever. That is the tribulation of which the unspeakable horrors of Jerusalem's fate are but a faint emblem. But those who have heeded the warning and waited for Him in daily watchfulness and prayer, fled out of this world and taken refuge in Him, will lift up their hearts, for their redemption is drawing near. The Epistle for this day tells us that neither those who have fallen asleep nor those who are alive at our Lord's coming will see anything of the destruction, but will be caught up in the clouds to meet Him in the air, and so we shall always be with the Lord.

D. Therefore We Flee to the Mercy That Never Fails. There is mercy in the warning that aims at securing man's escape from the tribulation. There is mercy in the exhortation to prayer, which implies God's readiness to hear and help. There is mercy in the divine providence that shapes all things for the welfare of the faithful.

1. The obvious purpose of pointing to the desolating abomination in the holy place as the sign of the coming doom and of giving earnest warning to flee from the approaching destruction was to arouse to a sense of danger and to invite to escape. It was the divine compassion yearning to save from ruin. The compassion extended even to the people whose sin was bringing about the ruin. It is tenderly expressed in our Lord's words: "O Jerusalem, Jerusalem, killing the prophets and stoning those who are sent to you! How often would I have gathered your children together as a hen gathers her brood under her wings, and you would not!" The multitude remained impenitent, and the tribulation came, but His mercy continued to all who were willing to embrace it; for He said: "If those days had not been shortened, no human being would be saved; but for the sake of the elect those days will be shortened." These elect were the Christians who by faith had accepted Christ as their Savior and those among the Jews who were yet to be brought to faith. They were His own, elected by grace to be the Lord's possession before the foundation of the world. The days of tribulation were shortened, not by the prayers of the faithful, but for their sake, for their good, that they might be delivered. The tribulation caused by war and famine and pestilence was not permitted to run its full course. There were some among the Jews who were to be saved, won for Christ later. For the sake of these, whom He had chosen, those days were shortened. "For the sake of the elect, whom He chose, He shortened the days" (Mark 13:20).

2. This mercy is great toward us also. It is that mercy which moved our Lord to give warnings which today are set before us for our learning. He would have us realize that the end is coming and that we must be ready. His mercy has provided a way of escape from the ruin that will overtake His foes and now calls upon us to flee from the wrath to come (Heb. 3:12-15). The announcement that the end of all things is approaching is designed to arouse us also to be ready every day and hour for the coming of the Son of man, the more so as we know not the day and hour when He will appear. We should be prepared at any moment.

The signs of the coming tribulation are given us that we may be incited to make no delay in preparing. "Wherever the body is, there the eagles will be gathered together." A dead, putrifying body is the gathering point of the vultures who remove the carcass. We are to recognize the mercy of God in giving us warning and offering us the needful grace to escape the coming ruin, the mercy He shows in shortening the days of distress for the saints on earth. The desolating abomination is a constant temptation to sin and leads many to destruction. While it is a mercy to the ungodly that God postpones the Day of Judgment in order to give them time for repentance, it is a mercy to His people that He shortens the time of delay in order to remove them from the temptations and afflictions to which they are subject in this wilderness of probation. For the sake of the elect those days will be shortened. Therefore the saints love the Lord's appearing and fervently pray: "Even so, come, Lord Jesus!" For the mercy of God that has provided for their salvation from sin and death has prepared for them a home of bliss eternal in the heavens. But before that home is reached, we must pass through the trials of this earthly life.

E. The Dangers That Beset Us. "Then if anyone says to you, Lo, here is the Christ! or There He is! do not believe it. For false Christs and false prophets will arise and show great signs and wonders, so as to lead astray, if possible, even the elect. Lo, I have told you beforehand. So, if they say to you, Lo, He is in the wilderness, do not go out; if they say, Lo, He is in the inner rooms, do not believe it."

1. Before the destruction of Jerusalem these words were literally fulfilled. There were false Christs who deceived many and led them away from the living springs to cisterns that held no water. There were false prophets who set forth their own vain fancy which could only lead astray. They showed great signs which had the semblance of miracles and deceived many. This, too, belonged to the tribulation of those dreadful times.

2. There are false Christs and false prophets showing great signs and wonders now, so as to lead astray, if possible, even the elect. Error in a thousand forms is spread among the people. The danger is all the greater because Satan has blinded the eyes

of the multitude, even of those who profess to be followers of the Christ, so that they do not see the ruinous consequences of false doctrine. When vigilant and earnest men lift a warning voice, this is attributed to bigotry and uncharitableness. There is a clamor for union without putting away the error that separates. Indifference to truth is preying upon the vitals of the Church. The desolating abomination has appeared, warning us that the end is approaching, and the perilous times of the last days are upon us.

Be ready, for the Lord is surely coming, perhaps very soon (2 Peter 3:3, 4, 9, 10). The destruction of Jerusalem shows us that the judgment must come. The Word of God announces the final judgment upon the world. Be ready that when the end comes, you may be safe in Jesus Christ.

THE TWENTY-SIXTH SUNDAY AFTER TRINITY

This Sunday is the second of a group dealing with the Last Things. If it is the last Sunday of the Church Year, the Introit and the Collect for the Twenty-third Sunday after Trinity shall be used, according to the Rubrics. The holy Gospel brings our Lord's own description of what will happen in the Final Judgment. Both the *Common Service Book* and *The Lutheran Hymnal* offer a choice of two Epistles. In the first St. Peter exclaims: "Since all these things are thus to be dissolved, what sort of persons ought you to be in lives of holiness and godliness, waiting for and hastening [earnestly desiring] the coming of the Day of God!" "Be zealous to be found by Him without spot or blemish and at peace." In the second, St. Paul gives thanks that the church at Thessalonica is growing in faith and love for one another in all their persecutions and afflictions. He assures them that the just God will repay and inflict vengeance on the day when the Lord comes in glory to be glorified in His saints.

The Introit. "Save me, O God, by Thy name, and judge me by Thy strength. Hear my prayer, O God; give ear to the words of my mouth. He shall reward evil to mine enemies; cut them off in Thy truth."

The text is from Psalm 54. This Introit first appears in Lutheran sources. It sings of the Christian assurance of salvation. Reference to the second Epistle for this day is evident in the words: "Vindicate me by Thy might." Also: "He will requite my enemies with evil; in Thy faithfulness put an end to them."

The Collect. "O God, so rule and govern our hearts and minds by Thy Holy Spirit that, being ever mindful of the end of all things and the day of Thy just Judgment, we may be stirred up to holiness of living here and dwell with Thee forever hereafter."

This prayer is unique in that it comes from a Swedish source, first appearing in 1639. Apparent is the connection with the first

Epistle: "In lives of holiness and godliness" and "stirred up to holiness of living here."

The Epistle, 2 Peter 3:3-14 or 2 Thessalonians 1:3-10.

The Gradual. "He shall call to the heavens from above and to the earth that He may judge the people. The heavens shall declare His righteousness, for God is Judge Himself. Alleluia! Alleluia! The ransomed of the Lord shall come to Zion with everlasting joy upon their heads; they shall obtain joy and gladness, and sorrow and weeping shall fly away. Alleluia!"

Here is assurance for the people who wait for and earnestly desire the coming of the Lord: "He will call to the heavens above and to the earth, so that He may judge His people." The heavens will declare His righteousness, be witnesses to God's judicial rectitude, for on this occasion God Himself will act as Judge (Ps. 50:4, 6). The holy Gospel is connected with either of the Epistles: "The ransomed of the Lord shall return and come to Zion with singing, with everlasting joy upon their heads; they shall obtain joy and gladness, and sorrow and sighing shall flee away" (Is. 35:10).

The Proper Sentence. "Alleluia! O Lord, deal with Thy servant according unto Thy mercy, and teach me Thy statutes. I am Thy servant, give me understanding, that I may know Thy testimonies. Alleluia!"

Or: "Alleluia! Blessed be the Lord God of our fathers; praise Him and highly exalt Him forever. Alleluia!"

The Gospel, St. Matthew 25:31-46. This is the conclusion of our Lord's discourse two days before His death, in which He instructed His disciples, upon their request, regarding the end of the world. He spoke to comfort and admonish His believers and to warn and to fill with dread the others who might be helped. This passage may be given the theme "The Last Judgment and Its Four Stages": the gathering of all nations before the judgment seat of Christ; the separation of sheep and goats; the twofold verdict; and the final lot of both groups, eternal punishment and eternal life. The judgment of the world may also be regarded as the permanent separation of the people of earth and considered under three heads: The Judge of all the earth will determine the eternal weal or woe of all men on that Day; He will separate men according to faith and unbelief; and He will prove the righteousness of His verdict by the works of faith or their lack. Or the preacher may impress the twofold truth that the merciful will receive mercy, the unmerciful, however, will be judged unmercifully.

The Proper Preface. "Who with Thine only-begotten Son and the Holy Ghost art one God, one Lord. And in the confession of the only true God we worship the Trinity in Person and the Unity in Substance, of Majesty coequal."

SERMON ON THE FIRST EPISTLE

With this Sunday we have reached the end of the Church Year. It reminds us of the end of all things, of time, of life, and of the world. We consider a portion of the Holy Scriptures which the ancient Church appointed as the Epistle for one of the last Sundays of the Church Year. The subject is:

The Delay of the End

St. Peter introduces the subject: "This is now the second letter that I have written to you, beloved, and in both of them I have aroused your sincere mind by way of reminder; that you should remember the predictions of the holy prophets and the commandment of the Lord and Savior through your apostles." He is referring to the end of the world and reminds his readers that the prophets and the Lord Jesus had predicted the final destruction of this world. The prophets had spoken hundreds of years before. This letter was written thirty years after our Lord's ascension. Yet there was no indication that the end was any nearer. Therefore St. Peter found it necessary to arouse the believers. For the delay was apt to result in complacency and apathy.

"First of all you must understand this, that scoffers will come in the last days with scoffing, following their own passions and saying, Where is the promise of His coming? For ever since the fathers fell asleep, all things have continued as they were from the beginning of creation." We know from several letters of the New Testament that the early Christians expected our Lord to return almost immediately. Yet the first generation of Christians was dying away, and still the world did not come to an end. The scoffers asked mockingly: "Should men still look for Christ's Second Coming? The laws of nature are still working with changeless uniformity. There is no indication of any change through all these years." This scoffing was done because these mockers followed their own passions. They would permit no consideration to interfere with their self-indulgence. Their skepticism was born of the wish that was father to the thought.

St. Peter continues: "They deliberately ignore this fact, that by the word of God heavens existed long ago, and an earth formed out of water and by means of water, through which the world that then existed was deluged with water and perished." By their own will the fact escapes them that there was a change. They willfully ignore the fact that God by His omnipotent Word created the world. By His Word He caused the dry land to be separated from the water. This was a mighty change. The scoffers say that all things have always been as they are. They deliberately ignore the fact that by the Word of God a stupendous change was once brought about.

They also willfully ignore the fact that a mighty change was brought about through the Deluge, when the earth perished in water. The word of Almighty God caused the earth to be covered with water and perish.

"But by the same word the heavens and earth that now exist have been stored up for fire, being kept until the Day of Judgment and destruction of ungodly men." This same word that brought forth the earth out of water and destroyed it by water is now keeping the world in existence. God has said that He will fully destroy it by His word at some future time. But this time the destruction will not be by water but by fire. By His word God is keeping the heavens and the earth against the day when ungodly men will be judged and destroyed.

How does St. Peter explain the delay? He is not writing to ungodly men and scoffers and skeptics and agnostics but to believers. People who do not want to believe God, who willfully ignore facts, who refuse to have any consideration to interfere with their self-indulgence, will brush St. Peter's explanation aside. "But do not ignore this one fact, beloved, that with the Lord one day

is as a thousand years and a thousand years as one day." The
Lord is not bound by the element of time. He speaks from the
viewpoint of eternity, where there is no time, no day, no year.
To Him one day can be a thousand years to us, and a thousand
years to Him can be a day to us.

"The Lord is not slow about His promise as some count
slowness, but is forbearing toward you [on your account], not
wishing that any should perish but that all should reach repentance." In His own mind God has determined the exact
moment. From His side there is no delay. What seems a delay
to the scoffers is not that. Men are slow in fulfilling their promises
from various, often selfish motives. The only motives God has are
love and long-suffering. He does not wish that any should perish.
He has set judgment into the future so as to give opportunity for
repentance. He is willing to receive all to repentance. St. Peter
expresses the same thought in his First Letter when he writes that
"God's patience waited in the days of Noah, during the building of
the ark." But in spite of Noah's warning the ungodly scoffed as
the years passed and the Deluge came upon them unexpectedly.

"But the day of the Lord will come like a thief, and then the
heavens will pass away with a loud noise, and the elements will
be dissolved with fire, and the earth and the works that are upon it
will be burned up." The Day of the Lord will come as a surprise,
without special warning, without further previous announcement.
All, believers and unbelievers, will be surprised. Our Lord impressed the unexpected suddenness of His return upon His disciples,
and St. Peter here, and also St. Paul, and St. John twice in the
Revelation, emphasize this feature. Then will come the crash of
a falling world and the roar of destroying flames. The framework
of the world will be dissolved. The earth and all the works of God
and man in it will be burned up.

"Since all these things are thus to be dissolved, what sort of
persons ought you to be in lives of holiness and godliness, waiting
for and hastening [earnestly desiring] the coming of the Day of
God, because of which the heavens will be kindled and dissolved
and the elements will melt with fire! But according to His promise
we wait for new heavens and a new earth in which righteousness
dwells." Seeing that all these things (!) are being dissolved, that

the process of dissolution is even now going on and will be completed unexpectedly, knowing that the end may come at any moment and put an end to all, what sort of people ought we to be? The natural reaction would be fear and uneasiness. The unbeliever, the scoffer, willfully and deliberately ignores all, because he will not be disturbed in his self-indulgence. In this way he keeps fear from overwhelming him. But we see and know from God's Word that all things will be destroyed by fire suddenly. What sort of persons ought we to be?

Not fearful people! The believer has nothing to fear. We shall not come into judgment but shall be removed from this earth before things begin to crash. St. Paul tells us that if we are alive, we shall be caught up to meet Christ in the air. The dead in Christ will rise first and go to meet the Lord also. So there is nothing to fear. Or should the thought that the things of this world will burn up sadden and depress us? This would indicate that we overemphasize things. However, that is why the Lord is waiting, to give time for repentance, for a shift of emphasis to the things that will endure forever.

St. Peter does not mention fear. We ought to be people in lives of holiness and godliness, people who wait for the coming of the Day of God. The Day of God will bring fulfillment of His promise to create new heavens and a new earth in which righteousness dwells. Eagerly we look forward to the day when this world, falling to pieces and dying a miserable death, will be replaced by a new world ruled by righteousness. This life is the school in which we are prepared and trained for the new world of righteousness. So we live in holiness and godliness. Holiness is separation from the service of sin and evil, from the godless world that serves sin and self. Godliness is the service of God, the reflecting of God in our lives.

St. Peter writes that we ought to hasten the coming of the Day of God. The coming of this Day is being delayed to give men time and opportunity to turn to God. The Lord is forbearing, not wishing that any should perish but that all should reach repentance. Then the coming may be hastened by making further delay unnecessary, by repenting, by turning from the perishable things of this world to holiness and godliness.

The Day of God may be hastened also by leading others to repentance. The Lord is delaying with His coming because the number of the elect must be complete. There are people who must be saved, and this world is still standing for the one purpose of saving them. When they are won for Christ, the end will come. Christ works and saves only through us. So we may make further delay unnecessary and hasten the Day by winning others to Christ and leading them to repentance. There is a terrible urgency about our mission work. That neighbor of ours, that relative, that acquaintance, may be the one whom we must win by our personal efforts. God wants to use us in adding him or her, and then the number of the elect will be full, and the end will come.

"Therefore, beloved, since you wait for these," since you wait for the coming of the Lord, for the restitution of all things, for the new heavens and the new earth, "be zealous to be found by Him without spot or blemish, and at peace. And count the forbearance of our Lord as salvation." The scoffers say that the delay is slowness. The beloved count it salvation. It is for the salvation of the elect that the judgment tarries. So be earnest to be found without spot or blemish when the Lord appears suddenly. While waiting for the Lord to come, we must strive to be like Him, to imitate Him who is the Lamb without blemish and without spot, and to be found blameless in His sight. And at peace! Peace in its fullest sense, peace with God and man, the peace that Christ gives, the peace of God that passes all understanding. "In peace" was a common inscription on Christian graves. In peace, whether you live or have fallen asleep when the Lord comes.

Against the background of these words we celebrate the Lord's Supper today. As we in memory enter the Upper Room, we hear our Lord say: "I will not drink henceforth of this fruit of the vine, until that day when I drink it new with you in My Father's Kingdom." We recall that St. Paul wrote: "As often as you eat this bread and drink the cup, you proclaim the Lord's death until He comes." Our thoughts go not only to the past but also to the future. As we do this in remembrance of Him, we look back to the death of the Son of God for our salvation. But we look forward also to the return of the Son of God in glory, when the heavens will pass away with a loud noise and the elements will be dissolved with fire and the earth and the works that are upon it will be burned up. We look forward to the day when there will be new heavens and a new earth in which righteousness dwells. We look forward to the day when our Lord will take us home to the marriage feast in heaven and when He will drink the wine with us new in the Kingdom of His Father.

To this coming feast of victory and reunion we look forward as we celebrate the Lord's death in the Holy Communion at the end of the Church Year and are reminded of the end of all things. After this life of suffering and sorrow, of struggle with temptation, after the turmoil of strife and the conflict of battle, we shall meet our Savior in the new creation of righteousness, and shall drink of the fruit of the vine new with Him in His Father's Kingdom. Today we hear our King say to us: "You weary men and women, I am coming again to take you out of this miserable world into the new world of righteousness. Let your thoughts go forward confidently and joyously to that hour. As surely as I meet you here invisibly in the Holy Sacrament, so surely shall I meet you visibly on that Day." As we leave His Table, we shall be what St. Peter said we should be: in lives of holiness and godliness, waiting for, hastening the coming of the Day of God, waiting for new heavens and a new earth, zealous to be found before Him without spot or blemish and at peace.

SERMON ON THE HOLY GOSPEL

At the end of a year of grace the Church reminds her children of a fact that is ignored and ridiculed by the unbelieving world. She declares that a day is coming when all things will be destroyed by fire and this great world structure will be reduced to nothingness. She impresses upon her children that the Day of Judgment will bring not only the disappearance of all we see but also the revelation of all that is not seen. St. Paul calls it "the day of wrath when God's righteous judgment will be revealed." The Lord Jesus speaks of it so in the text.

On that day, Christ will be revealed. Now He is not seen. He was on earth centuries ago as a humble and despised man. Only few knew then that seeing Him they were seeing God. Then He withdrew His visible presence and ascended to heaven. He is now present on earth only invisibly, in and through His Word and Sacraments, in His Church. It seems as though our Lord does not live and rule. He has His way in the hearts of His believers, but this is hidden from others. Even His beloved at times feel only little of His abiding presence. Therefore the unbelieving world ignores, despises, blasphemes the unseen Christ, and all who serve Him faithfully are looked upon as odd and foolish.

When our Lord withdrew the body He had taken from the Virgin Mary, He said He would continue His life and work on earth through another body. As its invisible Head, He would rule and direct the members of this body. This body is His Church, the Communion of Saints, the Communion of Separated People. Every believer is a member of this body. The Church is the body of the living and invisible Son of God on earth. The Church is Christ on earth.

This fact is disregarded by most. The great majority are not in the least concerned about the welfare of Christ's body. Even people who profess to be members often fail to function as the Head directs. Because the Lord's displeasure is not immediately apparent, they imagine Him either indifferent or powerless. So they go on, secure in their disregard of the unseen Christ, who is living on earth in the body of His believers.

The text reminds us that this will not continue forever. "When the Son of man comes in His glory and all the angels with Him, then He will sit on His glorious throne." The invisible Lord will come to earth visibly a second time, as a true man, but this time not in humility. He will come in His glory, and all His holy servants, all the kingdoms of angels, ten thousand times ten thousand, will accompany Him. "Then He will sit on His glorious throne." Until that moment, He was the great High Priest, pleading men's cause before God that time and opportunity be given for turning to Him. But now He comes as the King in majesty and glory, to judge the world in righteousness. Now He descends from heaven with a shout of command, with the archangel's call, and with the sound of the trumpet of God, and on His robe and on His thigh a name inscribed, King of kings and Lord of lords.

"Before Him will be gathered all the nations." All who lived on earth from Adam to the end must appear before Him, the angels gathering all before the throne. We, too, shall stand there, you who hear these words, and I who proclaim this truth to you. "And He will separate them one from another as a shepherd separates the sheep from the goats, and He will place the sheep at His right hand, but the goats at the left." Here, in this life, believers and unbelievers are mingled together. True believers may go unrecognized and misjudged. Some godless may pass for Christians. But on that Day there will be a clean-cut division, without the possibility of a mistake. Every man's true self will be revealed in a moment, all false fronts will be torn away.

The sheep are placed on the right hand. The picture of the Good Shepherd and His sheep reaches beyond time into eternity. "The Lord is my Shepherd." "My sheep hear My voice, and I know them, and they follow Me; and I give them eternal life." The believers stand on His right. They are His sheep. They heard Christ's Word, they obeyed His voice, they followed His directions.

The goats are put on the left. Apart from their odor the outstanding characteristic of goats is their unreasoning stubbornness that leads them to butt their thick heads against a stone wall. They on the left are goats because they willfully, stubbornly refused when God graciously invited them: "Come now, let us reason together; though your sins are like scarlet, they shall be as white as snow." They insisted on going their own way and would not be led and guided by Christ's Word. Whenever His Word threatened to interfere with their selfish way of life, they reared and charged head on. They obstinately refused to follow the Good Shepherd, who laid down His life for them.

This separation and division takes place immediately. There is no examination, no trial, no presentation of evidence, no sentence by the court. This is not a trial or the passing of a sentence. This is a judgment, the carrying out of a sentence already passed. The trial is over, all the evidence is in, the sentence was determined in this life. The Judgment is merely the carrying out of the sentence that fell here in this life. You and I may know in this hour where we shall stand on that day. Our Lord told us on what basis a man is judged. "The word that I have spoken will be his judge on the last day." Our attitude over against Christ's Word, the Word we read in the Bible and hear preached by human lips, this attitude here in life determines. Our Lord also said: "Truly, truly, I say to you, if anyone keeps My Word, he will never see death." Again: "Truly, truly, I say to you, he who hears My Word and believes Him who sent Me, has eternal life; he does not come into judgment but has passed from death to life." To hear Christ's Word means to hear it effectually, to accept it, to trust in it, to act upon it, to obey it. Our Lord promises with an oath: Be My sheep in this life, hear your Shepherd's voice, follow your Shepherd's directions, feed on the pasture of God's holy Word, and there can be no question where you will stand on the Last Day.

This immediate division, this revelation of sheep and goats, will cause much surprise on the left. The goats paid no attention to Christ's Word and, being ignorant to the last, will even now continue to butt their heads against everything they do not like. They will not like the judgment. Many will think that they do not belong on the left and that others they see on the right have no business there. All their life the goats stubbornly insisted that they were at least just as good as the simpletons who heard Christ's Word regularly. So the King must justify His judgment and prove before all the world that it is righteous.

He turns first to the sheep: "Come, O blessed of My Father, inherit the Kingdom prepared for you from the foundation of the world." In life you believed in Me, followed Me, loved Me. You were children of God, My brothers and sisters. Your Big Brother has come to give you your inheritance. What proof does He present that they believed in Him and loved Him? They gave Christ food, drink, welcome, clothing, and they visited Him. Now there is surprise on the right hand. When did they ever do all this to Him? They loved Him, yes; and because they loved Him and wished to imitate Him, they showed kindly love to humanity wherever needed. But they never did it to Him! Then the righteous will answer Him, Lord, when did we ever do this to Thee? "And the King will answer them, Truly, I say to you, as you did it to one of the least of these My brethren, you did it to Me." You did it to My brethren, for My sake. You showed that you loved Me, obeyed Me, followed Me, imitated Me. You did it because you knew I would do it under the same circumstances. Your attitude proves that you are My sheep.

"Then He will say to those at His left hand, Depart from Me, you cursed, into the eternal fire prepared for the devil and his angels." By your attitude you proved in life that you did not love Me. There was only selfishness. So your place is where there is no love for Me, for only there will loveless, selfish people be at home.

The goats make an attempt at defense: "Lord, when did we see Thee hungry or thirsty or a stranger or naked or sick or in prison and did not minister to Thee?" If we had ever seen Thee in need, we would have ministered to Thee, for we knew it would pay off and be to our advantage. But we never saw Thee. Thou wast far away and absent. "Then He will answer them, Truly, I say to you, as you did it not to one of the least of these, you did it not to Me." Naturally, you never saw Me, because you paid no attention to My Word, and therefore did not know that out of love for Me you were to imitate Me. When you saw a needy fellow man, you never asked what your Lord would do under the circumstances. You were so wrapt up in self that you saw nothing but whatever would bring you profit and advantage. You belong where you are, on the left, among the goats.

"My brethren." The Son of man is speaking, the human Christ. All humanity is no doubt included in the term "My brethren." Yet there are people who are the Judge's brothers and sisters in a special sense. They are united with Him not only by the bond of a common humanity but by the bond of a common sonship. They are His believers, His sheep, the children of God. They have the same Father with the Son of God, they are members of God's family, and therefore the Judge's brothers and sisters in a special sense. Surely the words apply to them in even greater measure: As you did it to My brethren, you did it to Me. As you did it not to these, you did it not to Me.

These brothers and sisters of the Judge the Holy Spirit gathers about the Word and Sacraments, and this communion of believers is called the Communion of Saints, the holy Christian Church. This congregation assembled here today is the outward manifestation of this invisible organism, Christ's Church. St. Paul calls the Church Christ's body and every believer a member of the body whose Head is Christ. Our Lord called the Church His bride. He said that on the Last Day He, the Bridegroom, will come to take His bride home to the eternal wedding feast. Surely, it is in the sense of the text when we say: As you did it to My Church, My body, My bride, you did it to Me; as you did it not to My Church, My body, My bride, you did it not to Me.

Then He will say to those on the left, the goats: "Depart from Me, you cursed, into the eternal fire prepared for the devil and his angels." Hear them as they are hurled down into the pit: "I never dreamed that God was really serious about the Word I heard. I never thought that my reaction to the Word had anything to do with being a sheep or a goat. The preacher often warned, but I imagined that he was out to build up the congregation or had a disturbed liver or disordered stomach and was too serious." Or: "If I had only realized that a church as that of which I was a member outwardly, is composed of members of Christ's body in which He continues His life and work on earth, I would have given my time and efforts and money. But I was so busy looking out for myself that I never thought how impossible a lifeless, deformed member is in the holy body of the living Christ." Or: "If I had only believed the word that the Church is Christ's bride, then I would not have ignored and neglected her and treated her so shabbily. I would have cherished her as the bride of Christ, tenderly and lovingly ministered to her, taken time to serve her. But now I must hear: You did it not to her; therefore you did it not to Me."

Then He will say to those on the right, the sheep: "Come, O blessed of My Father." As you did it to My Church, My body, My bride, for My sake, you did it to Me. On this note we shall end the Church Year. Every minute spent for His Church, every attempt to win a soul, every visit made on the King's business, every effort to build Christ's Kingdom, is noted, and the King will on the Last Day acknowledge all profusely. We have today seen the picture of the text in a local setting and frame. So ends another Church Year, another year of grace, perhaps our last. It is possible that also this warning of a righteous Judge will not affect the loveless attitude of some toward Christ, toward His body, toward His bride, toward His brethren. But the indifference of some must not discourage the sheep and cause them to grow weary in welldoing. There will come a day of revelation when the Christ they love and serve through their fellow men and brethren will declare before the world: "As you have done it for My sake to My Church, My body and bride, you have done it to Me. Thereby you proved your faith and love. Blessed of My Father, inherit the Kingdom which the Father has prepared for His children from the beginning of the world." Then the righteous will enter into the life eternal.

THE TWENTY-SEVENTH SUNDAY AFTER TRINITY

The Epistle and the holy Gospel are the same in *The Lutheran Hymnal* and the *Common Service Book*. The former has the rubric: "The Introit and Collect for the Twenty-third Sunday after Trinity shall be used on the last Sunday after Trinity in each year." The latter offers a complete set of Propers, the Collect being that for the Twenty-third Sunday, and the rubric directs: "The Introit, Collect, Epistle, Gradual, and Gospel here following, shall be used the Last Sunday after Trinity of each year."

The Introit. "I know the thoughts that I think toward you, saith the Lord, thoughts of peace and not of evil. Then shall ye call upon Me and pray unto Me, and I will hearken unto you; and I will turn your captivity and gather you from all nations and from all places. Lord, Thou hast been favorable unto Thy land; Thou hast brought back the captivity of Jacob."

This is the Introit appointed for the Twenty-third Sunday after Trinity, and comment on it is found under that Sunday. The *Common Service Book* has the following Introit: "I am the Alpha and Omega, the beginning and the ending, which is, and which was, and which is to come, the Almighty. Behold, the tabernacle of God is with men, and He will dwell with them; and they shall be His people, and God Himself shall be with them and be their God. Lift up your heads, O ye gates; and be ye lift up, ye everlasting doors; and the King of Glory shall come in."

The Collect. "Absolve, we beseech Thee, O Lord, Thy people from their offenses that from the bonds of our sins which by reason of our frailty we have brought upon us we may be delivered by Thy bountiful goodness."

This is the Collect for the Twenty-third Sunday after Trinity and appointed by both *The Lutheran Hymnal* and the *Common Service Book* for use on the Last Sunday.

The Epistle, 1 Thessalonians 5:1-11. At the end of the year, the Church brings anxious warnings and lessons. She is terribly earnest in her desire to bring home to every heart the wonder of the one, great, last opportunity. The Epistle warns to keep awake and be sober, to put on the armor not of offense but of readiness. Then something sweetly peaceful reaches the heart, that dispels the awe filling the heart at the thought of the Last Day. For God has not destined us for wrath, but to obtain salvation through our Lord Jesus Christ, so that we might live with Him. "Therefore encourage one another, and build one another up."

The Gradual. "The King's daughter shall be brought unto the King; the virgins, her companions that follow her, shall be brought unto Thee. With gladness and rejoicing shall they be brought; they shall enter into the King's palace. Alleluia! Alleluia! I saw the holy city, New Jerusalem, coming down from God out of heaven, prepared as a bride adorned for her husband. Alleluia!"

Another Gradual is offered in the *Common Service Book:* "I am the Light of the world; he that followeth Me shall not walk in darkness, but shall have the light of life. The Spirit and the bride say, Come, and let him that heareth say Come. And let him that is athirst come. Alleluia! Alleluia! Even so, come, Lord Jesus. Alleluia!"

The Proper Sentence. "Alleluia! O Lord, deal with Thy servant according unto Thy mercy, and teach me Thy statutes. I am Thy servant, give me understanding that I may know Thy testimonies. Alleluia!"

Or: "Alleluia! Blessed be the Lord God of our fathers; praise Him and highly exalt Him forever. Alleluia!"

The Gospel, St. Matthew 25:1-13. This is a parable of warning. It pictures readiness against unreadiness, preparedness against unpreparedness, watchfulness against sleep. All ten maidens seem to be of the company-to-be, all go to the wedding, all go to meet the bridegroom, yet five of them were wise and five foolish. "Those who were ready went in with him to the marriage feast; and the door was shut." This note of finality is new. The door is not opened again. Be ready!

The Proper Preface. "Who with Thine only-begotten Son and the Holy Ghost art one God, one Lord. And in the confession of the only true God we worship the Trinity in Person and the Unity in Substance, of Majesty coequal."

SERMON ON THE EPISTLE

The desire to discover and ferret out what God has left hidden from man is characteristic of perverse human nature. Instead of being content with what is revealed in the works of creation and God's Word, men delight in occupying themselves with unnecessary and useless questions. Speculation regarding the future holds particular attraction. It is not surprising, therefore, that the end of the world is a frequent subject of investigation. Even while our Lord was still on earth, His disciples wished to know exactly when He would return. A few decades after His ascension, people in Thessalonica believed that the Last Day was imminent and therefore neglected their daily work. Of them St. Paul wrote: "We hear that some of you are living in idleness, mere busybodies, not doing any work." To this day, enthusiasts undertake to set the time of the Last Day and mislead and frighten many.

Christians are to beware of such speculations. St. Paul wrote to the believers in Thessalonica: "We beg you, brethren, not to be quickly shaken in mind or excited, either by spirit or by word, or by letter purporting to be from us, to the effect that the day of the Lord has come. Let no one deceive you in any way." Not only does he warn against paying attention to speculations as to the time of our Lord's return, but he is also deeply concerned that the Christians be in constant readiness for the Last Day, not become secure but expect it any and every day. Of this continual readiness he speaks in the Epistle appointed for this Sunday. We speak, then, of

The Right and Constant Readiness for the Last Day

A. Why Constant Readiness Is Necessary. "As to the time and the seasons, brethren, you have no need to have anything written to you." The Apostle refers to what he wrote at the end of the previous chapter, the Epistle for the Twenty-fifth Sunday after Trinity, where he described the resurrection of the dead and

the events of the Last Day. Now he speaks of the time and hour
when what he has described will take place. He declares there is
no need to write anything regarding the time, "for you yourselves
know well that the day of the Lord will come like a thief in the
night." You know well that no man, no apostle, no angel, can say
when the end will come, for it will come unexpectedly, suddenly,
and without special foregoing signs. A thief does not announce
his coming in advance, but comes unexpected, unnoticed, noiseless,
under cover of darkness. So will be our Lord's coming. No one
can know when the Last Day is coming, but like lightning out
of a clear sky, like a snare, it will come upon all who dwell upon
the face of the whole earth (Luke 21:34, 35), and even the faithful
will receive no special warning. A snare is laid secretly. So God
has prepared the Last Judgment without revealing the time to the
world, to any living soul, to any angel, or to any creature. The
great and terrible Day is near, but no one can foretell the hour
and moment of its coming. Our Lord said to His disciples: "Of
that day and hour no one knows, not even the angels of heaven,
nor the Son [in His state of humiliation], but the Father only."
Again: "The Son of Man is coming at an hour you do not expect."

If, then, we know, know well that the Day of the Lord will
come, and come suddenly and unexpectedly, this knowledge is to
keep us in constant readiness. Because no man knows the time,
all men are to be in a state of readiness at all times, every day
and hour. Woe to him who says, "My master is delayed." He is
like that wicked servant, and "the master of that servant will come
on a day when he does not expect him and at an hour he does
not know, and will punish him and put him with the hypocrites;
there men will weep and gnash their teeth" (Matt. 24:48-51).
If we knew that thieves are in our neighborhood, it would be
culpable negligence not to be constantly on guard, with eyes and
ears open. Though we do not know the day and hour when the
Lord will come, we know that He is coming; certain signs proclaim
that He is near; we know that He may come at any moment.
It would be inexcusable if we were not in a constant state of
readiness. In the text the Apostle gives us definite signs by which
we know that the Day of the Lord is near and may come at any
time. "When people say, There is peace and security," the Thessa-

lonians were to know that the end is near. When we hear people speak so today and the feeling of security becomes more pronounced, we are to know that the Day of Judgment is near. Our Lord described the time immediately preceding the end. "As it was in the days of Noah, so will it be in the days of the Son of Man. They ate, they drank, they married, they were given in marriage, until the day when Noah entered the ark and the flood came and destroyed them all. Likewise as it was in the days of Lot — they ate, they drank, they bought, they sold, they planted, they built, but on the day when Lot went out from Sodom fire and brimstone rained from heaven and destroyed them all — so will it be on the day when the Son of man is revealed" (Luke 17:26-30).

When we see our times against the background of our Lord's picture, we must conclude that everything points to the nearness of the Judgment, that we may expect it to come at any moment. Therefore we are to be ready always. With every year the world sinks deeper into security. Never did the conception of a Day of Judgment seem so ridiculous to the world as now. Evidently this is the time of which our Lord spoke. It is close to the world's midnight, and the alarm bell is ringing. The signs of our times clearly indicate that God is about to put the burning torch to the structure of this world and set it to burning in the fire of His wrath. The archangel has put the trumpet of judgment to his lips and is awaiting the signal. Intently our times call to us: "Make ready!" All we read in the newspapers, all we hear by radio, every day cries to the Christian: "The Day of the Lord is coming! The Lord is near!"

However The world is oblivious to it all. It lies in deep sleep with eyes and ears shut tight. Natural man lies in spiritual sleep and sees not the approaching end, hears not the footsteps of doom. He is steeped in deepest darkness of night and senses not the danger threatening him. He sees not the bright light of the Gospel that illumines the world with a brightness greater than that of the sun. "But you are not in darkness, brethren, for that Day to surprise you like a thief. For you are all the sons of light and sons of the day; we are not of the night or of darkness." We have been roused from sleep. The Word of God, like a loud voice from heaven, has entered our ears and driven spiritual sleep from our

the Word of God has

soul, awakened us to a new life. We must now prove ourselves to be children of light and of the day. How we are to do this, St. Paul tells us in the following.

B. Wherein Constant Readiness Consists. "So, then, let us not sleep, as others do, but let us keep awake and be sober. For those who sleep sleep at night, and those who get drunk are drunk at night." Sleep is for the night and not for the day, when everybody is alert and has his eyes open. So Christians, as children of the day and of the light, must not sleep, for in sleep we are powerless and at the mercy of our enemy. But when we are awake and watchful, no one can surprise us or take us unawares. The sentry who knows the enemy near does not permit sleep to dull his senses but keeps a sharp lookout. So the Christian must be alert and watchful.

To be watchful, the believer must be sober and avoid everything that might make him listless or may befuddle or intoxicate his senses. In this midnight hour it is required that he be free from the spirit of this world, that his heart and mind be in no way distracted, hindered, or burdened. The world is carousing and reveling according to its maxim "Let us eat, drink, and be merry, for tomorrow we are dead." Shameless and brazen sin has become the vogue, as though there were no God and no Judgment to be feared. A dissolute intoxication has gripped most people so that they no longer see, hear, or understand what God speaks to them by Word and signs. Of this senseless revelry we are to beware.

That is not enough, however. We should also be prepared at all times. St. Paul writes: "Since we belong to the day, let us be sober and put on the breastplate of faith and love and for a helmet the hope of salvation." He pictures the equipment of those whom the Last Day will not surprise. They have put on the spiritual armor of defense, not of offense. "The breastplate of faith and love." The breastplate was the chief part of the Roman legionary's equipment. It protected against the enemy's thrust or blow. The spiritual breastplate consists of faith and love. In the Christian's heart there is a living faith. This faith is not a mere outward pose he has assumed, but a living fire that breaks forth in works of love. Only when composed of these two, faith and love, is this armor a protection against the attacks of Satan, only then will it deflect all the fiery darts of the Evil One. God alone can supply this equipment. A self-made armor, be it yet so bright and shining, cannot keep a man fit to stand before the Son of Man. A Christian never puts off this armor even for a moment, but stands and walks and lives in it, lest his Lord come on a day when he does not expect Him.

What is it that keeps the Christian awake and watchful and ready? It is hope. "Put on . . . for a helmet the hope of salvation." The confident expectation of the eternal inheritance on the day of his Lord's return makes it possible for him to look forward joyfully, hour after hour, to the day of deliverance and salvation, knowing that this hope will never make him ashamed. Like the soldier who is on guard at a dangerous post, who knows that help is not far away and that he may be relieved at any moment, the believer waits hopefully and confidently, for God's Spirit has given him the assurance that he will stand before the throne of God and inherit eternal salvation.

"For God has not destined us for wrath but to obtain salvation through our Lord Jesus Christ, who died for us so that, whether we wake or sleep [that is, whether the Day of the Lord comes by day or at night], we might live with Him." The joyous certainty of his election from eternity, and that his salvation is secure in God's hands, imbues the Christian with ever new courage and strength. He does not grow weary and sleepy, but remains awake and patiently courageous, waiting every day and hour for the coming of his Lord in glory and power.

It is not enough, however, that each Christian be wakeful and watchful for and by himself and himself put on the armor and helmet, but the Christians are to keep one another awake and alert. St. Paul writes at the close of the Epistle: "Therefore encourage one another, and build one another up, just as you are doing." In this hour, when the hands of the world's clock are approaching twelve, when the children of this world are sleeping in darkness, we must be concerned not only about ourselves. We dare not fail to prove our faith by love of the brethren. We must perform the service of love by showing deep concern for the brethren. Throughout the Church Year we have had it impressed upon us that we cannot love God without loving our brethren. Sentries call to one another to keep one another awake. When the fighting becomes desperate, soldiers draw closer to one another. Every Christian congregation is a band of soldiers on guard duty who must be wakeful and alert. How welcome and inspiring is every word of encouragement! Every Christian congregation is a group of soldiers *on guard duty* defending themselves against the attacks of the common enemy. When one of us appears to be growing weary, sleepy, less watchful, we all are to help and encourage him. A Christian congregation is what it should and must be only when every member is concerned not only about his own salvation but also about the salvation of each fellow member. In the previous chapter St. Paul wrote to the Thessalonians about the resurrection of the dead and the Judgment, and he concluded: "Therefore comfort one another with these words." We are to talk about these things with one another, to watch over and admonish and encourage one another, to pray for one another. The smaller the band of the truly faithful becomes as the end draws nearer, the closer we are to draw to one another. Would to God that St. Paul could say also of us: "Just as you are doing." God grant that this become true of us more and more. Then we may look forward to the Day of Judgment confidently and joyously.

NOTES ON THE HOLY GOSPEL

With this Sunday we have reached the end of another Church Year. At the end of the year the merchant takes stock and balances his books to determine the state of his business. If he finds it unsatisfactory, he will plan improvements. If he discovers mistakes, he will resolve to avoid them in the future. The holy Gospel calls upon us to take stock of ourselves at the end of another year of grace whether we have true and saving faith. The end of the Church Year reminds us of the end of the world and the return of our Lord to take His believers home. Will He find in us the faith with which alone we can stand before Him? Are we ready and prepared to meet Him? The Epistle calls to us: "Put on the breastplate of faith and love, and for a helmet the hope of salvation." The holy Gospel brings a parable of our Lord that ends with the warning "Watch therefore, for you know neither the day nor the hour."

We are here dealing with a parable. In applying it we must first determine the point of comparison. All parables are embellished with details which serve merely to heighten the interest and enliven the story but contribute nothing of importance to the teaching and truth presented. Also the parable of the Ten Maidens dare not be interpreted in detailed allegorical fashion. It has only one point of comparison.

In the twenty-fourth chapter of St. Matthew's Gospel our Lord speaks of the signs that will precede the end of the world. "Then the Kingdom of Heaven shall be compared to ten maidens who took their lamps and went to meet the bridegroom." Then, in the last days before the end, the Church of God here on earth will be like ten maidens who took their lamps and went to meet the bridegroom. According to old Jewish custom, the bride awaited the groom in her home, surrounded by youthful companions. The groom came in company of his friends to meet her here and to lead her in procession to the wedding. As he approached, the maidens went to meet him. Then the joyful procession wended its way through the streets to the place where the marriage feast was prepared. The maidens entered the hall of feasting with the rest of the bridal company. Weddings were celebrated in the evening; therefore the maidens carried lamps to light their way in the darkness.

So it will be in the Church when the Bridegroom comes to take His bride to the heavenly marriage feast. Ten maidens will wait for His coming, with lamps in their hands, to meet the Bridegroom and to join the bridal procession. All will appear to be ready, apparently all will be adorned with festive decorations and ornaments, all will carry lamps. Outwardly there will be no difference. All in the communion of the Church will profess faith in the Lord, all will know that the Bridegroom is coming to take His bride to the eternal home. All will act like Christians, talk like Christians, and imagine themselves to be ready for the Bridegroom and fit to enter the marriage hall. All will be waiting to meet the Bridegroom and to be present at the wedding feast. All will appear to be Christians, all will have lamps and the same dress and ornaments.

But there will be a difference, although this will become apparent only later. Our Lord points out the difference. "Five of them were foolish, and five were wise." The folly of the five consisted in this, that they took their lamps but no oil. The wisdom of the other five consisted in this, that they took a supply of oil in flasks. At this point it is to be noted that the parable does not speak of the bride. Our Lord impresses upon us that there is a distinct difference and division in the Church on earth at His coming. Among those who wait for His appearance some are foolish. They have the outward earmarks of a Christian, they carry the symbol of watchfulness, the lamp, but they have no oil. They are without true, heartfelt faith. They are not equipped for watchful waiting. They lack the one quality that will make them acceptable as wedding guests at the marriage of the Lamb. They shut their hearts against the constant supply of the Holy Spirit. They fail to put on "the breastplate of faith and love, and for a helmet the hope of salvation," as the Epistle puts it.

The others are wiser. While there was yet time, earlier in the day, they acquired a supply of oil, real faith. They permitted the Holy Spirit to perform His work in them, to have His way with them, to direct and rule their conduct and life. They put on the breastplate of faith and love, the helmet of hope. They had not only the outward appearance of Christians but believed in fact, in their innermost heart.

The difference between the maidens became apparent in due time. "The bridegroom was delayed." The maidens waited and waited. The parable does not state whether their lamps were burning throughout the period of waiting and therefore the oil in the lamps of the foolish maidens consumed. More important is that all the maidens fell asleep. All ten slept. We must remember that our Lord is presenting a picture of the Church in the last days before the end. Even true Christians, even the faithful, fall asleep while waiting for the Bridegroom. In the days of the early Church, the Christians waited eagerly and longingly for His coming. In Thessalonica some discontinued working for their livelihood and idly awaited the Lord's immediate appearance. Modern Christendom occupies itself far less with thoughts of Christ's return. Concern for the things of this world is generally closer to our hearts than seeking the Kingdom of God and His righteousness. The faith of many has grown weak and their love cold. In the atmosphere of the last days even true believers find wakefulness and watchfulness most difficult.

"At midnight there was a cry, Behold, the bridegroom! Come out to meet him!" When all were asleep, when all the world lay in the slumber of security, when preoccupation with sinful indulgence was at its height, the bridegroom came unexpectedly and suddenly. At the cry all the maidens rose and trimmed their lamps. Were the lamps of all ten merely smoldering by this time, and did the fresh supply of oil revive the flame of the wise maidens' lamps, while the lack of oil caused the lamps of the foolish maidens to go out? Be that as it may, the foolish found that their lamps were going out. When they attempted to trim the wick, they discovered that they had no oil in their lamps. Their lamps were going out at the very time they were to serve their purpose. They had no oil to replenish the lamps. How foolish not to have provided oil! They could not go to meet the bridegroom without lamps. In their dilemma they turned to the wise maidens and said: "Give us some of your oil!" These refused, since the supply would not reach. So the foolish maidens rushed out to buy oil from some dealer. This was hopeless, for at this time of night all shops and markets were closed. While they vainly tried to acquire oil, the bridegroom arrived at the home of the bride. The wise maidens met him when he approached, with their lamps burning brightly. "Those who were ready went in with him to the marriage feast; and the door was shut." Later the foolish maidens came, after a vain search for oil, and pleaded: "Lord, lord, open to us!" But the bridegroom answered from within, without opening the door: "Truly, I say to you, I do not know you."

The parable teaches important truths. One is that it is not enough that we are outwardly members of a church and identify ourselves with God's people. Oil is essential, an absolute necessity. There must be true, inward faith. Without oil the foolish maidens could not face the bridegroom. Again, no man can believe for another. No man can be saved by another's faith. All must have their own oil, have oil in their own flasks and lamps, and must see to it that their flasks contain oil before the advent of the

Bridegroom. Again, when the Bridegroom comes, it is too late to acquire faith. The time of grace has come to an end. Again, when the Bridegroom has come and led His bride to the marriage feast, the door is shut, never to be opened again in all eternity. Again, the Bridegroom says to the maidens who had no oil, "I do not know you." The Bridegroom knows only His own, who are united with Him by true faith. Unbelievers, faithless pretenders, have no claim on Him when He comes.

Our Lord applies His parable: "Watch therefore, for you know neither the day nor the hour." The Bridegroom will come, but we do not know when. Therefore we are to watch at all times, always be ready to meet Him. This is the great lesson the parable teaches, and the preacher ought not to stress unduly the particular details of the story. Possible outlines are suggested.

True Christian Watchfulness. 1. Wherein it consists. Not in confessing Christ outwardly, nor in giving the appearance of godliness, like the foolish maidens, but in having the oil of true faith by God's grace and in persevering to the end. 2. How necessary it is. a. We do not know when the Bridegroom will come. b. While He is delayed, we are in danger of relaxing. c. At His coming it will be too late to make ready. 3. Its gracious reward. a. The terrible fate of the excluded. b. The joy of the faithful at the marriage of the Lamb.

Be Prepared for the Revelation of the Bridegroom! 1. Many who wait are not prepared. 2. Also true Christians are in danger of becoming sleepy. 3. On that day it is too late to prepare. 4. Life and salvation is at stake.

The Five Wise Maidens. 1. Their wisdom. a. They see to it that they have oil. b. Therefore they are prepared to meet the Bridegroom. 2. Their gracious reward. a. The foolish maidens are excluded. b. The wise go with the Bridegroom to the marriage.

The Solemn Warning of the End of the Church Year. 1. The Bridegroom will come, but we do not know when. 2. Always be ready to meet Him in faith that you may not be excluded from the heavenly marriage feast.

A DAY OF GENERAL OR SPECIAL THANKSGIVING

A day of thanksgiving may be observed whenever a local congregation or the Church at large is moved to thank God for His gifts in general or for some special gift of His grace and mercy. In the United States of America such a day of general thanksgiving is observed on the fourth Thursday of November and in Canada on a date annually fixed by proclamation. The Church willingly follows the suggestion of the State but always reserves the right to observe the day in her own way, without disregarding the usual forms of worship. The *Common Service Book* has the rubric: "The proper Service for this Day is the Order of Matins; but when The Service is used, the following Propria are appointed." *The Lutheran Hymnal* offers a complete set of Propers without further comment or direction. On the national Thanksgiving Day, the Order of Matins should be used rather than some order arranged by the pastor. Matins and Vespers are minor services of praise and thanksgiving, the one preparing for and introducing The Service, the other being the Amen to The Service. The Canticle on this day is the Te Deum Laudamus.

If the Order of Matins is not used, wholesome, historical, liturgical usage calls for the Holy Communion as part of The Service also on this day. Many will hesitate to celebrate on the Day of National Thanksgiving. One reason may be that visitors and nonmembers are expected to be present in unusually large number. It is well that we call to mind that a congregation performs a liturgy not for the sake of visitors, but for the members, the household of faith. Consideration for the occasional visitor is permitted to interfere with the worship of the faithful also on other occasions. The Nativity of our Lord is commemorated without Holy Communion because the "Christmas Christians" may not wish to "sit that long." The Resurrection of our Lord is observed without the celebration of the Holy Sacrament because some

"Easter Christians" may resent being excluded. Also a Day of General or Special Thanksgiving must be observed without the Eucharist, the Feast of Thanksgiving and Praise, because casual or occasional visitors may not approve. There is no valid reason that compels elimination of the Holy Sacrament. *The Lutheran Hymnal* appoints a full set of Propers, which are liturgically parts of The Service, the Holy Communion. Therefore a celebration of the Feast of Thanksgiving and Praise is quite in order on the Day of Thanksgiving. Care must be exercised, however, to make clear that our sacrifice of praise and thanksgiving is not a part of the Sacrifice we commemorate, that we are celebrating a Sacrament and not bringing a sacrifice. In the Holy Sacrament God alone is active, God alone offers. Our offering of thanks and praise is merely the fruit of the complete Sacrifice Christ offered to God once. If The Service is used, the Te Deum may be sung in procession before the Holy Communion.

The Introit. "Let everything that hath breath praise the Lord! Praise ye the Lord! Praise Him for His mighty acts; praise Him according to His excellent greatness! Praise ye the Lord! Praise God in His sanctuary; praise Him in the firmament of His power!"

The service opens with a call to everything that breathes to praise the Lord for His mighty deeds, according to His exceeding greatness. The assembled congregation is to praise God in His sanctuary, and all creation in His mighty firmament (Ps. 150: 6, 2, 1).

The Collect. "Almighty God, our heavenly Father, whose mercies are new unto us every morning and who, though we have in no wise deserved Thy goodness, dost abundantly provide for all our wants of body and soul, give us, we pray Thee, Thy Holy Spirit that we may heartily acknowledge Thy merciful goodness toward us, give thanks for all Thy benefits, and serve Thee in willing obedience."

We confess that we in no wise have deserved God's goodness. In spite of our unworthiness His mercies are new every morning, and He provides for all our wants of body and soul. We pray for the Holy Spirit that He may lead us to acknowledge God's merciful goodness, give thanks, and in gratitude and love serve Him in willing obedience.

The Epistle, 1 Timothy 2:1-8. St. Paul urges that supplications, prayers, intercessions, and thanksgivings be made for all men, for rulers in high positions of responsibility and authority, so that our common life may be lived in peace and quiet. Phillips translates "Supplications, prayers, intercessions, and thanksgivings should be made on behalf of all men . . . so that our common life may be lived in peace and quiet, with a proper sense of God and of our responsibility to Him for what we do with our lives. . . . Therefore, I want the men to pray in all the churches with sincerity, without resentment or doubt in their minds."

The Gradual. "The eyes of all wait upon Thee, and Thou givest them their meat in due season. Thou openest Thine hand and satisfiest the desire of every living thing. Alleluia! Alleluia! Bless the Lord, O my soul, and all that is within me, bless His holy name. Bless the Lord, O my soul, and forget not all His benefits. Alleluia!"

In the Collect we prayed for the Holy Spirit "that we may heartily acknowledge Thy merciful goodness toward us." Here we heartily acknowledge God's merciful goodness and call upon our soul to give thanks for all His benefits, to bless His holy name, the reputation He has established as the Provider of food in due season (Ps. 145:15), and not to forget all His benefits (Ps. 103:2).

The Gospel, St. Luke 17:11-19. This Gospel is appointed also for the Fourteenth Sunday after Trinity, when it was intended to illustrate the cleansing power of Christ. Today it is to teach a lesson in regard to gratitude and ingratitude.

The Common Preface.

SERMON ON THE HOLY GOSPEL

The Lord Jesus was on His way to Jerusalem, traveling along the borders of Samaria and Galilee. As He entered a village, He was met by ten lepers, who stood at a distance and cried: "Jesus, Master, have mercy on us!" Immediately He said: "Go and show yourselves to the priests." The priests were the health officers who had to pronounce lepers cured before they could return to their homes and mingle with people. "And as they went, they were cleansed." On their way to the priests they noticed that they were healed.

So far all ten were alike. They were all lepers, suffering from
the same disease. All ten faced the same ghastly death, dying by
inches. All were outcasts, shut out from the consolations of the
church, their friends, and their home. To all appearances one was
just as hopeless as the other.

They were alike also in their faith. There is evidence that
they had faith. They had heard strange rumors that this Man of
Nazareth could heal all manner of diseases. Of course, they found
it hard to believe that He could cure even leprosy. But in spite
of doubts they went in a body to this amazing Healer. That was
faith. When the ten came as close as they dared, they appealed
for help. That was prayer. Their prayer was marked by a beautiful humility. They did not ask for justice or for benefits they
deserved. In simple faith they pleaded: "Jesus, Master, have mercy
on us!" Then they gave the supreme test of faith, obedience. Our
Lord did not heal them at once, but He gave them the bewildering
command to show themselves to the priests, to submit to an
examination by the department of health. Lepers were to go to
the priests when they believed themselves to be free of their disease.
The ten went with their loathsome sickness, they obeyed before
they had any evidence of their cure.

Finally, they were all alike in that they found healing. "As
they went," before they had gone far on their way to the priests,
something happened. They felt new life pulsating in their veins.
Each looked with wide-eyed wonder into the face of the other,
seeing what seemed too good to be true.

Like these ten lepers, so we all are alike in many respects.
For one, we all are lepers before God. Leprosy is frequently used
in God's Book as a picture to describe our sinful state. Sin makes
us utterly unworthy of the least of God's gifts. In this day's Collect
we confess that we have in no wise deserved God's goodness and
plead for mercy. We can never be truly grateful until we realize
our unworthiness and that we have forfeited every claim on God's
consideration.

No doubt, we are also alike in this, that we all have suffered,
some more, some less. As we think back over the years, we recall
worries, sicknesses, griefs, bereavements, separation. Surely, we are
alike also in this, that in our need we went to God for help.

As time went on, it became clear to us that man's help was at an end, that only God could help under the circumstances. So we prayed to God and asked for mercy.

We are alike also in that we have enjoyed God's merciful goodness. We acknowledge in the Collect that His mercies were new every morning and that He abundantly provided for all our wants of body and soul. First of all, the Great Physician healed the leprosy of our sin. For Christ's sake God cast all our sins behind His back and will remember them no more. Also in a material way we have enjoyed God's mercies. Many of us complained much, others feared the direst calamities. Yet here we are, none has starved, we are dressed warm or at least moderately well; we still have a roof over our heads. We are alike in that our worst fears never materialized.

However, there is a point where the likeness ends. The ten lepers in the text were all alike in many respects, but soon a difference appeared. Having discovered that they were healed on the way, they came to the priests in high spirits to be declared clean officially. Then the group scattered. Nine hurried to their respective homes and forgot all about the Man who had healed them. Only one went back to our Lord. He turned back, praising God with a loud voice, and in an abundance of gratitude fell down at the Master's feet, giving Him thanks. *mankind at all time*

We have here a picture of the world, of ~~America, of many,~~ perhaps most, congregations today. Ten beg and plead, ten receive mercy, only one returns thanks. Ten enjoy God's blessings, only one thinks of saying "Thank You." The Church does wisely when she has us pray today: "Give us Thy Holy Spirit that we may heartily acknowledge Thy merciful goodness toward us, give thanks for all Thy benefits, and serve Thee in willing obedience." As in the text, so today the grateful are a small minority. The thankful Samaritan towers above the majority like Pikes Peak above molehills. What was wrong with the nine? Why do they seem such pathetic dwarfs? Not because they said any unkind word to their Healer. It is because they said nothing at all. They took their priceless gift and went their way in silence. We honor the nameless Samaritan, not because he was rich or clever, not because he had received more than the nine, but because he knew how to say that gracious and heartening word "Thank you."

Why was the one grateful and the nine not? Not because of any difference in their circumstances. If the one had been healed and the nine left to die, this could be an explanation. But all ten were cured. This points to the fact that real gratitude is seldom born of circumstances. If it were, the rich, healthy, successful could be put in one group and the poor, weak, unsuccessful in another, and we could say: "The children of good fortune are thankful, the unfortunate are not." But many who are comparatively well situated complain and whine, while many less fortunate give thanks.

Could it be perhaps that the nine were grateful but less demonstrative? Perhaps they reasoned that our Lord knew without being told that they were appreciative? This explanation will not serve. That type of gratitude brings no joy, dries no tears. Perhaps our friends and benefactors know, but as a rule they do not. Even if they know, they are greatly heartened by hearing us say so. This was true of our Lord. In His Book He tells us: "Let the redeemed of the Lord say so" (Ps. 107:2).

The nine may have become so absorbed in the gift that they forgot the Giver. When they received a clean bill of health, they all talked excitedly. "I have not seen the old farm for years," said one and hurried away. "I must run and see how my business fared in my absence," said another. "It's been years since I saw my family last; the baby must be a big boy by now," and off he ran. How different the Samaritan! He thrilled over his gift just like the nine. Yet his joy was greater than theirs, because he rejoiced not only in the gift but even more in the Giver. Instead of allowing the gift to become an obscuring mist to hide the face of the Healer, he made it a veritable sunrise to give him a clearer vision of that face. He could not think of his blessing without thinking of God, and never think of God without giving Him thanks.

Another reason for the ingratitude of the ten may have been that they forgot both gift and Giver in their contemplation of the terrible tragedy they had passed through. They had suffered in body and mind. Their sickness had brought financial reverses. They found themselves in the rear of the procession. They had such a fine business, but their sickness ruined it. They could not forget. They fixed their mind on their losses. This is a common blunder also today. People are far from want, in fact, doing rather well. But they still lament what they suffered and lost and missed in the past. Think where they would be if they had not suffered this or that loss. The attitude of the Samaritan was different. He, too, had suffered, had through dull, gray days and bitter, black nights, experienced tragic losses. But now that he was cured, the bitterness of his yesterdays was all forgotten or remembered only to add to the sweetness of today. His heart was so filled with the glory of the gains that had come into his empty hands that there was no room for a single pang over his losses.

It is even possible that the nine took their healing as a matter of course. It came rather suddenly and soon after their appeal to our Lord's mercy. But how could they know whether their recovery was not a natural process, had been going on for some time, and happened to become apparent just at this time? Did the Master of Nazareth really have a part in it? The priests, who were bitter enemies of our Lord, perhaps strengthened them in this foolish notion in order to discredit the Nazarene. It would have happened anyhow. In our day many persuade themselves that God has nothing to do with their improved condition. Every affliction is bound to run its course. All one need do is to wait for the end. Conditions always improve sooner or later. Because God's blessings come through natural law or through human hands, without unusual display of power, they are taken for granted. The nine might take their cure as a matter of course. Not so the Samaritan. He took it as a gift of God. Not because he was blinder or more superstitious, but because he was more clear-eyed and saner. To read God out of the affairs of men is not a display of wisdom or intellectuality. Some men of great ability have missed God, but their ability was not the cause. This Samaritan had received something, and with St. Paul he asked: "What have you that you did not receive?" (1 Cor. 4:7). Nothing. All comes from God, even though it is usually mediated to us through human hands or natural law.

Possibly the real reason why the nine were wanting in gratitude was their conceit. They were Jews, of God's chosen people, and had a claim on God's consideration. It was proper for the cursed Samaritan to be grateful for undeserved mercy, but you can't down a child of Abraham. How many are going through life today with such a mental swagger in their attitude! Americans are smart and enterprising. When others lose their heads and their shirts, they keep cool and ride out the storm. They have the know-how. For such people this day is an occasion for congratulating God on the wonderful assistance He has been getting from them. They sprain their arms patting themselves on the back. Conceit and gratitude do not dwell in the same heart. The Samaritan was truly humble. Giving all glory to Christ, he turned back and with a loud voice praised God. He was not ashamed to admit that God had a hand in his affairs. He was the only one who gave joy to our Lord. There was a touch of tears in His voice as He expressed His disappointment in the nine. Surely there was an abounding joy in His welcome of the one who turned back to give thanks.

Our Lord demands gratitude. It is part of a Christian's equipment. In almost every letter St. Paul admonishes Christians to have a spirit of gratitude, and not merely that they give thanks for a particular favor done them, but far more that a spirit of gratitude characterize their entire life. Generally speaking, a noble person can be known by how he excels in the matter of appreciation and gratefulness. A Christian especially has reasons to be continually grateful, because he has been deluged with favors by his heavenly Father. From the midst of thousands he has been snatched out of darkness and hopelessness and transferred to the realm of light and grace. The cleansing of the ten lepers forcefully reminds us that in Holy Baptism our leprosy of sin was healed, we were justified and endowed with sanctifying grace. We must live in a wicked world and in the ordinary pursuits of life. But we have appointed days and occasions when we turn back to Christ in order to thank Him for the favor of having cleansed us from sin and enriched us with grace. The grateful leper in the holy Gospel is a symbol of the Christian who returns to Christ in the house of God, praises God with a loud voice, falls on his face, and gives thanks.

This day is such an occasion for baptized Christians to praise God and give thanks. We have gathered to celebrate the Eucharist, to perform the Liturgy of the Service of Thanksgiving and Praise. The Holy Communion is the finest and loftiest service of thanksgiving, and for this occasion we have added the Te Deum Laudamus. We give thanks for all the favors we have received from Almighty God, in particular for having been chosen to be children of God. We begin by calling on one another, yes, on all that breathes, to praise the Lord. We pray for the Holy Spirit that He may lead us to acknowledge God's merciful goodness, to give thanks for all His benefits, and to serve God in willing obedience. In the Kyrie we acknowledge that we are utterly dependent on mercy, and in the Gloria in Excelsis we glorify, praise, and give thanks. In the Epistle we are told how we may serve God in willing obedience. In the holy Gospel the Lord Himself opens His mouth, just as He spoke of old on the mount or from the boat. The ceremonies of the Liturgy demonstrate that in the Gospel Christ really speaks to us, for when it is announced, we rise and chant: "Glory be to Thee, O Lord!" After the reading we chant: "Praise be to Thee, O Christ!" The offering and the Offertory are expressions of offering ourselves and of our consciousness that we are united with God, and they include our work, our sorrows, our prayers, and our firm will to serve God and to follow His admonitions. This was expressed much better in olden times. The housewife and mother of a family used to bake a loaf of bread embossed with the sign of the cross. In this loaf she enclosed, as it were, the cares and necessities of the family, their love of God, and their trust in Him. On the following Sunday, at the Offertory procession, she laid this gift on the table of offerings, in token of the self-sacrifice of her family, and from time to time she had the joy of seeing her bread chosen for the element of the Eucharist. The money we offer today is certainly not as beautiful and expressive a symbol.

The celebrant admonishes us, "Lift up your hearts," and we respond, "We lift them up unto the Lord." Next we declare that it is meet and right to give thanks unto the Lord, and the celebrant introduces the Sanctus and Benedictus with the words: "It is truly meet, right, and salutary that we should at all times and in all places give thanks unto Thee, O Lord, holy Father, almighty, everlasting God, through Jesus Christ, our Lord. Therefore with angels and archangels and with all the company of heaven we laud and magnify Thy glorious name, evermore praising Thee and saying" . . . The congregation then chants the angels' hymn of adoration from the sixth chapter of Isaiah and the song with which our Lord was greeted when He came to Jerusalem on Palm Sunday. As we kneel at the altar, our Lord comes and together with the Bread and Wine gives us His Body to eat and His Blood to drink. Christ says to us: "I gave My Body for you, I shed My Blood for you." He gives Himself to us as our very own and assures us that we are beloved children of God through Him. He gives us food for the life of grace. Our Holy Communion becomes a great commingling of love. Most appropriately the Eucharist ends with, "O give thanks unto the Lord, for He is good," and the response, "And His mercy endureth forever."

The Order of the Holy Communion is the finest prayer of thanksgiving we have. May God grant us what we ask in the Collect for this day! May the Holy Spirit inspire us to celebrate the Eucharist with heartfelt fervor and thanksgiving and to be strengthened by our Holy Communion in our resolve to serve God in willing obedience!

Bibliography

Bouyer, Louis. *Liturgical Piety.* Notre Dame, Ind.: University of Notre Dame Press, 1955.

Brenner, Scott Francis. *The Way of Worship.* New York: The Macmillan Company, 1944.

Cabrol, Fernand. *The Year's Liturgy.* Two Volumes. New York: Benziger Brothers, 1938.

Chapman, Michael Andrew. *Sundays of the Saints.* London and St. Louis: B. Herder Book Company, 1928.

Clarke, W. K. Lowther. *Liturgy and Worship.* New York: The Macmillan Company, 1944.

Dix, Dom Gregory. *The Shape of the Liturgy.* Westminster: Dacre Press, 1947.

Freeman, Philip. *The Principles of Divine Service.* Oxford and London: James Parker and Company, 1873.

Gaillard, Jean. *Holy Week and Easter,* trans. William Busch. Collegeville, Minn.: The Liturgical Press, 1954.

Gerhard, Johann. *Postille.* Three Volumes. Original editions of 1613, 1616, and 1663. Leipzig: J. C. Hinrichs'sche Buchhandlung, 1877.

Gibson, George M. *The Story of the Christian Year.* New York and Nashville: Abingdon-Cokesbury Press, 1945.

Gueranger, Abbot. *The Liturgical Year,* trans. Dom Laurence Shepherd. Westminster, Md.: The Newman Press, 1949.

Hellriegel, Martin B. *Vine and Branches.* Volume I — *Vine.* St. Louis: Pio Decimo Press, 1948.

Horn, Edward T. III. *The Christian Year.* Philadelphia: Muhlenberg Press, 1957.

Lawrence, Emeric. *Meditating the Gospels.* Collegeville, Minn.: The Liturgical Press, 1957.

Lindemann, Fred H. *In Remembrance of Me.* New York: The Lutheran Press, 1937.

————. *Thy King Cometh*. New York: Ernst Kaufmann, Inc., 1948.

Loehr, Aemiliana. *Das Herrenjahr*. Regensburg: Verlag Friedrich Pustet, 1955.

Lochner, Friedrich. *Der Hauptgottesdienst*. St. Louis: Concordia Publishing House, 1895.

Mather, F. V. *The Saints' Days and the Holy Eucharist*. London: Sheffington and Son, 1888.

McGarry, William J. *He Cometh*. New York: The America Press, 1947.

Parsch, Pius. *Das Jahr des Heiles*. Three Volumes. Klosterneuburg bei Wien: Verlag Volksliturgisches Apostolat, 1952.

————. *Sermons on the Liturgy*, trans. Philip T. Weller, Milwaukee: The Bruce Publishing Company, 1953.

Reed, Luther D. *The Lutheran Liturgy*. Philadelphia: Muhlenberg Press, 1947.

Schmidt, C. C. *Weg des Lebens*. St. Louis: Concordia Publishing House, 1915.

Scott, Melville. *The Harmony of the Collects, Epistles, and Gospels* of the Sundays of the Church Year. London: Bamrose and Sons Ltd., 1905. (Since this book is out of print, a distinct service is rendered by making a number of sermon outlines available. At times some liberty was taken as to adaptation and changes, but the source and origin of the outlines are hereby gratefully acknowledged.)

Seiss, Joseph A. *Lectures on the Gospels and Epistles for the Minor Festivals of the Church Year*. Philadelphia: Lutheran Bookstore, 1893.

Sermons for the People, Second Series. Volume IV of *Plain Sermons for the Christian Year*. By Various Contributors. London: Society for Promotion of Christian Knowledge, 1906.

Snyder, A. W. *The Chief Days*. Milwaukee: The Young Churchman Company, 1899.

Strodach, Paul Zeller. *The Church Year*. Philadelphia: The United Lutheran Publication House, 1924.

Viator. *He Is Faithful*. London: Burns, Oates and Washbourne Ltd., 1937.

Webber, F. R. *Studies in the Liturgy*. Erie, Pa.: Ashby Printing Company, 1938.